BIO
ROOSEVELT ☑ **P9-DHQ-640**

Hazelgrove, William Elliott, 1959-
Forging a president : how the wild
West created Teddy Roosevelt
05/17
33950010597356   ISL

P.65 "smudge" noted 2-14-19

MANATEE COUNTY
PUBLIC LIBRARY SYSTEM
BRADENTON, FL
ISL

FORGING A PRESIDENT

FORGING A PRESIDENT

HOW THE WILD WEST CREATED

TEDDY ROOSEVELT

WILLIAM HAZELGROVE

REGNERY
HISTORY

Copyright © 2017 by William Hazelgrove

All rights reserved. No part of this publication may be reproduced or transmitted in any form or by any means electronic or mechanical, including photocopy, recording, or any information storage and retrieval system now known or to be invented, without permission in writing from the publisher, except by a reviewer who wishes to quote brief passages in connection with a review written for inclusion in a magazine, newspaper, website, or broadcast.

Regnery History™ is a trademark of Salem Communications Holding Corporation; Regnery® is a registered trademark of Salem Communications Holding Corporation

Cataloging-in-Publication Data on file with the Library of Congress
ISBN 978-1-62157-476-7

Published in the United States by
Regnery History
An imprint of Regnery Publishing
A Division of Salem Media Group
300 New Jersey Ave NW
Washington, DC 20001
www.RegneryHistory.com

Manufactured in the United States of America

10 9 8 7 6 5 4 3 2 1

Books are available in quantity for promotional or premium use. For information on discounts and terms, please visit our website: www.Regnery.com.

Distributed to the trade by
Perseus Distribution
www.perseusdistribution.com

For
Kitty, Clay, Callie, and Careen

CONTENTS

*Now look, that damned cowboy is
President of the United States.*

—Republican insider Mark Hanna

The romance of my life began here.

—Teddy Roosevelt, on returning to the West

PREFACE

The "romance of his life," as Theodore Roosevelt described his relationship with the American West, lasted from 1883 to 1887.[1] He would write seven books on the West, and later, as president, he would set aside millions of acres of western land for future generations. The "vigorous life" that characterized Teddy Roosevelt had its roots in his time spent out West. The third transcontinental railroad, the Northern Pacific, made it possible for people to travel in comfort to the northwest territories (first mapped by Lewis and Clark in 1803–1805) while reading dime novels filled with Western heroes like Kit Carson and Jim Bridger. It put areas like the Badlands (a smaller Grand Canyon, carved out of the earth sixty million years ago) within reach of men like New Yorker Teddy Roosevelt.

There really would be no America without the West. It gave great scope to American avarice, later justified as Manifest Destiny. For many, the simple phrase, "Go West, young man," was enough to send young men and women on their way into a virtually unknown world. The

United States simply didn't have the manpower to control the land that came with Jefferson's Louisiana Purchase. Even today Americans are fascinated with the idea of people heading into the unknown. The movie *Wild* chronicles the story of a woman who hikes the Pacific Crest Trail after her life disintegrates. She emerges a year later a changed person. This is what the West offered people in the nineteenth century, even more so than now—a chance to start again and remake oneself.

We associate Theodore Roosevelt with what would become his famous, larger-than-life persona: the barrel-chested, teeth-snapping, Big Stick–wielding, swaggering cowboy expansionist who exemplified the vigorous life of the early twentieth century. The vigorous life was the creed by which Roosevelt lived, and for him the cowboy was its apotheosis. Through Roosevelt's influence the idea of the cowboy made an indelible mark on American culture. "Peril and hardship, and years of long toil broken by weeks of brutal dissipation, draw haggard lines across their eager faces, but never dim their reckless eyes nor break their bearing of defiant self-confidence," he later wrote, elevating the cowboy to his ideal, a sort of Nietzschean plainsman.[2] Eric Foner writes of the enduring myth of the cowboy: "The image of the courageous, spirited horseman living a dangerous life carried with it an appeal that refuses to disappear. Driving a thousand to two thousand cattle hundreds of miles to market; facing lightning and cloudbursts and drought, stampedes, rattlesnakes, and outlaws; sleeping under the stars and catching chow at the chuck wagon—the cowboys dominated the American galaxy of folk heroes."[3]

Roosevelt himself was far from this cowboy ideal. He often pointed out that "once a cowboy is a good roper and rider, the only other accomplishment he values is skill with his great army revolver."[4] But even after years out West, Roosevelt never became really proficient with a lariat, though he once rescued an Englishman from a river with an amazing lasso throw; and his eyesight was such that he never became the dead-eyed shot of legend, though he did once manage to drill a grizzly between the eyes.

The truth is that Theodore Roosevelt became what he was not—a cowboy—through sheer will. When he first came out West, he was a sickly, weak young man who suffered so much from asthma that, when he was a boy, his father would take him on fast buggy rides just to force air into his lungs. Many doubted he could survive to adulthood. But survive he did. Roosevelt became a delegate-at-large to the Republican National Convention and was a progressive reformer on the rise, when, in 1884, both his wife and his mother died within twelve hours of each other. The light in his life simply went out. Four months later, after a stinging political defeat, he headed out West and didn't give anyone a return date.

In 1890, the superintendent of the U.S. Census Bureau declared the American frontier finally closed. Frederick Jackson Turner affirmed this and claimed that the frontier experience, more than any other, had shaped America's character; it had given the pioneer "a new field of opportunity, a gate of escape from the bondage of the past."[5] Teddy Roosevelt went to the Badlands of the Dakotas at the tail end of the Wild West. The asthmatic with thick spectacles who stepped off the train in the town of Little Missouri bore little resemblance to the man who would return years later thick of chest and ready to tackle the world. He came back as the Teddy Roosevelt we now recognize.

The West *remade* Roosevelt, just as it had remade the country. Basically lawless and churchless, the West offered freedom unbounded if you were tough enough to take it. As he later wrote, "For cowboy work there is no need of special traits and special training, and young Easterners should be sure of themselves before trying it: the struggle for existence is very keen in the far West, and it is no place for men who lack the ruder, coarser virtues and physical qualities.... "[6] This held great appeal for young Roosevelt, who would find the essence of America in the frozen and baking terrain of the Badlands. Here the character of America presented itself to Roosevelt, and he essentially *became* that character.

The West delivered this one-hundred-and-twenty-five-pound man, this "dude," a great adventure: he faced down gunmen, grizzly bears, thieves, rustlers, unscrupulous ranchers, ruthless outlaws, and Indians. He had the breath knocked out of him by overturned horses, cracked a rib, dislocated a shoulder, and nearly froze to death more than once, getting lost in the hell that is the Badlands—all while fighting chronic asthma and ignoring a physician's admonition to protect his weak heart and lead the sedentary life of a recluse.

To recover from the twin blows of losing both his mother and his wife on the same day, and in his quest to find his way again, Theodore Roosevelt would push himself to the point where his broken heart would either heal or stop forever. The West was just the place for such a contest.

THE BULL MOOSE
1912

Teddy Roosevelt had just finished dinner at the Gilpatrick Hotel in Milwaukee and was walking to his car—he was to give a speech in the Milwaukee Auditorium. The election of 1912 had been vitriolic with Roosevelt bolting the Republican Party and forming his own third party, the Bull Moose Party. Roosevelt was sure he could beat the incumbent William Howard Taft and the Democratic candidate, the former Princeton President, Woodrow Wilson. He reveled in giving speeches and attacking Taft as incompetent, and Wilson as an egghead who had the demeanor of a "druggist." He now planned to deliver another rousing speech and had the fifty-page manuscript stuffed in his coat pocket, folded twice behind his steel glasses case.

John Schrank, a thirty-six-year-old psychotic and former New York saloonkeeper, approached Theodore Roosevelt. Schrank believed that deceased President McKinley had spoken to him in his dreams, proclaiming that no man should run for a third term. Schrank had bought a fourteen-dollar Colt .38 and fifty-five cents worth of bullets, and had been following Roosevelt through New Orleans, Atlanta, Charleston, and Tennessee, ever since the dead McKinley had risen in his coffin and pointed to him and said, "Avenge my death." While waiting to shoot Roosevelt in Milwaukee, he had passed the time drinking beer in a local bar and smoking Jack Pot cigars. Now his opportunity came. Roosevelt had just sat down in an open car in front of the hotel. Schrank approached him and Roosevelt rose to wave to the crowd when the assassin raised the .38 caliber pistol and fired. Roosevelt fell back into the car as the bullet entered his chest after piercing the steel glasses case and the folded manuscript pages of his speech.

The bullet entered under his right nipple and lodged in his ribs. The ex-President immediately took out a handkerchief and dabbed his mouth to see if his lungs had been hit. He then proclaimed he wouldn't go to the hospital, but would deliver his scheduled speech. Dr. Terrell, his physician, insisted he go to the hospital. Roosevelt would have none of it. "You get me to that speech. It may be the last one I shall deliver, but I am going to deliver this one!"

Theodore Roosevelt went to the auditorium and spoke for more than ninety minutes while bleeding under his coat—thundering to the crowd the immortal line, *"It takes more than a bullet to stop a bull moose!"*[1]

The crowd loved it. And when Roosevelt went to the hospital, the doctors opted to leave the bullet lodged in his chest. He sent a telegram to his wife Edith, informing her that he was not nearly as badly hurt as he had been falling from a horse. He boarded a train for a Chicago hospital and changed into a clean shirt and asked for a hot shave. He hummed as he shaved and then climbed into the train compartment bed and fell asleep, sleeping like a child.

In the press, people expressed astonishment that a man who had been shot at point-blank range could give a speech for an hour and a half. But they truly expected no less from Teddy Roosevelt. The sickly, asthmatic son of a rich man in Manhattan was born in the East; the Bull Moose who spoke for an hour and a half with a .38 caliber bullet lodged in his chest, well, he was born in the West.

1

BADLANDS, DAKOTA TERRITORY

1885

Theodore Roosevelt was out farther than he liked, looking for a lost horse. Riding across the "Badlands" with its primal geological formations gave him pause. There had been reports of Indians attacking men from Little Missouri in the Dakota Territory. Worse, there had been reports of gruesome torture that prompted men to carry rattlesnake poison in a vial in case of capture. Theodore Roosevelt was in the Badlands in the year 1885 with his pony and Winchester—in his mind, already a cowboy, but to others a dude from New York with thick glasses, a small frame, and an asthmatic cough.

This "hell with the fires out" part of the Dakota Territory was still a no man's land.[1] The frontier wouldn't be declared closed for eight years, and a man could still go there and become lost and emerge remade, if he survived. But Roosevelt thought of none of this as he crossed the hot plain, staring straight ahead. He was thinking about the five Indians who had just emerged on the ridge beyond and were now riding toward him with their rifles drawn.

1

Roosevelt swung down from his pony Manitou and raised his Winchester. He positioned himself behind his horse. The five Indians riding in a deadly gallop were almost upon him. It had been ten years since Custer's Last Stand at the Battle of Little Bighorn, and Geronimo was still on the run. The Indian Wars had simmered down, but atrocities still occurred on both sides. Roosevelt would later write, "There is always danger in meeting a band of young bucks in lonely, uninhabited country—those that have barely reached manhood being the most truculent, insolent, and reckless."[2]

Roosevelt knew he might die if he stood his ground, but he would surely die if he gave up his rifle or tried to outrun the Indians. He cocked his Winchester and took aim over the saddle of his horse. His glasses hit the stock and sweat tickled his nose. His hat was pulled low. The Indians whooped and shrieked with their rifles over their heads. Roosevelt breathed in the heated air of the Badlands and the ropy smell of his saddle.

Later he would write, "The level plain where we were was of all places the one on which such an onslaught could best be met."[3] Being in the open gave him an advantage. Roosevelt drew a bead on the Indian in the middle. Men who knew they might die would think twice before charging someone with a rifle aimed at their chest. Still, Roosevelt knew the Indians had the odds. He might take one of them—but of course the others would kill him. Maybe take his scalp or hack him to pieces as they had left others. All he could really do was wait. He was a man from New York who just a year earlier had frantically taken a train in the middle of the night to find his destiny. It was a murderous world there, too.

2

THE MIND BUT NOT
THE BODY
1869

The boy was sick again. The family was on the Grand Tour of Europe and Theodore Roosevelt Sr. didn't know what to do for his son. They were now in Vienna, and it was always in the nighttime when the dreaded disease came on. They didn't know what caused it or really what to do about it. The carriage rides in the middle of the night in New York, after having walked up and down the hallway with the boy in his arms, were the acts of a desperate man. Call the servants and get the carriage and then rush through the night with the boy's mouth open to the wind.

But now they were in a foreign land and his son was literally suffocating before his eyes. His father resorted to experiments to try to stop the swelling bronchial tubes that wouldn't allow air in or out. As Roosevelt's mother wrote, "it came to a point where he had to sit up in the bed to breathe. After a strong cup of black coffee the spasmodic part of the attack ceased and he slept...had the coffee not taken effect he would have gone on struggling through the night.... "[1]

The Roosevelts were at the mercy of the medical theories of the day, which were often contradictory. An attack could be brought on by a fall, something the boy saw, bad air, good air, or rain. Some said asthma was hereditary and came from the mother. Others said that patients themselves brought on the attacks, that they were in some way psychosomatic and that the sufferer was to blame. A "nervous temperament" was sometimes diagnosed. The nervous young boy suffered at a time when an English physician, Henry Hyde Salter, published a study (1864) declaring asthma a "nervous condition."

Salter cited patients who had attacks from seeing a fire or a horse and patients whose asthma disappeared when they neared a doctor's office. Depression seemed to kick off many attacks. Then Salter veered and claimed exercise was the most important thing a person could do to ward off attacks: "Organs are made for action, not existence; they are made to *work*, to work, not to *be*; and when they *work* well they can *be* well."[2] Roosevelt's father took this as gospel and preached it to his son with the fervor of the converted. Action and more action was to be used against this disease brought on by the mind...a vigorous approach to life.

But Teddy was apparently a weakling. He seemed incapable of action, and so the crude pharmaceuticals of the day were used to stop the attacks. But the attacks were horrible. Drowning was often invoked as a comparison—slow drowning. Waterboarding might be its contemporary equivalent. "The sensation of an acute asthmatic attack is that of being strangled or suffocated, only infinitely more complex. The whole body responds.... The trouble is not just in the lungs. The central nervous system is involved, the endocrine system, both sides of the brain, possibly the stem of the brain as well. The agony is total.... And the largest part of the agony is psychological—inexpressible terror, panic."[3]

Ten-year-old Teddy was too sick to write about it in his diary; he could only say he was "very sick" and there were "witches in my chest."[4] And it was always at night when the attacks came on. First the tightening of the chest, then a dry hacking cough. Eventually, the child had to sit up just to breathe. And "Soon he is unable to speak or move, except with the utmost difficulty. He is battling for breath, for life, tugging, straining, elbows planted on his knees, shoulders hunched high, his head thrown back, eyes popping."[5] He was in hell and there was no end in sight.

Teddy's parents reached for the only remedies available at the time. Strong black coffee was given until he could drink no more; then a cigar, with the child taking deep breaths, holding the smoke in until he collapsed; then potions of garlic and mustard seeds. If these didn't work then an enema, or a cold bath, or a shot of whiskey, or some gin, or wine mixed with opium, or chloroform, or marijuana, or burning nitrate paper. Anything to break down the child and knock him out and stop the attack. It was not unlike chemotherapy, where they try to kill the disease without killing the patient.

Teddy's parents tried many of these, and because they were rich they would whisk him off to seashores or country estates or take him for rides behind fast-moving horses—anything to break the awful strangling beast that could easily kill him.

"I sat up for six hours and papa made me smoke a cigar," he wrote in his diary.

The bronchial tubes just didn't work right; they would fill with mucus and the ventilating action would cease. The boy was suffocating, with spoonfuls of air being pulled in and even less being expelled. If the attack got worse, he would turn blue, with his chest pounding and his back and chest muscles fighting to get air. He would look cadaverous, and without ventilators or strong bronchodilators, he could asphyxiate; and so the desperate measures continued.

And Teddy Roosevelt fought for his life during these nights of terror. He was not just an asthmatic but *an acute asthmatic*. Then psychological factors were again dragged to the bar. Great stress was said to bring on the attacks. Separation from the mother was pointed to as a cause. Melancholia was another. It didn't matter. Teddy learned at an early age that life is literally a battle to breathe. Nothing would be as bad as this and he must always be prepared for the worst.

And he must fight back. "It is as if having experienced asthma, he finds other pains and discomforts mild by comparison."[6] He was either a victim or a conqueror, and Teddy had to choose to be the latter or die. Salter wrote, the asthmatic "knows that a certain percentage of his future life will be dedicated to suffering." Or, put another way, suffering is life, and so to suffer from extreme hardship or turmoil or intense physical challenges is considered within the realm of the normal. "I am to do everything myself,"[7] Roosevelt wrote as a child. The words from Salter and Teddy's father became like a dirge that the child, and later the man, would convert into the creed of the "vigorous life," one that will push the man to do things no sane person would even attempt.

After the trip to Europe, the asthma attacks continued. His father grew increasingly frustrated and wrote his wife, "I am away with Teedie again much to my regret.... He had another attack, woke me up at night and last night to make a break, I took him to Oyster Bay."[8] Roosevelt's father was basically running him around trying to catch the best air; Oyster Bay had a sea breeze that could be a balm to release the grip on the boy's lungs. But he could not keep this up forever. "Teedie had an attack of asthma on last Sunday night and Papa took him to Oyster Bay where he passed Monday night and Tuesday night."[9] The attacks returned and mother and son were off to "take the waters" at Richfield Springs and would go again and again, accompanied by Uncle Hilborne. They were getting desperate; even the rich didn't have enough summer homes and spas and boats and carriages to combat the mucus-laden attacks against the boy.

"The spasms yielded," Theodore's mother, "Mittie," reported, "but [he] passed a wheezy miserable night and I have concluded to leave...for New York tomorrow, with the feeling that this last week Teedie has lost all he gained ... and the sulfur baths and water proved no good."[10] What Teddy needed was a good "bronchial inhaler," something people with asthma take for granted today, but there were no steroidal therapies at the time, just the quackery and guesswork that passed for medicine in the closing years of the nineteenth century. President James Garfield, for instance, would die from gunshot wounds, but not from the bullet itself—it was from the doctor's unwashed probe and then his finger inserted into the bullet hole. The doctor literally injected bacteria into Garfield's body; and even though some were beginning to believe in the radical theory of germs and the need for sterilizing instruments and washing hands, many did not.

So that left the coffee, the waters, the cigars, the chloroform for the desperate parents, until young Theodore's father had had enough. As Mittie later recalled, the patriarch called his son to him and cast the problem in such a way that it would change Theodore Roosevelt Jr. forever. "Theodore, you have the mind but you have not the body, and without the help of the body, the mind cannot go as far as it should."[11] He then gave Teddy his charge: "You must make your body. It is hard drudgery to make one's body, but I know you will do it."

And in this way the Roosevelts really stumbled upon the only cure that would work for the boy who, otherwise, could find no relief. Exercise would induce breathing, and this would open his lungs and develop his weak body. Teddy declared to his father that he would build up his body. Daily workouts began at once under Mr. John Wood, a sort of personal trainer for the Victorian rich, whose clients included Sloanes, Goelets, and Vanderbilts.

Mittie went with her son to the gymnasium while Teddy wrestled with a weight machine and hoisted free weights from the floor. He sweated and grunted and began the brick by brick process of trying to construct what God had left out of his build. It was drudgery punching away at punching bags and working his body back and forth on horizontal bars—this at a time when exercise was seen as something almost eccentric, if not totally useless. It was clearly not for the upper caste of New York society.

But what other choice did a sickly boy have? Roosevelt began to work out on his own piazza after the equipment was set up. His sisters watched their skinny brother huffing and puffing, trying to get his body to swing between the parallel bars and mostly not succeeding. He was the invalid child who was forever being taken for carriage rides or to the shore or enduring cigars or coffee or spending days in bed with doctors huddled around him. Now he was out of doors and swinging back and forth.

Teddy was intent on self-realization as he struggled to bring muscle to arms that had none. He was underweight and undersized, and one could imagine doctors thinking at times that he would never reach adult-hood. People much healthier died habitually in the 1870s, and here was this severe asthmatic with spindly legs struggling to do what another boy his age could do with ease.

In Maine, a confrontation took place when Teddy was bullied by two boys. He tried to defend himself and was beaten. It shocked him that when he fought back they could "handle me so as to not hurt me too much and yet...prevent my doing any damage whatever in return."[12] In other words, he was so weak his attackers didn't even take his resistance seriously. Worse, they might have felt sorry for the sickly boy.

So he continued with his weights and his punching bags and his parallel bars, all the while creating a secret world of action through his reading: David Livingstone's *Missionary Travels and Researches in South Africa*, and *Robinson Crusoe*, and the adventures of Captain Mayne Reid whose heroes went West in search of adventure. Reid was an Irish-man who had exchanged the soft life of a tutor for that of a trapper and trader out on the frontier. His books, *The Scalp Hunters*, *The Hunter's Feast*, and *The Boy Hunters*, were adventure stories set beyond the Mississippi in the unexplored regions of the West.

The Scalp Hunters begins, "Unroll the world's map and look upon the great northern continent of America. Away to the wild West—away towards the setting sun—away beyond many a far meridian.... You are looking upon a land...still bearing the marks of the Almighty mold, as upon the morning of creation. A region, whose every object wears the impress of God's magic. His ambient spirit lives in the silent grandeur of its mountains, and speaks in the roar of its mighty rivers. A region redo-lent of romance—rich in the reality of adventure."[13]

Teddy Roosevelt longed for Reid's world, where a boy could remake himself and become a strong adventurer. The West was transformative in Reid's stories, and the asthmatic boy, who had been killing himself with weights and punching bags, would sit dreaming in a big chair or on a wicker sofa on the porch and travel in his mind to places his body could not go.

"What with the wild gallops by day, and the wilder tales by the night watch fires, I became intoxicated with the romance of my new life.... My strength increased both physically and intellectually. I experienced a buoyancy of spirits and vigor of body I had never known before. I felt a pleasure in action. My blood seemed to rush warmer and swifter through my veins.... "[14] So says one of Reid's characters, and the sickly boy in New York was swept up with visions of the Wild West, the place where all things are possible. And then in 1872, as he galloped through the West in his mind, Teddy Roosevelt received a gun and a pair of spectacles. The twelve-gauge rifle from his father was a double-barreled, French-made shotgun with a big kick. With his new spectacles, the boy who could not see beyond thirty feet found the world opening up. "I had no idea how beautiful the world was.... I could not see, and yet was wholly ignorant that I was not seeing."[15] He would never be without his glasses from then on, through war and peace and to death. And now he had a gun that brought down every bird he pointed the double-barreled buckshot toward, and the world of the hunter came to the boy.

Roosevelt was now thirteen and was steadily building himself up with one eye toward the West. The old warrior, Indian Red Cloud, was in a parade in the middle of Manhattan. He passed the boy and then passed into history. Teddy Roosevelt would eventually find himself in the sacred lands that the old Indian had lost.

3

THE DAY THE LIGHT WENT OUT

1884

Theodore Roosevelt clutched the two telegrams, shifting uncomfortably in the train—leaning forward, tapping his foot, trying to hurry on the frustratingly slow steam engine. Roosevelt was a man with a beautiful wife, a new baby, a brilliant political career, and the patronage and wealth of an aristocratic family behind him. Now, all this seemed in danger. The young assemblyman from Albany was making his way 145 miles south to Manhattan, where his wife and his mother both lay dying.

On a clear day the train ride from Albany to Manhattan took five hours, but a heavy fog had been hovering over New York for days, seeming to portend what lay ahead for him. Teddy Roosevelt tapped his foot impatiently and stared at the first telegram. *You have a baby girl. Congratulations.* The second telegram told a much different story. *Come at once. Mother and Alice gravely ill.* The light went out for Roosevelt that day as he ran for the train. The man who valued action above all else could now do nothing but wait to be delivered to destiny.

Roosevelt stared out the window. The fog reminded him of when he was a boy and he would sleep sitting straight up because his asthma squeezed his small chest. On such nights, his father would take him out in his carriage. They would ride like the wind through the streets of New York.

"Open your mouth Teddy! Open your mouth!" his father instructed. "Let the air in!"

And, as in a primitive oxygen ventilator, he would open his mouth and feel the cool air go down his throat and inflate his lungs. The image of a man frantically driving a black, rain-slicked carriage through the night streets of New York, and a boy hanging off the side with his mouth open to the heavens—it was all his father could do, after walking up and down the hallway with him all night. The rich man's son could get no air, and his father could only admonish the boy to open his mouth while he sped the horses savagely along.

"Faster! Faster! For my son must breathe!"

Now the train was pulling into Grand Central Station. The young dandy ran for his home in a fog so thick he could only grope his way toward 57th Street, where the lordly Roosevelt mansion commanded the street. Finally, he ran up the stairs to where his young wife, Alice, lay in bed. She was dying of Bright's disease, an affliction of the kidneys causing fever, vomiting, terrible back pain, and bloody urine. They had just married three and a half years before, but now the love of his life was dying in his arms.

They had recited poetry and written love letters to each other. Alice Hathaway Lee was the young beauty of a prominent Boston family who had fallen in love with the man with thick glasses and teeth that snapped words in half. Alice was just seventeen when Theodore first saw her on October 18, 1878. "As long as I live I shall never forget how sweetly she looked and how prettily she greeted me."[1] Roosevelt was smitten. He had found his true love and often walked the six miles from Harvard to Chestnut Hill to see her. His grades fell as he courted her with rides in the woods and long days spent reciting poetry. He asked her to marry him his junior year, and after an arduous courtship he won her. Now...now, incredibly, she was leaving him.

Roosevelt hit his knees and held his wife. Bright's disease, combined with complications from childbirth, was robbing the world of Alice Lee, and in the late nineteenth century there was little anyone could do. The fog outside the windows was so heavy it was as if the world was cloaked in a thick blanket.

"What can I do for you my love?"

"Teddy..." She was very weak by now. "Teddy."

The long labor had robbed her of any fight, and Roosevelt saw clearly she was moribund. At that precise moment, he heard a voice from outside the room—it belonged to his brother Elliott.

"Teddy. Come at once if you want to see mother one last time."

It was Elliott who had declared, on realizing his mother and sister-in-law were dying on the same day, "There is a curse on this house."[2] It was the same house in which he had helplessly watched his father writhe in agony from stomach cancer years before. The same sense of helplessness possessed the two brothers now. Men of action could do nothing against the primitive state of medical science.

Roosevelt reluctantly left his barely conscious wife and rushed downstairs to see his mother. Mittie Roosevelt was dying of typhoid fever. There were no antibiotics, and one in ten people died from complications stemming from the symptoms of 104-degree fever and chronic diarrhea. At age forty-eight, Mittie was still a Southern beauty with a cream-white complexion and dark glossy hair. She barely recognized Teddy as he kneeled down and held her hand. Even now, he could scarcely believe that just seven hours earlier he had been leading a reform movement in the halls of Albany, a young crusader with a brilliant political future and a wife and new baby.

Kneeling there, in his suit pants with dirty cuffs and hair tousled from the humidity and six hours on the train, Roosevelt felt at a complete loss. Could this be his mother, whom he so depended on? And could that really be his wife, who lit up his world in a way he never thought possible? Could she really be leaving him in this dark, fog-soaked world to forge ahead by himself? Why, he had a daughter! But where was she? How would he raise her? No answers came—Theodore Roosevelt simply couldn't think anymore as he ran back and forth between two dying women in the hell of that long night.

At three o'clock in the morning, his mother, Martha Stewart "Mittie" Roosevelt, died. The fog didn't lift. Roosevelt then devoted himself to holding his semi-comatose wife and willing her back to health. *Will. Will. Will.* This was his mantra. He had beaten back death with will. He had pushed through life as a sickly child with will and she must do the same. But Alice Lee wasn't her husband and barely clung to life through the morning. The fog lifted briefly; then the rain came, followed by the sun—then clear cool air poured down from the northeast. Roosevelt cradled Alice Lee and refused to give up hope. It was for naught.

At two o'clock in the afternoon on February 14, 1884, Alice Hathaway Lee, the mother of his first child, died. Teddy Roosevelt had lost the second light of his life and could see only darkness. He stumbled through the funeral. Some said he was like a child now, and they worried about his sanity. He seemed dazed and unable to think. He gave his newborn daughter to his sister, and when the last funeral had passed, Roosevelt headed back to Albany to throw himself into his work as the reforming politician. "I have never believed it did any good to flinch or yield for any blow," he later wrote. "Nor does it lighten the pain to cease from working. ... Indeed I think I should go mad if I were not employed."[3]

Roosevelt had always been an insomniac, and now he slept even less. He had taken on the corrupt bosses of Tammany Hall, but this blow made that look like nothing. He didn't sleep. People heard him pacing back and forth. No one was allowed to mention his wife or mother. People worried he might just collapse or have a nervous breakdown.

Roosevelt didn't collapse, but his political career did. He literally worked around the clock as an assemblyman and as chairman of the city investigating committee. He split his time between New York and Albany, rewriting a fifteen-thousand-word Investigative Report on corruption during hearings in Albany. "He feels the awful loneliness more and more," his sister Corinne wrote to his brother Elliott, "and I fear he sleeps little, for he walks a great deal in the night."[4] Roosevelt introduced nine bills related to his findings and submitted two more reports of a million words of testimony. He was a man running from himself as he headed to the Republican National Convention in Chicago.

As if to actualize his feeling of isolation from the world, he joined the Mugwump faction of his own party against the nominee James G. Blaine. Roosevelt's candidate, George F. Edmunds, lost to Blaine, and Roosevelt was seen as a traitor. When all was lost and the Stop Blaine movement collapsed, the Mugwumps then swung around to support Grover Cleveland, the Democratic Nominee, and demanded Roosevelt join them. Roosevelt equivocated and considered abandoning the Republican Party. He further alienated Republicans by telling a reporter from the *Evening Post* that rather than vote for Blaine he would give "hearty support to any decent Democrat."

After the reform movement was handed a resounding defeat, Roosevelt found no more interest in politics, or anything else for that matter. He was going one place and one place only. He was going to the South Dakota Territory—that unsettled swath of country where Indians roamed and men with six-shooters settled scores. In a letter to the editor of the *Utica Herald*, he confessed his weariness with politics, if not life, and his ambivalence about his future:

> I wish to write you a few words just to thank you for your kindness towards me. ... Although not a very old man, I have yet lived a great deal in my life, and I have known sorrow too bitter and joy too keen to allow me to become either cast down or elated for more than a brief period. ... I have very little expectation of being able to keep on in politics. ... I feel both tired and restless; for the next few months I shall probably be in Dakota ... [5]

In the year 1884, four months after Theodore Roosevelt's wife and mother died, there was still a Wild West; and though it would end soon, there was yet room for one more man who had lost everything. Roosevelt boarded a train in the middle of the night. The engine chugged out of the station as he stared out at the fading lights of the East. He didn't hurry the train along this time. He was leaving and heading into the unknown darkness. His last words to a *World* reporter were that he was heading West and "what I shall do after that I cannot tell you."[6]

The twenty-four-hundred-mile journey took him first to Chicago, where he switched to the St. Paul Express, which then plunged into the great flat plains of the American Midwest. When he crossed the Red River at Fargo and slipped past the Western Boundary of the United States, Teddy Roosevelt knew he had reached the vast Dakota Territory.

Roosevelt stared out into the flat darkness and saw the moon glimmering on the Missouri River as the train clattered over the trestle. He sat back in the train car, heading for the one place he could be alone. Life had divested itself of him and now he would divest himself of life. He stared into the darkness hiding the geological formations of cliffs, ravines, and buttes, volcanic fire still smoldering up from the rocks. Hell was outside the window as he slept and traveled farther into the last bit of land not claimed by men. He dreamed of the first time he had taken the journey. It was much like this, and just a year before.

4

THE FIRST TIME WEST
1883

Commander Gorringe had decided at the last minute not to go, and this left Teddy Roosevelt to hunt buffalo alone. Gorringe was an entrepreneur who oversaw a grand hunting lodge in the Badlands, playing to New York's upper crust. So far he had only one client; and that twenty-six year old had boarded the train out of New York alone. When he switched to the St. Paul Express for the twenty-four-hundred-mile journey, Roosevelt wired his mother, Mittie, that he felt "like a fighting cock again"[1] as he left the United States for the Dakota Territory for the first time. The darkness masked the geological malformations of the Badlands passing by his window, with its glowing lignite fires and ancient waters that had carved stone, blasted gullies, and formed rivers.

Then Roosevelt was blinking in the darkness of two a.m. after the warmth of the Pullman car—a dapper young man who stepped off the train directly into the wet sagebrush of Little Missouri in the Dakota Territory. The train rolled away, leaving white smoke and the train whistle's lament. Roosevelt breathed heavily, his asthmatic wheeze not unlike the huffing steam locomotive fading into the night. His new boots were stiff, his hat tight, his collar itchy. The new clothes he had bought in New York felt all wrong, but they were the latest in Western outdoor apparel. There was no sound save for the yips of coyotes out in the darkness beyond the town.

The town wasn't much. Little Missouri had come of age rapidly when the railroad arrived and would die just as quickly. Such was the boom and bust of railroad towns in the West. Roosevelt stared at a dilapidated sign reading "PYRAMID PARK HOTEL," behind which slouched a recently painted white structure leaning toward the street. Roosevelt hoisted his Sharps rifle and duffel bag and began to walk in the cool darkness. A coyote howled in the distance again; then he heard the thin musical note of running water. Roosevelt saw moonlight glimmering on the Little Missouri River, whose waters whispered softly in the night. The train had since faded into the darkness, heading for the heart of the Badlands. Teddy Roosevelt was in the middle of nowhere with a recommendation to see a man who might be able to help him.

If someone had asked him why he had gone West when he was about to marry, he would have replied he had come to shoot buffalo and see if the myth of the Wild West still existed. What was the Wild West this well-to-do man hoped to find? Was it the Wild West of dime novels and legend? Were the Indians still out there? Geronimo? Sitting Bull? Custer was dead, but his legend lived on. The railroad ran to the coast now, yet the legends still lived in a young man brought up to embrace the "vigorous life," which seemed to demand going to the last great frontier.

For now, it was still the Wild West, open to anyone who had the guts and some money to lay claim to the land. But time was running out fast. By 1889, North Dakota and South Dakota would be admitted as the thirty-ninth and fortieth U.S. states. Montana and Washington would soon follow. More significantly, in 1890, the U.S. Census said they would no longer track Westward Expansion by moving the line and declaring how much territory had been "claimed" from the wilderness. The fact was there was no more claiming to be done; the West had filled and the frontier was essentially closed.

But Roosevelt had squeaked in. The period of the Wild West dated from the Louisiana Purchase in 1803, and was officially over in 1890, a period of less than ninety years. Interrupted by the Civil War, the real settling of the West took place between the years 1865 and 1890. In 1881, two years before Roosevelt first descended into the sagebrush, Billy the Kid had been gunned down and the gunfight at the OK Corral had taken place. Then in 1882 yet another notorious outlaw met his demise when Jesse James was murdered by Bob Ford. Things were settling down, although the Apache renegade Geronimo was still out there and would not surrender until 1886. Indians and settlers were still fighting it out, with massacres and murders on both sides. And in 1883, a man could still go into the Dakota Territory and find buffalo if he had a guide.

Roosevelt continued through the sandy sage to the porch where the words "Pyramid Park Hotel" were hammered to the door. He knocked politely and adjusted his glasses, looking around the deserted town—if the assortment of buildings could even be called that. A saloon next to the hotel called *Big-Mouthed Bob's Bug-Juice Dispensary* was quiet and dark, and on the other side of the railroad was a store and some shacks; a graveyard glowed white and high in the moonlight on the aptly named Graveyard Butte.

Roosevelt began to turn away when the door was swung back by a whiskery old man. Frank Vine stared at the bespectacled "dude" who looked like he had just come from New York City.

"What in the hell do yer want?" he growled.

"My name is Theodore Roosevelt. Commander Gorringe recommended I speak to you about shooting buffalo."

The man he was facing stared at him and spat. Vine scratched his cheek and squinted at the man in the thick glasses and new clothes. Gorringe had bought property and owned an abandoned army cantonment along the banks of the river. Always open to an opportunity, Vine figured this was a man who had money, and that was enough to give this "dude" some consideration.

"He did, did he? ... Then come on," he grumbled. "You can sleep in the bullpen tonight."

"Well, that's just fine," Roosevelt replied.

Roosevelt followed the swinging suspenders hanging from both sides of the man's legs. They mounted wooden stairs, boots clunking in the night. Gruffly, he guided the young man upstairs where men were bunked in a large room of cots with blankets. It was a "bullpen" of snoring cowboys and drunks and traveling souls. Here was the myth of the West—a roomful of cowboys bunked down for the night. One can only imagine that Roosevelt was beginning to see reality and myth becoming one. He was, after all, the pampered son of a rich New York aristocrat, and here was adventure coming alive.

The man rubbed his leathery, whiskered cheek and spat in the corner. Body odor, must, alcohol, and tobacco offended and stimulated Roosevelt's senses.

"Two bits and that cot there is yours."

Roosevelt swung down his duffel bag and took out his wallet.

"Bully!"

Vine stared and took the money. "Strange accent," he muttered. The man's labored breathing was heavy and he sure was skinny—looked like the wind might blow him over any minute. Still, two bits was two bits, and Vine descended the stairs with his footsteps receding. Roosevelt listened for a moment to the men snoring. The coyotes howled wildly outside the open window. A door creaked. Nothing. Just the long silence of the still moment. Roosevelt fell onto the cot, which, after the train, felt like heaven. He looked up at the rafters and breathed in the cool, foreign air scented with the dust of the Badlands. He took off his glasses and excitedly thought of buffalo and the vast darkness outside—he thought of the Unconquered West. Myth and reality blended once more in his mind until there was no telling where one left off and the other began.

"By God...By God..." he murmured.

He fell heavily asleep.

Brilliant sunshine greeted him upon waking, and Roosevelt found himself in one of those dime novels—hay, sawdust, coffee, cigar smoke, dung. Roosevelt heard the call to breakfast downstairs and the stampede of men hurriedly washing up, drinking coffee, and eating eggs and flap-jacks. In the daylight, he took in the town again and saw the saloon, *Big-Mouthed Bob's Bug-Juice Dispensary*, then the same shabby bungalows; and then the white crosses in Graveyard Butte—the result of the carnage that was Little Missouri in 1883. The denizens called it "Little Misery"—but to Roosevelt, it was the perfect Wild West town. The railroad rated it one of the roughest on the line with the nearest sheriff 150 miles to the east and the nearest U.S. Marshal 200 miles to the south. Men were on their own to settle scores with Colt revolvers, Winchesters, fists, knives, arrows, pipes, bricks; and like the future ghost towns, they did not expect to live long.

Just the day before, the "Golden Spike Special" had come through with ex-president General Grant aboard. As he whisked through the depot with his stovepipe hat, people strove to catch sight of the man who had won the Civil War. He was headed toward an event in Montana celebrating the completion of the Northern Pacific Railroad Corridor. The country had just been stitched together, but the threads were weak and snapped in the violent places. Teddy Roosevelt was a man with one foot in the past, in the Wild West town of sixty souls called Little Missouri, and one in the present, three thousand miles to the east in New York.

Frank Vine suggested a man named Joe Ferris as a guide to hunt buffalo. In reality, there weren't a lot of buffalo left in 1883. The mythology pushed by newspapers back East, and by men like Gorringe, suggested the West was teeming with these animals. But the government had encouraged the Sioux to slaughter buffalo, and recently five thousand had vanished on the east side of the Badlands. Kill the buffalo and you kill the nomadic Indians was the rationale of the United States government. There were so many rotting, hideless carcasses left cooking under the Badlands sun, it seemed impossible there could be any buffalo left. The telegraph companies had joined in the slaughter when they realized buffalo like to rub against the telegraph poles to relieve their fly-infested hides. The poles eventually fell. So now there was the government, the Indians, and the telegraph companies shooting buffalo as fast as they could.

Teddy Roosevelt wanted just one, for the coveted head he pictured mounted and hanging in the brownstone he bought for him and his new bride Alice Lee, but the trick was to find that elusive lone buffalo. He needed a man who could find the creature, and Joe Ferris was such a man. Frank Vine took Roosevelt to the general store he ran in Little Missouri. It was a dim, dusty, coarse-planked establishment of nails, barrels of whiskey, ammo, implements, and one tobacco-chewing Joe Ferris.

Ferris was short, Canadian, and built like a bull dog, with a drooping cowboy mustache that hid a tight-lipped mouth. He was the same age as Roosevelt, but he didn't take to the man with glasses and the strange nasally accent. Joe had worked for the railroad, had logged, and now was guiding a succession of hunters toward buffalo. The man imploring him to find a buffalo seemed like a dude from New York, just another rich man come to claim and bring home his part of the Western myth in the form of a buffalo head. But the dude had money, if nothing else, and Ferris agreed to help him find his buffalo. Ferris and Vine decided a good base camp for the hunt in the Badlands would be the cabin of the Scotsman, Gregor Lang, on the Cannonball Creek fifty miles up the river.

They loaded up a buckboard with provisions, and then Roosevelt and Ferris rolled out of town following the railroad to the north, with the trestle casting a long shadow in the setting sun. Ferris spat tobacco juice and said little, the reins held loosely in his hands, as Roosevelt stared into the primeval landscape of buttes and gullies that amazed him. He saw nothing less than God's Creation in Genesis, in the wide sky and the slanting silhouettes. He found it "hardly proper to belong to this earth," and felt once again the exhilaration of being away from New York in the land of myths, the *Badlands*.

To French trappers the area had been simply *les mauvaises terres à traverser* or "bad lands to travel through." David McCullough writes in *Mornings on Horseback*, "It was as if the rolling prairie land suddenly gave way to a weird otherworld of bizarrely shaped cliffs and hummocks and tablelands, these sectioned and sliced every which way by countless little ravines and draws and by the broad looping valley of the Little

Missouri River. ... a kind of Grand Canyon in miniature, the work of millions of years of erosion on ancient preglacial sediments. Stratified layers of clay, clays as pale as beach sand, were juxtaposed against brick-red bands of scoria or sinuous dark seams of lignite. Some formations had the overpowering presence of ancient ruins."[2]

The captain of a force fighting the Sioux called it "hell with the fires out" but actually the fires were still lit in some places with lignite smoldering and burning. Many a hapless cowboy saw it as hell on earth, and there were bones of men to prove it, poor souls who had frozen or been killed by 140-degree heat. George Custer was blunter in his assessment calling it "worthless country," and Frederick Remington would later say it is a "place for stratagem and murder."

But to Teddy Roosevelt it was pure adventure. The only problem was he had brought a Sharps rifle with a faulty hammer and a Winchester. Ferris knew the Winchester could do nothing against a charging buffalo and stopped at the bungalow of gunman Eldridge "Jerry" Paddock, who had dispatched a few strangers and become the right-hand man of another rich man looking for fortune if not adventure in the West: Antoine-Amédée Marie-Vincent Amat Manca de Vallombrosa, Marqui de Morès et de Montemaggiore. Marquis De Mores...or simply, "the Marquis," which later became, "that son of bitch of a Marquis."

Roosevelt may have even passed the well-dressed, mustache-waxed Marquis, who looked like a modern-day movie star and who declared upon arrival, "I am weary of civilization." A man of considerable wealth and distinguished lineage, the Marquis had come out from France to corner the cattle market and had already employed Paddock as his enforcer for people who got in the way of his establishing a cattle empire. The two dudes might have recognized the same qualities of good family and thirst for adventure, but they would meet later and not under good circumstances.

But for now, only the buffalo mattered. The Badlands truly amazed Roosevelt. Here was a part of the country with extreme temperatures ranging from 116 to -40; there were skulls, giant rock formations, crevices, ravines, cliffs, baking slopes still smoldering from ancient fires. The extremes of the Badlands would mirror the extremes of Roosevelt's own life—a sickly young man who remade himself into a man of action. There was no sign of human life among the geologic contortions brought about by fire and water colliding over thousands of years, except for a lone log cabin in the distance.

They passed the settler's log house, the Custer Trail Ranch; so named for the immortal Custer who had camped there in 1876. Then they came to a small log cabin in a valley. Joe told him this was the Maltese Cross ranch that belonged to Bill Merrifield and Joe's brother, Sylvane Ferris. They tied up the buck wagon and then walked to the rough-cut cabin. Roosevelt looked out from the porch and noticed the underground lignite fires glowing in the early darkness of the Badlands. The crescent moon pearled the early evening blue of the Western sky with a few cold stars. A coyote howled as Roosevelt breathed in the cooling, lung-expanding air—the ultimate tonic for an asthmatic.

"By God...By God," he muttered.

5

THE DUDE
1883

Sylvane Ferris stared at the dude from New York. Tough as tree bark, the Canadian had just begun to make a living with his partner Bill Merrifield out on the Dakota frontier. Now he had this skinny, wheezing man with a patrician accent and thick glasses who wanted to borrow a horse. This cabin was the last stop to get a horse, so Roosevelt stood there expectantly, watching the lignite fires burning. The bearded men stared at him suspiciously and shook their heads. No, they could not see their way clear to giving a horse to a man they didn't know.

Sylvane Ferris and Bill Merrifield had been hunting and trying to survive with their 150 head of cattle. They had ridden out on the free passage the railroad had given to emigrants. Merrifield had made money by shooting buffalo and selling the venison to the Northern Pacific at five cents a pound for their dining cars. Sylvane Ferris took out contracts to cut cordwood and drive mules. Merrifield once found himself thirsty and flagged an express train to take a drink of ice water from the dining car. The conductor was speechless, but Merrifield, with six-shooters bulging from his waist, just thanked him and rode off.

Sylvane and Merrifield then took to raising cattle for two Minnesota investors, buying more cattle of their own on credit. They were not unlike sharecroppers of the South and were paid a portion of the profit by absentee landowners. The small log cabin was not much of a ranch, but they could dream. They called their ranch the Chimney Butte, and everyone else called it the Maltese Cross after their brand. They were men who risked life and limb to come out West and dream, and here was another dreamer with his new clothes…what…come to hunt buffalo?

"No sir, we don't have no horse to sell you," Merrifield replied to the persistent man with the squeaky voice.

Teddy didn't want to ride across the West in a buckboard. It was bumpy and it didn't fit with the novels and the newspapers accounts and the myth of the West. Roosevelt had beaten back his asthma and graduated Harvard a rich man's son, but he was sickly in the era of muscular Christian men. His skinny frame, glasses, chronic asthma, and undiagnosed heart condition made him an unlikely cowboy. But he at least needed a horse.

TR's antidote would be simple: he would handle this the way he did his chronic illness as a young man—when through unremitting, strenuous activity beginning with weight training, boxing, rowing, and hiking, he put himself to the test against every physical challenge he could find. This had included a Grand Tour of Europe with his parents, which nearly put him under from asthmatic attacks, and a strenuous hunting trip in Maine. Teddy Roosevelt had begun to practice "his policy of forcing the spirit to ignore the weakness of the flesh."[1] Much later, he would spell out his credo and admitted his fears in the early days ranged "from grizzly bears to mean horses and gun fighters, but by acting *as if I was not afraid I gradually ceased to be afraid.*"[2]

So he was not about to cross the Badlands in a buckboard wagon, even though the two ranchers saw no reason to give "Four-Eyes" a horse. And there was something else, too: Roosevelt was very interested in ranching. He had actually invested five thousand dollars in a Cheyenne

Wyoming beef company years before. So the operation of a ranch was something in his blood, but Sylvane and Merrifield were close-lipped. They didn't know this "dude" from Adam, and after a game of Old Sledge failed to break the ice, the atmosphere in the cabin became smaller and more uncomfortable until squawks from the chicken house interrupted the silence. The four men jumped up. A bobcat had gotten into the hen house, and the men chased him out, and in the ensuing melee found themselves joking and talking.

But they still wouldn't give Roosevelt a horse.

"Then I will buy one from you," he said, taking out his wallet.

Sylvane and Merrifield shrugged. Money was money. Joe Ferris would later say, "By Gosh, he wanted that saddle horse so bad we were afraid to let him have it. Why we didn't know him from Job's off ox. We didn't know but what he'd ride away with it."[3] Roosevelt now had his horse, Nell, and what was really his first investment in the West. Now he could be mounted properly for his buffalo hunt. He had wanted to go West before it vanished for good. Bedding down on the dirt floor, he felt he was getting closer to the cowboy life. Roosevelt stared up at the rough cabin roof with its fire-shadowing, listening to the crackle of the logs. Outside were the howling coyotes and the lignite fires glowing in the distance.

A young assemblyman with a spectacular future, a new wife, and soon a new baby, and now a horse named Nell, lay awake with his glasses reflecting the dying light. Tomorrow he would go further into the Badlands to find buffalo. The night settled down with the moon beaming over the lone cabin. Wolves scampered and Indians prowled. The West waited for Teddy Roosevelt just outside the cabin door.

6

INTO THE BADLANDS
1883

They started south in the early morning, following a faint wagon trail; Teddy in front with his mare Nell and Joe behind in the buckboard like some old painting, just two men and two horses on a moonscape of rock and sky. Roosevelt was now flying high as he stared at the landscape Edmund Morris described so well in *The Rise of Theodore Roosevelt*: "The nearer buttes, facing the river, were slashed with layers of blue, yellow, and white. In the middle distance these tints blended into lavender, then the hills rippled paler and more transparent until they dissolved along the horizon, like overlapping lines of watercolor. Random splashes of bright red showed where burning coal seams had baked adjoining layers of color into porcelain smooth scoria."[1] A picture of the Badlands' geologic rawness, where fire and water have combusted and pushed up rock and plates of earth in volcanic convulsions—a match for the volatility of the slouched rider bucking along slowly. Puffs of smoke·flew up from the ground where the fires still raged below, and then there were the rivulets and ravines and rivers formed from the rains over thousands of years. It was a red, scoriaceous world of grooved impressions running across a terrain baked by blistering heat. This world of rude contradictions cracked loose Teddy's Victorian restrictions even as it cracked open his lungs. He could breathe! The dry air was a tonic. Health would follow. Did he know "the romance of his life" had begun? He probably did, as he stared at primitive rock formations and the unending horizon stretching to infinity.

To some it is hell. There are no trees; only the brutal sun beating down on clumps of dark juniper and wild flowers here and there. The twenty-first-century mind sees merely a moonscape of odd rock formations and baked land with little grass or vegetation. But few modern men have grown up with a vast open space where one could go to start over and become a new wished-for self. Perhaps a few people have been able to achieve this by moving from one coast to the other. But for nineteenth-century Americans their chance was the Wild West as it existed in myth and fact.

Roosevelt turned around with Nell's hooves kicking up puffs of sand.

"Do you think we will see Indians?"

Joe Ferris spit off to the side, holding the reins loosely, jerking his head.

"Might. Better hang on to your scalp."

Roosevelt turned back around.

"Bully!"

The Indians had fallen back in the Badlands, with incidents on both sides setting a new low for barbarity. Roosevelt, at this point, saw them as part of the mythology of the West, no less than the buffalo. Later, he would take a positive view of the indigenous people; but Joe Ferris could only shake his head. Best they didn't see Indians. Joe had taken other rich men on buffalo hunts, and Indians had complicated the hunt and could be downright dangerous. The truth was there just weren't that many buffalo left after the Sioux had slaughtered most of them on the plains; and the open cars of the Northern Pacific had proven such a wonderful platform from which people could shoot buffalo, leaving them to rot in the sun.

But here was this thick-spectacled New York dude who wanted a buffalo. Fine. They would find a buffalo or give up when the "dude" had had enough. Joe had found after a few days in the Badlands people started not to care so much about finding their buffalo. They wanted to get out of the sun or the rain or the wind or the biting cold and back to their nice, cozy lives.

And this dude would be no different, he was sure. Joe watched Roosevelt stare across the rocky moonscape broiling under the hundred-degree midday sun. It was as desolate as it gets; a land of brutal extremes with life hiding from the sun until nightfall, when the temperature would sink down and freeze the same men it had baked before. And here was this dude sitting on his horse, his face lit up with wonder.

"By Jove, this is beautiful!"

Ferris held the reins loosely. He had never heard anyone talk like this. What the hell was a *Jove?*

Roosevelt stared at the landscape and broke into a toothy grin.

"Egad! It's good to be out here!"

Joe stared at the greenhorn and shook his head. The man even breathed strangely and sounded like a steam engine. *Beautiful?* This rocky landscape? This hell born out of millions of years of convolutions of water and fire, with its curved canyons created by rivers and ancient lakes? *Yeah, the sun on the far buttes…and the wide blue sky, that was alright,* thought Joe, *but you sure forget about beauty in a hurry when you don't have nothin' to eat or drink for three days, or your fingers are frostbit, or you're so soaked from the rain that your underwear feels like it's floating.*

"Bully! Just Bully!"

Joe eyed the dude.

What in the hell was a bully?

But Joe didn't have time to wonder too long. There was no more wagon trail, just sandy weeds that gave no trace of anyone passing. They had already forded the Little Missouri River six times and would do it seventeen more times before they reached the Lang Cabin, which would serve as their base for hunting. But now they had to pull the buckboard out of a bog and then the quicksand, and then struggle up steep banks that could topple man and wagon.

By dusk, the shack by Little Cannonball Creek seemed a forlorn structure against the backdrop of empty desolation. But it was something. Inside waited the very first pioneer Teddy Roosevelt would meet. Gregor Lang, a Scotsman, was a stocky, blue-eyed, mutton-chopped, whiskered man with spectacles. He had named his sixteen-year-old son after the great emancipator, Lincoln, and he'd built himself a sod cabin, with cattle coming in from Minnesota and his wife on the way.

He had originally been hired to keep an eye on Commander Gorringe's Little Missouri Land and Stock Company, but Gregor saw a chance to make his own fortune in the Badlands of South Dakota. Building his cabin on the Little Cannonball Creek, he and his son Lincoln hacked out an existence and waited for Providence to shine upon them— or at least for their cattle to arrive. What arrived first were the Cokebottle glasses of Theodore Roosevelt. Gregor's son Lincoln spoke of him years later, "Aided by the beam of light showing through the cabin door, I could make out that he was a young man who wore large conspicuous-looking glasses, through which I was being regarded with interest by a pair of twinkling eyes. 'This is my son, Mr. Roosevelt,' [Father] said. Then somehow or other I found both my hands in the solid double grip of our guest. Heard him saying clearly but forcefully, in a manner conveying the instant impression that he meant what he said … 'Dee-lighted to meet you, Lincoln!'"[2]

Gregor Lang was a well-read and politically-minded man. The young reformer from Albany was *dee-lighted* to find a man his equal in appetite for intellectual discourse and polemics. They talked through the night, while Joe Ferris went to sleep and the rain began to patter on the sod. Teddy Roosevelt learned about cattle ranching and the view of a Scotsman whose dreams were commensurate with the sweep of the land outside. Lang felt he had found an equal in this young patrician from New York; they were both men with the future before them who saw only the bright shining objects and none of the darkness.

Maybe Roosevelt told the Scotsman of watching Abraham Lincoln's funeral procession from the window of his uncle's home in Manhattan when he was a boy. Or about his mother Mittie, the Southern belle, who married his father, a New Yorker, but never really fit in. Maybe he told him about her love for Southern duels and feuds and her fondness for novels of chivalry and romance and the tales she told young Theodore of "men who love the name of honor more than they fear death." Or her neurasthenia and invalidism that put her into rest cures, and her habit of dragging her sickly son along, which gave him a horror of the life of the invalid, committing him forever to action.

It was his father, Theodore Sr., who picked up the slack and gave the young boy a disdain for anyone who didn't do their part. It was his sickly disposition and his invalid mother and his father's muscular Christianity—"the only man of whom I was ever afraid"—which drove him into the arms of the strenuous life. They talked into the wee hours with Lincoln asleep by the fire. In the morning, Roosevelt woke to a hard, steady, roof-pounding rain, with Joe Ferris advising against going out.

"Nonsense. We are going hunting buffalo," Roosevelt declared, every bit the man funding the expedition.

Even the Langs warned of the slippery clay that would cause horses to fall and wagons to fail. Never mind. "He had come to get buffalo and buffalo he was going to get, in spite of hell or high water."[3] With the same grit and determination Roosevelt used when fighting to breathe and conquering his fears, he would face the Badlands. At six a.m. they mounted up and headed into the streaming rain to finally find a buffalo for the dude.

7

HUNTING BUFFALO
1883

Shooting buffalo in 1883 was problematic. In John Williams' classic novel *Butcher's Crossing*, a young man, Andrews, goes out to participate in a buffalo hunt before it is all over. He discovers the treachery of a land that forces him to spend a night in a buffalo or freeze, and the brutality of the buffalo hunter who mows down the standing creatures like corn before a scythe. Then after days in the saddle going after buffalo, they almost die from lack of water. "Andrew's hands clung to the saddle horn; they were so weak that again and again they slipped from it, and he hardly had the strength to pull them back. ... Sometime during the night he discovered that his mouth was open and he could not close it. ... He remembered the sight of the oxen's tongues, black and swollen and dry..."

Hunting for buffalo was strenuous and could be deadly. The land and weather were constant hazards that could turn against a hunter. The days of the great herds were long gone, when someone could shoot from a "stand" and pile up their buffalo pelts. Even shooting a buffalo from a horse was a challenge merely due to the fact that the old bull might charge. A buffalo could cover a mile in a minute and would stampede on the scent of something in the wind. Or the buffalo could disappear and were impossible to track in the type of rain that Roosevelt and Joe Ferris were setting off in.

Much of the Badlands is like a great clay bowl, the runoff a sticky, slick gumbo. The two hunters left Lang's at first light and made their way across the Little Missouri and then entered a land from another world. "It was a wild region, bleak and terrible, where fantastic devil-carvings reared themselves from the sallow gray of eroded slopes, and the only green things were gnarled cedars that looked as though they had been born in horror…"[1]

A man with glasses who had to continually wipe his lenses saw a buffalo in every butte and rock formation only to have it dissolve into the hazy, watery distance. But this was Teddy Roosevelt's adventure, and they would find their buffalo or go down trying. Joe Ferris couldn't believe it when TR put mud on his face like a Lakota Sioux preparing for battle. Finally, they saw a buck and the new cowboy fired and missed with the animal bounding away. He loved to hunt, but because of his myopic vision he would never become a great shot. Ferris finished the job with a one in a million shot, and Roosevelt turned in the rain and shook his head.

"By Godfrey! I'd give anything in the world if I could shoot like that!"[2]

Back to the ranch then at nightfall they went; wet, tired, hungry, and covered in clay. The two men dismounted their slimed, red horses. Gregor Lang saw only the toothy grin of the "dude" from New York coming out of the rainy darkness. Joe Ferris turned in early, counting the days until "the dude" returned to his soft life, so he could get out of the rain. He fell asleep as Lang and Roosevelt solved the world's problems by the crackling fire.

The next four days brought incessant rain. Joe Ferris hoped the man from New York would just roll over in his blankets and pull out one of his books. The hammering on the roof foretold of misery outside the door, and Joe kept looking for something to slow the dauntless spirit of the "dude." But they went out and returned at night as two men of the earth, squishing into the cabin slathered with gumbo mud from head to toe. Roosevelt just beamed. "Returning at night, after another day fruitless, all save misery, the grin was still there, being apparently built in and ineradicable."[3]

And every day Roosevelt insisted they go out and every night returned with the toothy grin. "He nearly killed poor Joe,"[4] Lincoln Lang would later reflect. What Lincoln Lang didn't understand was that Roosevelt was far from home. As Kathleen Dalton wrote in *A Strenuous Life*, "Theodore grew up encased in iron cages of Victorian thought about cultural evolution, overcivilization, race suicide, class, mob violence, manliness and womanliness. As a child and a teen he was incapable of bending open those iron cages. Asthma and invalidism already imprisoned him so tightly that he had to worry about staying alive."[5] Years later, in a different century, Lincoln Lang would sum up Roosevelt as "radio-active."[6]

To Teddy Roosevelt, this trudging out into the rain and returning at night tired and worn out from the hunt was just dandy. Besides, it couldn't rain forever, and the conversations at night with the Scotsman were very interesting indeed. Take this ranching, for instance. Now that was a vocation for a man, and from the sounds of it very profitable, too. Little did Roosevelt know that he was giving Lincoln Lang the education of his life, and he would later write about the Rooseveltian philosophy as "the up building of a colossal pyramid whose apex was the sky. The eternal stability of this pyramid would be insured only through honest, intelligent interworking and cooperation, to the common end of all the elements comprised in its structure. Individual elements might strive to build intensively and even high; but never well."[7]

The Little Cannonball had become a classroom for the boy, and the animated man pacing the cabin was instructing him in the Rooseveltian code; it made the boy wonder for the first time that maybe, "the Lord made the earth for all of us, and not for a chosen few."[8] Egalitarianism aside, the Roosevelt spectacles shined with a different kind of light, a vision really. "Mr. Lang," he began. "I am thinking seriously of going into the cattle business. Would you advise me to go into it?"[9]

The Scotsman sucked on his pipe and puffed smoke into the darkened cabin, pondering the question put to him by the man from the East; he then looked Roosevelt in the eye. "As a business proposition, it is the best there is."[10] The dude pondered this remark through the rainy days of hunting for the elusive buffalo who left no trail in the shifting mud. Joe Ferris had taken to collapsing into his bunk while Roosevelt held court and fed the fire. He did have energy, that four-eyed sum buck.

Then on the sixth day came sunshine and the fresh hoof-print of the buffalo. They took off in pursuit as the clay earth heated and immediately turned from gumbo to dust. Roosevelt later described how the tracks dwindled and they searched a ravine:

> …as we passed the mouth of a little side coulee, there was a plunge and crackle through the bushes at its head, and a shabby-looking old bull bison galloped out of it and, without an instant's hesitation, plunged over a steep bank into a patch of rotten, broken ground which led around the base of a high butte. So quickly did he disappear that we had not time to dismount and fire. Spurring our horses, we rode to the butte and rode around it, only to see the buffalo come out of the broken land and climb up the side of another butte over a quarter of a mile off. In spite of his great weight and cumbersome, heavy-looking gait, he climbed up the steep bluff with ease, even agility, and when he reached the ridge stood and looked back at us for a moment.[11]

Then the buffalo galloped off and led Roosevelt and Ferris on a chase for miles, but they never caught up with him—the adventure was just beginning. They had now entered the eastern prairie, which was barren and hot. The Badlands, while only toying with the hunters those first days, now brought the heat, literally. They ambled through the stifling heat of one hundred and five, and finally saw three specks off in the distance. No doubt Roosevelt finally saw his vison of the West...buffalo in the distance.

To Teddy Roosevelt's delight, they left their horses once they closed the distance, and began to crawl through the sagebrush. Teddy's hand ended up full of thorns as they snaked along the ground. Roosevelt was breathing like a bull, his mouth inches from the soft heat rising from the ground, when he drew up at 300 yards and fired at the nearest buffalo. The bullet slammed into the thick torso, but the shaggy creature, followed by the other two buffalo, galloped off. Ferris and Roosevelt jumped back on their horses in hot pursuit.

The buffalo had a considerable head start, and the heat and the pockmarked land had worn down their ponies. But by sunset they caught up with the old bulls, and Roosevelt could see he had wounded one. By now the moon was rising and they were all in the false light of the passing day. Teddy got within twenty feet of the buffalo, but because of the uneven terrain he couldn't get off a shot. He missed again and this time the bull had had enough. The hairy demon wheeled and charged Roosevelt under the moonlight.

Roosevelt raised his rifle and knew he better not miss. "My pony, frightened into momentary activity, spun around and tossed up his head. I was holding the rifle in both hands, and the pony's head, striking it, knocked it violently against my forehead, cutting quite a gash...heated as I was, the blood poured into my eyes."[12]

Ferris reined around him and galloping past shouting, "You alright?"

"Don't mind me," Roosevelt shouted back. "I'm alright."

The bull took off after Joe Ferris, and like a Keystone comedy it took to the chase with its head just inches from the tail of Ferris's horse. Roosevelt tried to assist. "I tried to run in on him again, but my pony stopped dead short, dead beat, and by no spurring could I force him out of a slow trot."[13] But Joe Ferris had other ideas. He swung off his horse and on the run fired twice on the bull but missed in the moonlight, and the bull galloped off again, leaving the two men in the darkness.

They were too far out to return to Lang's and really didn't quite know where they were, as the hunt had taken them a long way from the Little Cannonball. Roosevelt, still bleeding, grinned in the night.

"Bully! Bully! Bully!" One can almost hear him now. "What a ride! What a show!"

Teddy Roosevelt was in the middle of the Badlands, in the middle of the myth of the Wild West, and there was no turning back. They needed water, for they had had nothing to drink for nine hours, and the best they could find was a slimy mud hole from which neither horse nor man could take more than a mouthful. There was nothing to do then but bed down for the night.

They camped under the pinwheel sky of stars. They each ate a horn-hard biscuit and went to bed thirsty. Ferris didn't like this. They were in bandit country, in danger of horse thieves—both Indian and white. No wood to make a fire and nothing to drink. They pulled off their saddles and made lariats out of their ropes, looping one end over the saddle horn and tethering their horses with the other. The saddle was their pillow under the blankets on the hard ground. Roosevelt grinned up at the night sky as he listened to the horse shuffling nervously, as there were coyotes and bobcats; and for Ferris and Roosevelt, there were men who would do them harm.

As Roosevelt later wrote, "Wild beasts or some such thing were about…we knew we were in the domain of both white and red horse thieves, and that the latter might, in addition to our horses, try to take our scalps."[14] And here again William Andrews, the protagonist of *Butcher's Crossing*, comes to mind. His buffalo hunt occurred in 1873, and William, like Teddy, was in his twenties and from the East. He felt a change coming over him when he entered the West—the same transformation that happened to Roosevelt as he slept under the stars. "Day by day he felt the skin of his face hardening in the weather, the stubble of hair on the lower part of his face became smooth as his skin roughened, and the backs of his hands reddened and then browned and darkened in the sun. He felt a leanness and a hardness creep upon his body; he thought at times he was moving into a new body."

They slept with their guns ready. The terror came at midnight when their saddles were pulled from under their heads. The two hunters had just drifted off, and then they were springing up with guns drawn as their horses galloped away in a white tornado of dust, dragging the saddles along.

"Maybe a wolf," Ferris muttered, gesturing to a shadow-figure in the distance.

Then the long walk across the sandy, rocky landscape, following the trail of their saddles in the moonlight. Roosevelt marveled that just weeks before he had been in Albany voting on reform measures, and now he was in the middle of the Badlands, in the middle of the night, chasing down his horse like in some cowboy novel with Indians and bad men about.

Joe Ferris turned to Roosevelt.

"Say, I ain't never committed any crime deserving that anything like this should happen." He turned. "Have you ever done anything to deserve this?"

"Joe," Roosevelt answered, "I never have."[15]

They followed the long path of their dragged saddles and finally retrieved their horses and returned to their meager camp. Then a cold rain began to fall. They woke soaked to the bone, their blankets heavy, sodden creatures pushing down on them. Joe Ferris shook his head and wondered when the benighted buffalo hunt would end, and then he heard Teddy Roosevelt, who lay soaked on the ground with his rain-spattered spectacles facing up toward the early dawn, "By Godfrey, but this is fun!"[16]

The fun had just begun. Ferris and Roosevelt mounted up at dawn, after some cold biscuits, and using a compass headed back in the direction of the Lang cabin. And then the buffalo appeared again in the distance. It was chilly now with light drizzle, and Roosevelt's glasses were stippled with rain. Once again they crept forward for a shot, and Teddy felt he would get one this time. He rose up and fired and the band of buffalo took this as a warning and galloped away again.

"It was one of those misses a man regrets until his dying day," Roosevelt would write much later.[17] On cue, the rain came back and continued all day and tortured man and horse through another night. The sun did return, but their prospects for buffalo didn't brighten.

"Bad luck followed us," Joe Ferris remarked, "like a yellow dog follows a drunkard."[18] Then Joe's horse nearly stepped on a rattlesnake, and Nell stepped into a hole and sent Roosevelt into a cartwheel. He had just remounted when Nell found a trap of quicksand and the earth left beneath her. They pulled the horse out with a lariat and continued on. Joe had figured any minute the dude would throw in the towel and catch the next train east in Little Missouri. But he was wrong.

"He could stand an awful lot of hard knocks and he was always cheerful. You just couldn't knock him out of sorts."[19] They finally returned to Lang's, and that night Roosevelt told Joe that a doctor out East had told him he didn't have much longer to live and that any kind of strenuous exercise would kill him.

"See you bright and early in the morning," Roosevelt sang out then.

Joe Ferris wondered if the tenderfoot wasn't just a little crazy.

8

CATTLE RANCHER
1883

In the small cabin in the flickering firelight, Teddy Roosevelt declared his intentions. "I have definitely decided to invest, Mr. Lang. Will you take a herd of cattle from me to run on shares or under some other arrangement to be determined between us?"[1] Gregor Lang could hardly believe a man could just make a decision like this. In his world, men did not just proclaim they wanted to start a cattle ranch and offer to make him partner. But he was already committed to another man for his investment in cattle.

"I am more than sorry Mr. Roosevelt,"[2] he said, with real regret.

But Roosevelt had decided that he was going to do this thing one way or another. One can only guess at the changing tides of his mind. He had become an assemblyman after studying for law had lost its flavor, and he had briefly considered the "literary life." Ranching was something he could do that would tie him permanently to the West. The truth was Roosevelt, along with a Harvard classmate, had already put money into a ranch north of Cheyenne, the Teschmaker and

Debillion Cattle Company. The Badlands had been recently discovered as prime cattle country, resulting in a bit of a stock market frenzy to investing in the West. Add to this the short-lived cowboy culture based on the frontier and driving cattle, with its emphasis on mobility, custom, and survival of the fittest, and there was an ideal realm for a young man craving adventure and the tonic of rude existence. Texas Grangers had started driving toward the Dakota territories in 1883 when they found the cattle loved northern-range grasses and realized cattle could survive the blue winters. The cowboys followed and now Roosevelt was one of those cowboys looking for his piece of the cattle empire.

He adjusted his glasses and clapped his teeth together.

"Then who could you recommend?"

Lang stroked his beard.

"About the best men I can recommend are Sylvane Ferris and Bill Merrifield. I know them quite well, and I believe them to be good square fellows who will do right by you if you give them a chance."

Roosevelt nodded.

"Done!"

Young Lincoln saddled up and went to fetch the two Canadians to the cabin to meet their potential new boss. Roosevelt had come into his money recently and was building a house for his young bride, preparing for his future life. So why not add a ranch to that life? He and Joe headed out on two more rainy days, and Ferris had by now taken a liking to the tough, skinny man with the oversized glasses. On the evening of September 18, Sylvane and Ferris were waiting for Roosevelt in the cabin when he came in from another unsuccessful hunt. They went outside to talk business. Roosevelt sat down on a log and asked how much it would take to stock a cattle ranch.

"Depends what you want to do, but my guess is, if you want to do it right, it'll spoil the looks of forty thousand dollars," Sylvane replied.[3]

Roosevelt pushed up his glasses.

"Bully. How much would you need right off?"

"Oh…a third would make a start."

Roosevelt nodded again.

"Can you boys handle the cattle for me?"

Sylvane and Merrifield exchanged glances and then Sylvane nodded.

"Why yes, I guess we could take care of 'em, bout as well as the next man."

Merrifield then piped up.

"Why, I guess so."

Roosevelt nodded to the men.

"Well, will you do it?"

Sylvane then explained he and Merrifield were committed to another outfit with cattle on shares.

Roosevelt brushed it aside.

"I will buy those cattle."

Merrifield and Sylvane looked at each other.

"Alright. Then the best thing for us to do is go to Minnesota and get released from our contract," Merrifield replied.

"Bully! How much do you need to get started?"

Merrifield rubbed his chin.

"About 14,000 dollars should do her."

Teddy Roosevelt then withdrew his checkbook from a leather pouch and wrote a check for fourteen thousand dollars. They were sitting on a log outside the cabin and Merrifield took the check. Fourteen thousand dollars in today's money is over two hundred thousand dollars.

Merrifield eyed Roosevelt.

"Don't you want a receipt?"

Roosevelt shook his head.

"Oh, that's alright."

People in 1883 didn't just casually write checks for fourteen thousand dollars outside of cabins in the Badlands. Roosevelt had inherited 125,000 dollars from his father, but he was not a good businessman and didn't really understand how to make money. He had made dubious investments before, but it wasn't the prospect of a great investment that motivated Theodore Roosevelt to write a check to men he had just met for an enterprise he knew nothing about. It was buying a piece of the West that appealed to him.

Already he knew there was something out in the rain-soaked Badlands that grabbed his spirit, something in the extremes of the lawless
West he needed in order to make himself. And yet he had no idea what
providence had in store for him; he was simply possessed with creating
a life in the West and not losing another day. Roosevelt would become
a rancher; he would add that to the role of politician, a role he had
recently adopted after deciding that being a lawyer was too boring.

The men shook hands all around and that was that. Lincoln Lang,
writing about the event much later, gave his take on why Roosevelt
plunked down a check on a life he knew nothing about. "Clearly I recall
his wild enthusiasm over the Badlands.... It had taken root in the con-
genial soil of his consciousness, like an ineradicable, creeping plant, as
it were, to thrive and permeate it thereafter, causing him more and more
to think in the broad gauge terms of nature—of the real earth."[4]

Maybe it was simply the freedom the West offered a young man, a
place where you could remake yourself and nobody told you how to live
or what to do. "Go West, young man!" as a motto seems hackneyed, but
it summed up an essential American value—the infinite ability to remake
oneself. American literature from *The Adventures of Huckleberry Finn* to
The Great Gatsby celebrates this ideal, and that is what the West offered,
the chance to remake oneself, to become an entirely different person.

One can only marvel at this type of freedom now. Modern man
would have to go to the moon to find this kind of *tabula rasa* of the
desert, a place to rewrite one's life story. Roosevelt might have had a
strange prescience that he would need an anchor in the future. Time
would prove that an anchor alone would not suffice for the tragedy
awaiting him.

At any rate, it was time to find the damn buffalo. Roosevelt and Ferris
set off at once the next morning, this time heading toward Montana. They
were looking for "lonesome Georges," buffalo that had strayed from the
herd because they were sick or couldn't keep up. Soon after they passed
over the line, the horses began to snort toward a coulee. Roosevelt slipped
off his horse, went up the ravine, and looked over and saw a bison.

...there below me, not fifty yards off, was a great bison bull. He was walking along, grazing as he walked. His glossy fall coat was in fine trim, and shone in the rays of the sun; while his pride of bearing showed him to be in the lusty vigor of his prime. As I rose above the crest of the hill, he held up his head and cocked his tail in the air.[5]

Joe was right behind him and pointed to a yellow spot on the old buffalo

"Hit him there," he whispered. "And you'll get him through the heart."

Roosevelt raised his Sharps rifle, and this time he was cool and deliberate. He had his ranch and now he would get his buffalo. He squeezed the trigger and heard the report. "I put the bullet in behind his shoulder." The buffalo didn't seem to care and bounded up the ravine with blood frothing his mouth and pumping from his nostrils. The two men scrambled up the ravine after him and in the gully the bull lay as dead—Joe Ferris would later say—"as Methuselah's cat."

And then Teddy Roosevelt did a war dance. He whooped and shrieked around the dead buffalo with his rifle held high like an Indian celebrating his kill. The myth the boy had read about all his life became reality and *he* was the warrior now. He was so excited he handed old Joe a hundred dollars. Joe Ferris could only stare openmouthed. "I never saw anyone so enthused in all my life."[6] But what he was seeing was the realization of a dream and that boy-man inside of it; victory over asthma, victory over death, now victory over the buffalo, and soon, victory over the West.

But for now they had to cut off the head and bring the buffalo back to the Langs' where they would feast. Roosevelt, ever the carnivore, would later write, "the flesh of this bull tasted uncommonly good...for we had been without fresh meat for a week; and until a healthy, active man has been without it some time, he does not know how...hungry for flesh he becomes..."[7]

On September 21, Teddy Roosevelt began the fifty-mile journey back to Little Missouri. Roosevelt's buffalo hunt was now officially over, and Gregor Lang and his son watched the buckboard rattle away. Lincoln, writing years later, recorded what he heard his father say, words historians would quote again and again: "...he is the most extraordinary man I have ever met. I shall be surprised if the world does not hear from him one of these days."[8]

And Teddy Roosevelt on Nell, trotting back to his life in triumph, had no idea what was waiting for him, and how soon a very different man would be returning West. He traveled back to New York on the Northern Pacific with his buffalo head wrapped in burlap, weighing about thirty-five pounds. One has to wonder if he kept the buffalo head in the Pullman car with him when he slept—the boy with his prize.

9

BUFFALO BILL'S WILD WEST SHOW
1883

In 1883, the same year Teddy Roosevelt went west for the first time, William Frederick Cody, a.k.a. Buffalo Bill, opened the Wild West show in Colville, Nebraska. To open the show, the mayor was riding in the coach that rumbled in a circle with Indians in hot pursuit. The plan was for Buffalo Bill and his cowboys to rescue the stagecoach from the Indians and prove once again the bravery of the American cowboy. The problem was nobody told the mules. When the Indians attacked, the mules went into high gear and went about as fast as mules can go. Then Buffalo Bill with his cowboys came charging in with guns blazing. The mules found new life and became like things possessed, trying to get away from Cody and his men.

Inside the coach there was terror. The mayor and everyone in the stagecoach held on for dear life. The mayor screamed out from the runaway coach: "STOP! HELP! STOP! LET US OUT!" Cody and his cowboys could do nothing. The mules were on a tear and the Indians had not been told when to stop and so continued in hot pursuit. The mules finally slowed from exhaustion, with the mayor "leaping out of the coach and making for Buffalo Bill ready for a fight."[1] The mayor never did get to Cody and eventually calmed down, as the crowd loved the spectacle and cheered the authentic show of cowboys and Indians and a runaway stagecoach. The Wild West show had arrived for an American public growing increasingly nervous with industrialized, modern urban life.

Teddy Roosevelt did eventually see the Wild West show and was part of the show—not literally, but as a man who would push the myth of the West through books and later as the "cowboy" president. As mentioned before, the frontier would be declared closed in 1890, but for Cody and others it had closed long before, with the biggest bonanza of the West being *the selling of the West.* And this coincided with a new modern malaise affecting Americans and one grief-stricken Teddy Roosevelt. A man named George M. Beard wrote about the new affliction in his *American Nervousness.* Another generation would knock it down to one word, "stress."

Beard saw a new affliction growing out of the sedentary life of modern Americans, who now lived more in cities than on farms. The Industrial Revolution, capitalism, the explosive growth of the country, and the lack of physical exercise had unleashed a series of nervous disorders and had produced a craving "for stimulants and narcotics…fear of responsibility, of open places or closed places, fear of society, fear of being alone, fear of fears, fear of contamination, fear of everything, deficient mental control, lack of decision in trifling matters, hopelessness…"[2]

Beard put a name to all of these afflictions: "neurasthenia." He believed that neurasthenia was the result of "labor of the brain over the muscles."[3] The victims were middle-class and upper-class men overburdened with commercial and managerial responsibilities, resulting in puny neurasthenic bodies. This new American malaise, that would kill thousands with heart disease and cancer, had arrived and people didn't know what to make of it. People had become "small and feeble," and, what was more alarming, the white race was being sapped of its virility. Beard said it was even direr than that: "there is not enough force left in neurasthenics to reproduce the species or go through the process of reproducing the species."[4]

In other words, people were becoming so stressed they could not even have sex, an existential threat for the White Race. This was a fearful prognosis for many late-nineteenth-century Americans who were already terrified by the million souls immigrating from Southern and Eastern Europe. In their xenophobic paranoia, they feared the White Race would soon be utterly submerged. The frontier was closing, a part of America that had given it a sort of national identity, and this made people wonder if the essence of the country was being lost. Enter Bill Cody and the Wild West show, where men were still men and more than that...still *white*.

Somewhere beyond the Mississippi, the real American was still out there. The cities were now polyglot, chaotic messes of disorder and disease that made little sense to the rural sensibilities of small-town Americans. So artists and writers began to rhapsodize about the frontier and the romantic struggle of Manifest Destiny, a phenomenon that was now apparently disappearing. These ideas were not lost on men like Teddy Roosevelt who had become uncomfortable with the contagion of modern America and the tragedies of death tied up with urbanity. Better to leave and go while the last open spaces were still out there.

The painter Frederick Remington did much to enhance the appeal of the West for men like Teddy Roosevelt. After leaving Yale and heading west in 1881, Remington returned to paint the West in famous oil paintings that would celebrate the vanishing frontier, offering it as an antidote to the corrupt bourgeois life of most Americans. His writings and paintings celebrated frontier virtues—especially *white* frontier virtues, pitting them against the vices of the immigrant hordes.

It is interesting to note the confluence of Teddy Roosevelt's flight West and the debut of the Wild West show built on the myth of a West that had all but vanished. One man went to find the myth, while another knew the myth was long over and that all that was left was to *re-enact* the past. The "vigorous life" that Teddy Roosevelt would later champion was the same that Buffalo Bill was selling under circus tents years earlier.

Both men spoke to a populace who wanted to find the men of action society had lost. Roosevelt would go on to publish many books about his exploits in the West, with the same return Cody experienced: people simply wanted to know what they were losing. Watching the Wild West show, a member of the Women's Professional League said, "Those are the kind of men that excite my admiration…big strong bronzed fellows! How much superior they are to the spindle-shanked, eye-glassed dudes."[5] One cannot help but hear an echo of Roosevelt's own sentiments.

William Cody created Buffalo Bill partly from the hell of his childhood. His father, Isaac Cody, sold their farm in 1853 and moved the family to Fort Leavenworth, Kansas Territory. Isaac was against slavery and in Bloody Kansas before the Civil War this put him in grave danger. When he spoke at a local trading post, Rively's store, on the evils of slavery, the crowd became so angry a man jumped up and stabbed him twice with a Bowie knife. He never fully recovered and left Kansas for a time. On his return trip there was a rumor that anti-slavery men were waiting for him. Young Bill Cody rode thirty miles with a fever to warn him. Isaac went to Kansas to bring back thirty anti-slavery families, but he caught a respiratory infection that, combined with complications from the stabbing, led to his death in April 1857.

After his death, the family suffered, so Billy Cody took a job with a freight carrier, riding up and down wagon trains and delivering messages to drivers. At age fourteen, in 1860, he headed for the gold fields in Colorado but ended up signing with the Pony Express. When the Civil War broke out, Cody joined the famous Red Legs, putting the flame to homes up and down the border. After the war, Cody drifted and ran freight, then went west, where his myth began. Cody claims to have ridden for the Pony Express and to have led the life of a cowboy—rustling cattle, fighting Indians, and hunting buffalo. Although his sister's biography tells a different story, the man who would become Buffalo Bill sensed that people were looking for Western heroes; and if truth was stretched into myth to satisfy them, then so be it.

What we do know is that he was Chief of Scouts for the Third Calvary in 1868 during the wars on the Plains. He fought in Indian battles and hunted bison (buffalo) for the Kansas Pacific Railway and sometimes the army. "Buffalo Bill," his alter ego, was born during this hunt for meat for the railroad. He was rumored to have killed 4282 buffalo, a real slaughter for the time. The Buffalo Bill legend was born when in 1869 he met Ned Buntline, who published a story on Cody's exploits in *Street and Smith's New York Weekly*. Buntline followed this with a novel, *Buffalo Bill, The King of the Border Men*, which had several sequels.

The Buffalo Bill Wild West show was spawned from a one-act production, *The Scouts of the Prairie*, that Buntline, now a fledgling showman, produced with Cody as his lead. Others were added to the show, including Wild Bill Hickok, and in 1893 the show was renamed for the star as Indians and more cowboys were added and the Wild West show began to tour the world.

In the show *Custer's Last Stand at Little Bighorn*, the famous battle was reenacted except for one little change: Buffalo Bill would come to the rescue and take his revenge on the Indians. It was not too much of a leap to see the Indians as stand-ins for the teeming immigrants flooding the cities and creating multifarious problems, but what the Wild West show really did was to make cowboys respectable. No longer were they thought of as grungy Mexicans who drank their wages away or got into gunfights or died destitute in skeleton towns or out on the lonely prairie. As Kathleen Dalton writes, "The Wild West show made cowboys into symbols of whiteness only through a balancing act, combating their border image on the one hand and portraying them as aggressively physical and autonomous on the other."[6]

But at the heart of the Wild West show was really the American middle class, represented by the lone frontier family in a cabin. In Cody's show, the family of women and children were portrayed alongside the father bravely fighting off the Indians, with certain doom closing in. Buffalo Bill and his cowboys would gallop in to save the day and not only save the family but save a way of life. The implications of this centerpiece of the show were enormous for Americans in the waning years of the 1880s.

The "Attack on a Settler's Cabin" tapped into a set of profound cultural anxieties. For nineteenth-century audiences, a home, particularly a rural "settler's home," was imbued with much symbolic meaning. The home itself presupposed the presence of a woman, particularly a wife. The home thus conveyed notions of womanhood, domesticity, and family. When the Indians rode down on the settler's cabin at the end of the Wild West show, they were attacking more than a building with some white people in it. To many in the audience, the scene conveyed an attack on family and domesticity itself. The Wild West show adapted the melodramatic rescue of the home for arena performance, allowing the cowboys and their leader to rescue the nation's domestic integrity from the threat of Indian captivity.

None of this was lost on Teddy Roosevelt. He had been knocked out of his domestic unity by the twin urban diseases of typhoid fever and Bright's disease. A pestilence of modern life had robbed him of his domestic happiness, and he would go West to slay the dragon and rescue his own self from the carnage wrought by modern life. The Indians were merely stand-ins for all that besieged the late nineteenth-century man, and Buffalo Bill galloping in on his white horse was the knight of old slaying the marauders and rescuing the white family from danger. As Louis Warren writes in *Buffalo Bill's America*, "[This] allowed urban men to think of themselves in new ways, to re-create urban manhood by looking to the simulacrum of the frontier West."[7]

As the suburbs began to take root, white men identified their homes with the frontier cabin. Women had been rescued from the scurrilous city and taken to the country to live in a home with children and to become "domesticated." By their isolation, suburban homes compelled much more family togetherness than did homes in the crowded city. White culture was being built around the bastion of male-dominated homes where the woman and children depended on protection from the marauding bands circling outside hearth and home.

Buffalo Bill's Wild West show celebrated this limited interaction with the world and protected it with his cowboys, allowing middle class and upper class men of the Gilded Age to participate vicariously in this world of cowboys and Indians, like knights battling dragons to rescue damsels in distress. No one participated in this more than Teddy Roosevelt, and no one was more susceptible to the myth of the West. It was the mythic possibilities that pulled him in during the closing years of the frontier to find the truth about the American West, and, more importantly, about himself.

10

FAR OFF FROM ALL MANKIND

1884

And so, a year after his hunting trip, on June 9, 1884, Roosevelt was back on the train. The lights in the world had gone out for the man watching the sagebrush turn purple in the dusk outside his window. News was the ranch had done well, and Roosevelt was thinking of buying another thousand head of cattle. But the black heart was upon him, and he knew only one type of self-medication: action and erasure of the wound. He had lost his political career, his wife, his mother, and essentially his child, whom he had given to his sister to raise because even the baby's name pained him, Alice Lee.

One may wonder why Teddy Roosevelt had suddenly bought a ranch when he was out hunting buffalo two years earlier, but it was not as serendipitous as it may seem. The Badlands cattle boom began in 1883, the year he plunked down his first 14,000 dollars. The "open range" policies of the Badlands and Dakota Territory meant that men like Roosevelt did not have to purchase the land, just the cattle. For many it seemed a lucrative investment; books like *The Beef Bonanza; Or, How to Get Rich on the Plains* fueled interest in investing west of the Mississippi. The availability of raw land, and the railroad with its hungry Eastern market, made raising cattle a high return investment. Or so it seemed. There were considerable risks; cattle often died from severe winters or drought or disease, and many small players like Roosevelt had been wiped out.

But the West, as a presence in young Roosevelt's life, seemed to be that one dynamic place where people could go to re-create themselves. And being a rancher was at the top of the Western pyramid. The truth was it was *in style* for well-to-do young men to have a ranch. And for many young men, owning a ranch was a romantic notion. "Ranching," wrote Roosevelt later, "is an occupation…having little in common with the humdrum, workaday business world of the nineteenth century…the free ranchman in his manner of life shows more kinship to an Arab sheik than to a sleek city merchant or tradesman."[1] Many "dudes" like Roosevelt went West looking for fortune, romance, and adventure; and of course these dudes had to be well-armed as ranchers: "every ranchman carries a revolver," Roosevelt would later write, "a long .45 Colt or Smith and Wesson, by preference the former. When after game a hunting knife is stuck in the girdle. This should be stout and sharp, but not too long, with a round handle. I have two double-barreled shotguns…. "[2] But besides carrying a weapon, the ranchman also had to look the part. Roosevelt was outfitted in New York:

> He spent a small fortune. … Besides the big hat, the buckskin shirt, chaps, bridle, and silver spurs, he had fancy alligator boots, a silver belt buckle, beautifully tooled leather belt and holster, a silver-mounted Bowie knife by Tiffany. His silver belt buckle was engraved with the head of a bear; the silver spurs had his initials on them. His Colt revolver was engraved with scrolls and geometric patterns and plated with silver and gold. On one side of its ivory handle were his initials, on the other side, the head of a buffalo to commemorate the one he had shot in 1883.[3]

At twenty-five years of age, Theodore Roosevelt was essentially starting over. And Little Missouri was as wild and untamed a place as any in the West. As Hermann Hagedorn wrote in *Roosevelt in the Badlands*, "Little Missouri was a terrible place. It was in fact 'wild and wooly' [according to Roosevelt] to an almost grotesque degree and the boom town was a little cruder than its twin across the river, Medora. The men who had drifted [there]... were, many of them, outcasts of society, reckless, greedy, and conscienceless, fugitives from justice with criminal records and gunmen who lived by crooked gambling and thievery of every sort."[4]

In 1884, Roosevelt went West with no definite plan as to when he would return. He no longer had a vocation, or really a life of any sort; the word *dispossessed* comes to mind. His wife, who was just seventeen when he first saw her, had been taken away along with his mother. Many times he must have gone over in his mind his courtship of Alice Lee: it had lasted over a year and had him so in knots he retreated to the woods one night and upon returning shot a neighbor's dog who barked at his horse.

The train rattled on into the Dakota Territory under a desolate moon. Gazing out the window, Roosevelt thought of his father, who told him that "being sick is a sin." He thought of his mother, who felt that ever since the Civil War the household had split in two and that she would never fit in with her husband's world—and never really did, taking refuge in one rest cure after another, her perpetual neurasthenia shielding her from the "Yankee world" she found so abysmal.

Roosevelt recalled the boys who beat him up at the private schools, and the asthma that could never be cured but "ignored through the will of the mind," along with the doctor's pronouncement that he should lead the life of a shut-in given his heart ailment. All that was falling away now, as the train plunged farther into the West. For it was 1884— Geronimo wouldn't be caught for another two years, and just three years before, Billy the Kid was gunned down and the famous gunfight raged at the O.K. Corral.

The frontier still existed, and a young man crushed by the twin pistons of disease and cutthroat national politics was going back to the only place the world made sense. Roosevelt thought again of his wife and mother, the black ice of depression nipping at the corners of his mind. The truth was Alice Lee was a lot like Roosevelt's mother. Mittie was the damsel in distress much of the time when Teddy was young. Rest cures were abundant, and Alice Lee could easily have slipped down the same path. Some in the Roosevelt clan would later say TR would have become bored with his vapid wife and her constant yielding to her husband's wishes. But of course the twenty-five-year-old Roosevelt would not have believed it. He simply wanted to go "as far off from all mankind" as he could get and mend his broken heart.[5]

A boyhood dream of going off into the wilderness by himself reasserted itself, and Roosevelt was even more determined to get away after meeting with the men running his ranch. It was quite possible he would never return to the East; instead he could have become one with the thousands of others who disappeared into the West—a sort of national safety valve for lives pummeled by the concussive pressures of capitalism, a developing country, and the onerous demands of emerging bourgeois life. Many just ran away and many had nothing to lose. Many were never seen again. The promise of land and a new life had lured them West. The East was stratified and money interests dominated, but if a man could survive in the West he might become wealthy in land and cattle.

Teddy had set up this promise of the "other life" marvelously on his first trip West, with the purchase of cattle and his staking claim to land in the age of "free range" (even though that age would be dead by 1890 along with all the concomitant rituals of cowboy culture that followed a free and open frontier). Why not? Why not just become a rancher, a cowboy, a wholly different person—a man who could no longer feel the horrible pain that made people worry he might never recover?

Teddy stared out from the train car at the dark landscape with its sliver of horizon light. He breathed deeply and blinked against the speckled stars of the great darkness. No lights now. No cities. The Dakota Territory was alive with rattlesnakes, coyotes, bears, Indians, murderers, and the great untamed will of a nation grappling with the last growing pains of an open frontier. Teddy Roosevelt was slipping away from civilization, and there were no cellphones, no landlines, just some puny telegraph lines knocked down by Indians who did not understand why men would risk their lives for a wire on a pole.

On June 9 Roosevelt arrived and was met at the station by Bill Merrifield and Sylvane Ferris. The Maltese Cross ranch was doing well and the boss had arrived. Accounts have Roosevelt meeting Arthur Packard at his printing office, home of *The Bad Lands Cow Boy*. Packard was young, like everyone else in Little Missouri, and had graduated from the University of Michigan and gone West to become the managing editor of the *Bismarck Tribune*. Bismarck, being a Wild West town, did not appreciate his editorializing; and besides having to do everything, which included setting type, Packard had to keep an eye out for crazed gunmen who took offence at his prose.

Packard, with the newspaper man's nose, had heard of the wild towns of Little Missouri and Medora and headed out for the story. He ran into Frank Vine and they went to the saloon. "You told me you'd never seen an honest to God cowboy..." Frank said, "see that feller at the far end of the bar...well that's a real cowboy."[6] Packard wrote about that "feller," describing his gun, hat, chaps. Vine went over and whispered to the man, who had noticed Packard's attention. After Packard had finished writing, he went out to ask the telegraph operator to mail the letter on the next train, but the black icy night made him think otherwise. The next day the man whom he had written about approached him outside of town.

"So you're a newspaper feller...I thought you was a deputy sheriff come to arrest horse thieves...if you had gone out last night I would have kilt you."[7]

Packard gasped and realized then he had alighted in a true Wild West town. He decided to start a weekly newspaper, *The Bad Lands Cow Boy*. It would immortalize the town forever. After Roosevelt's first trip West, he and Packard became fast friends. The office of the *Bad Lands Cow Boy* was a one-room building that served as office, bedroom, bath, and print shop. The boards were rough-cut and leaked air, and on this June night the woodstove glowed red while a thirty-degree wind was rasping under the door. Packard wrote later of his conversation with Roosevelt that night. "He gave us such a swinging description of the stirring scenes of the Republican convention. ... I can see him now as plainly as I did then, as he straightened up, his doubled fist in the air, his teeth glittering, and his eyes squinting in something that was far from a smile as he jerked out the words, 'By Godfrey! I will not be dictated to!'"[8] But no mention of his dead wife; or his mother; or the fact that he had a daughter. To Roosevelt that world seemed not to exist. A brief squib in *The Bad Lands Cow Boy* appeared days later: "Theodore Roosevelt, the young New York reformer, made us a very pleasant call Monday... New York will certainly lose him for a time at least... "

Unlike Little Missouri, the town of Medora was thriving. Founded by the Marquis and named for his wife, it had eighty-four buildings, and it was *there* the trains stopped and not at "Little Misery" across the river. There was a feel of lusty capitalism in the air as cattle ambled through the middle of town. The winter had been mild and the cattle were fat, and Roosevelt, in his new world with his new career, felt great excitement. The next morning he rode out to his ranch.

"The old stockade shack... [had] been converted into a stable, and a simple but substantial one-and-a-half-story log cabin had been built with a shingle roof and a cellar. ... An alcove... was set aside for Roosevelt's use as combined bedroom and study.... "[9] The buildings belonged to the two Canadians, as Roosevelt had only bought the cattle and horses. He grazed the cattle on land owned by the government and the Northern Pacific railroad. The open-range era allowed ranchers to graze their cattle on land-claims based on need. It was an honor system that frequently broke down, leading to range wars. It was based on the understanding that the ranchers were all in this together and cattle should be allowed to graze over "the line," a mutual courtesy. Roosevelt had lost twenty-five head of cattle in the winter from the cold and wolves, but after two days of surveying his ranch, he came to a decision. Cattle raising would be his regular business and he would buy another thousand head of cattle. He would be a rancher and this would be his life's work. This train of thought was in line with the ethos of the West: throw away who you were and become who you are. Teddy Roosevelt was about to use the last years of the "Wild West" to find out who he was.

He had always been reckless with his health, and this was part of his ongoing battle against his own frailty. Roosevelt would put himself to the ultimate test and become this other person or die trying. In his darkest moments, either outcome was fine by him. Roosevelt then went out to visit the Langs, who had moved seven miles closer to town and were living in a makeshift dugout. Much had changed since he had been on that buffalo hunt—the dude returned, carrying unimaginable tragedy like a backpack; Lincoln and McGregor worked on the ranch house, preparing it for Mrs. Lang and her two children.

Roosevelt did some business with Lang and worked on a contract for a thousand more cattle at a price of 26,000 dollars. Then he turned to young Lincoln. "Two things I want to do. Get an antelope and a buckskin suit." The boy took Roosevelt to a Mrs. Maddox, known for her skill in fashioning buckskin coats and her ability to banish husbands with a stove lifter. She was a dead-eyed shot; many called her "the first Calamity Jane." She lived alone with a hired man, Crow Joe, a suspected horse thief, in a mud-roofed hut on Sand Creek.

The strong frontier woman made the famous buckskin coat that Roosevelt would pose in years later in New York. One can only imagine what Roosevelt was setting himself up for. A man who wore coke-bottle glasses from the East now donning the "Buffalo Bill" attire of the West . . . it was not unlike buying the varsity football jersey before trying out for the team. But this was part of Roosevelt's transformation. He was shedding his old life, clothes and all, and donning the uniform of the West: chaps, neckerchief, boots, jeans, rope, Colt, Winchester. The man completely immersed himself in the new world, the new culture, and became a new man.

Of course, Roosevelt was also making himself one hell of a target. But that was Roosevelt, and after a dinner he and Lincoln rode back and found a couple antelope, with Teddy shooting the first one, then dropping his gun and whooping with his arms up in the air.

"I got him! I got him!" he shouted.

"Shoot the other one," Lincoln called out.

Apparently Roosevelt burst into laughter.

"I can't...not to save my life."

He was so exuberant over his kill he wanted to give his shotgun to Lincoln but the boy wouldn't accept it—not unlike his triumph over the buffalo when Roosevelt did a war dance and gave Joe Ferris a hundred dollars. There was something almost touching about the man who felt he had nothing to give but material goods; it was the magnanimous gesture of a rich man and purportedly he was hurt by Lincoln's refusal.

Roosevelt then headed out into the Badlands for five days of solitude, summing up his own prescription for life's troubles: "Black care rarely sits behind a rider whose pace is fast enough."[10] Now, among historical scholars there exists a theory that the death of Roosevelt's wife and mother were nothing more than isolated occurrences and that all his life decisions to follow were independent of that event. The Rooseveltian doctrine of "action cures all" was in play, and Teddy was a man who appeared to have no emotional baggage. Many historians have accepted this interpretation, glossing over the deaths and over his time in the West as if it were an Outward Bound trip by a patrician, merely a sort of extended vacation before going back and starting on the trajectory to the presidency.

Nothing could be further from the truth. A ranch woman who saw Roosevelt said he was "quiet and sad." In reality, he was extremely melancholic, even morbid, viewing his life as essentially finished. But because Roosevelt covered his tracks so well, and because later scholars treated the months after the death of his wife and mother as if they meant nothing more than a man going on a vacation, the impact of his personal loss is unduly minimized. Action was Roosevelt's credo, but he was a severely wounded man.

So he started with this lonely journey into the Badlands by himself for five days; and although it was no bird-watching expedition, Roosevelt, an ornithologist from his youth, wrote of the meadowlark with its "cadence of wild sadness, inexpressibly touching." The keening of the meadowlark was "laden with a hundred memories and associations."[11]

There was an elegiac tone to Roosevelt's writing. This was a solitary march into the wilderness to redefine existence and find out the worth of his life, but he still grieved over the losses of his past.

Roosevelt said to Bill Ferris, in an unguarded moment a year later out on a roundup, "I have nothing to live for now." Ferris gave him back Western logic at its best. "This too shall pass and then you won't need to be out here no more."[12] These grizzled cowboys had seen many come to the West to piece together shattered lives. The buffalo hunter Ferris understood more than Roosevelt that he was on a long journey of healing.

For now, on his first lone journey into the Badlands, he had a rifle, a book, a blanket, an oilskin, a metal cup, some tea and salt, and dry biscuits. This was a "Thoreau" trip off the beaten path; Roosevelt, on the slow canter of Manitou, his favorite horse, surveyed the desolate landscape that, while beautiful, also mirrored the desolation of his soul. He crossed ravines and clambered up rocky slopes with the tick of the horse hooves the only sound. Roosevelt would not speak of his depression, his grief, the blackness of his world, but one can detect it in his description of the world:

> Nowhere, not even at sea, does a man feel more lonely than when riding over the far-reaching, never-ending plains...their vastness and loneliness and their melancholy monotony have a strong fascination for him. The landscape seems always the same and after the traveler has plodded for miles he gets to feel as if distance were really boundless. As far as the eye can see there is no break; either the prairie stretches out into perfectly level flats or there are gentle rolling slopes...nowhere else does one feel so far off from mankind; the plains stretch out in deathless and measureless expanse, and as he journeys over them they will for many miles be lacking in all signs of life.[13]

Roosevelt writes in the third person, distancing himself from this "rider" who sees only "a deathless measureless expanse...lacking in all signs of life."[14] He was the proverbial rider in the valley of the shadow of death. He saw antelope and wriggles through cactus, but cannot get off a shot before they bolt. Meals of biscuits and water, and then bedding down for a siesta in the sun under his hat, and then up again.

Danger came in the form of quicksand that nearly took Roosevelt and his horse; only though a mighty struggle did they get clear. Quicksand—the best allegory nature can throw at a man who risks everything—yet still he did not take the hint and go back, but pounded on, looking for antelope because *action is all*. For a man of sorrow, it is the action taken that is important and nothing else. Action is the cipher for the riddle of existence.

Roosevelt shot an antelope and skinned the creature, cutting off the head and laying the meat across the pommel of his saddle. Around dusk, he found a spot and lit a fire "for cheerfulness" (irony upon irony), and had his feast; then, setting up his blankets under a cottonwood, he paused, "looking up at the stars until I fell asleep."[15] It is a scene reminiscent of Hemingway's short story "Big Two Hearted River," written forty years later, in which the hero Nick Carraway takes solace in the mechanics of camping after the hell of World War I.

Roosevelt, with his small fire under the cottonwood tree, was fighting for his existence in the biting cold plains of the West. He was a man at the end of an era, partaking in a life already past. Roosevelt was, by the magic of his ritual, dispelling the darkness. From the chaos of emotion comes order, and this is the order of the kill: a man eating his meat in the darkness and sleeping under the stars.

So he was up again in the cold morning with the prairie dogs. Rude sensation was good because it shook him out of himself, as he took his rifle to head out to the prairie for game. "Nothing was in sight in the way of game," he recalled later, "but overhead a skylark was singing, soaring above me so high that I could make out his form in the gray morning light."[16]

Roosevelt clearly embraced the natural world as an antidote to all that he did not want to recognize. Not unlike Hemingway's hero, who saw beauty in the rushing river and the tactile sensation of walking through the forest. *Action. Action. Action.* Then the hunter came in contact with a doe going down to the water near his camp, "her great sensitive ears thrown forward as she peered anxiously and timidly around."[17] Roosevelt then watched some ducks and never thought once of hunting. He would later write his sister Bamie of his experience:

> For the last week I have been fulfilling a boyish ambition of mine—that is I have been playing a frontier hunter in good earnest, having been off entirely alone, with my horse and rifle, on the prairie. I wanted to see if I could do perfectly well without a guide, and I succeeded beyond my expectations. I shot a couple of antelope and a deer—and missed a great many more. I feel as absolutely free as a man could feel; as you know, I do not mind loneliness; and I enjoyed the trip to the utmost. The only disagreeable incident was one day when it rained. Otherwise the weather was lovely, and every night I would lay wrapped up in my blanket looking at the stars till I fell asleep, in the cool air. The country has widely different aspects in different places; one day I could canter hour after hour over the level green grass or through miles of wild rose thickets all in bloom; on the next, I would be amidst the savage desolation of the Bad Lands, with their dreary plateaus, fantastically shaped buttes and deep winding canyons. I enjoyed the trip greatly, and have never been in better health.[18]

Remember, Bamie was caring for his daughter Baby Lee, so one can only wonder: Did Teddy ever ask how his daughter was doing? He did not and would not write of her for a long time. Certainly one would never guess this was a man who had lost his wife and his mother five months earlier. Perhaps he did inquire about the baby in a different letter, but, given his sectored view of the world, it is unlikely. There is present action and there is the unpleasant past. Clearly, the world was at bay, and the Wild West acted as a medicinal antidote to all that ailed a man who was looking for answers. It was enough, for now.

11

FOUR-EYES
1885

Glasses were not worn in the West. They were looked upon as a weakness and, what's more, they marked a man forever as an Easterner. The boy who could not see in 1870 because he did not have glasses supposedly saw Red Cloud, chief of the Oglala Sioux, riding down Fifth Avenue in an open carriage, "a real-life warrior from the Dakota prairies wearing a stove pipe hat."[1] In reality, the young Roosevelt could only see about thirty feet in front of him, and beyond that everything was a blur. He literally did not see the world as others did.

So Red Cloud entered and passed beyond the fuzzy, out-of-focus world of the asthmatic boy with chronic diarrhea, who was nervous and sickly—the antithesis of the Roosevelt apotheosis of action and determined thinking. Theodore Sr., his father, was a man who stood to inherit a million dollars upon the death of his father (ten million today); and yet for all his money, his son was half-blind and seemed as if he could strangle on his own breath.

And five years before the parade with Red Cloud, young Roosevelt had watched from an upstairs window as Abraham Lincoln's funeral procession passed by. This was not a proven fact until the 1950s when a scholar noticed in a photograph of the funeral two young faces in the window of what was determined to be the Roosevelt mansion; it was six-year-old Theodore and his brother. But one has to wonder how much young Teddy really saw as he had no glasses and would not until he was thirteen. (The delay in getting Teddy spectacles seems incredible, given how blind he was, but, then again, the young boy had other more pressing problems, like breathing.) His myopia was so bad it was later said he could not recognize his own sons without his glasses.

Gregor Lang wore glasses, but they were small and oval. Roosevelt's glasses were large and round, giving him the look of an owl under a cowboy hat. The nickname "Four-Eyes" would follow him and not as a term of respect. But Theodore Roosevelt was essentially blind without his glasses and could never be without them. This set him up as a man who was frequently underestimated. His hired hand Merrifield had galloped to town and was speaking with a man named Fisher, the superintendent of the Northern Pacific Refrigerator Car Company, who spotted Roosevelt talking to some cowboys. Fisher saw a "slim, anemic-looking young fellow dressed in the exaggerated style which newcomers on the frontier affected, and which was considered indisputable evidence of the rank tenderfoot." In short, Fisher saw another "dude" come West searching for adventure, with the assumption he would soon return to the comfort of home. Merrifield, a few days later, suggested to Fisher they take Roosevelt out on a hazardous trail known as the old Sully Trail. "We'll let on we're going for a little hunt."[2] Fisher agreed, thinking of the Sully Trail that ran dangerously along buttes and was barely a trail at all. Rain had recently turned it into slippery gumbo. The next day, Merrifield led the way, with Roosevelt following and Fisher behind. They came to a slope that dropped at a forty-five-degree angle into a dry creek bed.

"There goes a deer," Merrifield shouted and started down the slope at a full gallop.

Roosevelt followed, keeping up with the Canadian, when Merrifield went over the neck of his horse and landed in the creek bed. The dude was still on his horse and looked at his ranch hand. "Now see what you've done, Merrifield, that deer is in Montana by now." He burst into laughter, and Fisher wondered if the joke wasn't on them. He understood there was more to "Four-Eyes" than a buckskin coat.

Now the sun shimmered across the Badlands and reflected in the glasses of the man sitting on the rocker. His finger rested in the book on his lap, holding his page, as he stared at the surrounding countryside from his porch and looked out at "a wide, semi-circular clearing covered with sagebrush, bordered on the east by a ring of buttes and grassy slopes, ... Westward, not a quarter mile from the house ... the river [Little Missouri] swung in a long circle at the foot of steep buttes crested with scoria."[3] He was a long way from Manhattan and had thrown himself into the new life of rancher and cowboy.

Roosevelt really did not know what ranch life was, so he had to learn by doing. He was starting at the beginning of the beginning. A good horseman, Teddy had been on many foxhunts, but he was not a natural in the Western sense of the word, which meant you could ride anything with four legs. Roosevelt didn't like to "break" horses and some would have called him a fancy rider. He was the boss, though, and men twice his age called him "Mr. Roosevelt," never Theodore, and certainly not Teddy.

That is not to say Roosevelt had earned automatic respect. The parlance of a patrician poked through sometimes to hilarious consequence. One time he was assisting in rounding up some calves and called out to the men, "Hasten forward quickly there!"[4] The cowboys roared at his proper English, and from then on they threw aside their own "Head off them cattle," for "Hasten forward quickly there." The fact was that the boss in the buckskin coat and glasses was a bit of a joke. This was a world where men had to prove themselves, and all Roosevelt had proven was that he had the money to buy a ranch. Besides, there was another rich man who had left a bad taste in everyone's mouth and with whom Roosevelt would eventually clash—the Marquis.

Even his name was all wrong. The Marquis was a rich French noble-man, who had stepped off the train much like Roosevelt had, declaring he was weary of civilization. He immediately began to create a new civiliza-tion by settling on the other side of the river, breaking a bottle of cham-pagne on a tent spike, and calling it *Medora* in honor of his wife. His scheme was simple. Buy up all the cattle he could, slaughter them on the spot in his newly constructed slaughtering house on a Ford-Assembly-line scale, and ship the beef in refrigerated boxcars. This would cut out the middlemen transporting live cattle to holding pens and slaughterhouses.

The Marquis planned to invest millions and then take the profits and buy an army to overthrow France and take back his birthright—the crown of France. He was delusional, but the West inspired these types of dreams. Maybe it was the vastness of the plains or the fact the govern-ment was incapable of taking control. This left men like the Marquis and Roosevelt to move into the vacuum, but there the comparison stops. The Marquis was not a well-loved man and had already had trouble, result-ing in the death of a cowboy who had disputed the Marquis' claim to land. He was known to be a good shot with plenty of courage and had proven it more than once in duels. One reason he settled the town of Medora was that he was hated in Little Missouri and was often referred to as "that sonofabitch de Marquis."

Roosevelt and the Marquis ran in the same circles in New York, and they may have even crossed paths when the Marquis worked in a family bank. Strangely, it was the same Commander Gorringe who had encour-aged the restless Marquis to go west and find his fortune, if not his destiny. Certainly the popular phrase "Go West, young man," spoke to the spirit of both Roosevelt and the Marquis.

So the denizens of Little Missouri or Medora could be forgiven for looking at Roosevelt like another crazy rich man with pie-in-the-sky dreams. By the time Roosevelt arrived, Medora had prospered while Little Missouri had slid, and the train stopped now where the Marquis' slaughterhouse smokestacks blanched the sky. The two men would cross paths later and not under good circumstances, and it is worth saying their differences were greater than their similarities.

But meanwhile Roosevelt was learning to be a cowboy. Writing his sister again, he summed up his experiences this way:

> Well I have been having a glorious time here, and am well hardened now (I have just come in from spending thirteen hours in the saddle). For every day I have been here I have my hands full. First and foremost, the cattle have done well, and I regard the outlook for making the business a success as being very hopeful. ... In the autumn I shall bring out Sewall and Dow [men he had hunted with in Maine] and put them on a ranch with very few cattle to start with, and in the course of a couple years give them quite a little herd also. I have never been in better health than on this trip. I am in the saddle all day long. ... I am really attached to my two 'factors,' Ferris and Merrifield; they are very fine men. ... I have shot a few jackrabbits and curlews, with the rifle; and I also killed eight rattlesnakes.[5]

Interestingly, this letter betrays the tone of a man looking for something other than just the rancher life. Roosevelt was still suffering from asthma, chronic diarrhea, and insomnia. He was thrilled to be sleeping so well and boyishly boasted of being able to ride all day with the cowboys—almost like the movie *City Slickers* in which modern people pay to live the cowboy life for a week on a cattle drive.

But it wasn't just a game for Roosevelt; the threat of death was exceedingly real. In the real West, men were shot. They were knifed or impaled with an arrow. They often froze to death or died of thirst. They were thrown from horses, drowned, starved, or baked to death in 140-degree heat. Many times men who froze to death were found naked months later, having pulled all their clothes off in delirium. And all this is to say nothing about the Indian threat. Sometimes men attacked by Indians were found with their organs cut out, still breathing, or with their severed penis in their mouth, or carved up like cattle. Many men simply disappeared, their bleached bones found years later in the Badlands. Even routine ranching activity entailed serious risks. Roosevelt once wrote of a horse that bucked him before a roundup: "he bucked me off and I managed to fall on a stone and broke a rib…once, when I was not quick enough, he caught me and broke something in the point of my shoulder."[6] Ranching life in the Dakota Territory was not simply an entertaining holiday for the wealthy, and Theodore Roosevelt would come close to death more than once.

Roosevelt by now was eyeing property further west, wanting to build a proper ranch house that would give him more privacy. He intended to write a book, as he had already written a naval history that had received positive reviews and had earned him royalties. But the converted log cabin had too much activity for the man who had considered the life of a writer—or at least a scholar. Roosevelt was never without a book, even on roundups or hunting trips.

Yet, far from a bookish introvert, Theodore was nothing if not a good mixer. He had a real interest in other people far outside the patrician class of New York. Even his political career as a reformer in Albany was based on the idea that the rich and powerful must be brought to heel by law. The egalitarian West, where class mattered not at all, was very much the place for a man who made his way by deed and example; it was a budding meritocracy that rewarded the talent and determination of the individual.

Still Roosevelt had a sense of propriety and to him there were lines that should not be crossed. Once, he went to town to get his mail, visit Joe Ferris's new store, and shoot the breeze with Arthur Packard of the *Bad Lands Cow Boy*, when he bumped into Bill Jones, a legendary "hell-roaring" bad man of the area. He was a gunslinger with the build of a fighter—long arms, barrel chest, thick neck—with black eyes that gleamed under bushy brows. In short, he was the Wild West menace, the model for a hundred Western bad guys to come. Jones's favorite pastime was to hang out in the saloon and tell stories in the foulest language imaginable. One day, Jones was holding court in the office of the *Bad Lands Cow Boy* when Roosevelt was there. Roosevelt might be considered a prig. He drank in college but he would never admit it, and he never really spoke of sex outside the context of procreation. So for him, there were boundaries, and Bill Jones had crossed the line.

"Bill Jones," he said, looking into the other man's eyes. "I can't tell why in the world I like you, for you're the nastiest-talking man I ever heard."[7]

Bill Jones's hand went to his gun, and the cowboys in the office of the *Bad Lands Cow Boy* expected shooting. Silence reigned in the dusty-planked room, the grizzled gunfighter facing the four-eyed man from the East in his cowboy getup. Everyone knew it would be a one-sided fight, but then a strange thing happened. Maybe it was the unwavering eyes or the trace of hard bark in Roosevelt's demeanor. But whatever the reason, Bill Jones turned sheepish.

"I don't belong to your outfit Mr. Roosevelt, and I am not beholden to you for anything. All the same, I don't mind saying that mebbe I've been a little too free with my mouth."[8]

From then on they became friends. Roosevelt had passed an early test, though to him it was just a given that a man should not talk so foully. The code of the West was simply that a man had to back up what he said, and in this regard Teddy Roosevelt came well-armed. But still, Roosevelt could perhaps have felt a nervous sweat cooling on his brow as he walked out of that office. Things easily could have gone the other way.

And he might have passed a man on the street with long, dark curly hair and a waxed mustache—"that sonofabitch de Marquis." One can only wonder if these two men in this small town did pass each other. Both had come looking for adventure, and as a correspondent of the *Mandan Pioneer* wrote of the Marquis, "He was armed to the teeth. A formidable-looking belt encircled his waist, in which was stuck a murderous-looking knife, a large navy revolver, and two rows of cartridges, and in his hand he carried a repeating rifle." Roosevelt would doubtless have noticed such an ensemble of arms, so unlike casual attire on the streets of New York. This certainly was the Wild West.

12

THE NEWLY MINTED COWBOY

1885

Roosevelt found the site for his new ranch after a tip from a ranchman sent him north. He splashed across the Little Missouri River and found the spot on the opposite shore. He was driven once again in a search of solitude. The man who reads and writes must have space, and this was the spot. Roosevelt's view from an imagined veranda would be magnificent. He later wrote, "A range of clay hills which seemed to have been sculpted by a giant hand as preparatory studies for mountains, loomed steeply into the sky. A distant plume of lignite smoke, glowing pink as evening came on, hinted at the surrounding savagery of the Bad Lands."[1]

It was to be the Roosevelt Ranch Headquarters, complete with a rocker where a man could contemplate all that was his while reading great works or while writing. But he needed men to build the place, and so he turned to the two men with whom he had adventured in Maine after the death of his father: Bill Sewall and Wilmot Dow. Roosevelt paid four hundred dollars for the rights to the land and then enticed the two men to come join him. "I feel sure you will do well for yourself by coming out with me...."

Why did Sewall and Dow agree to go? The reason was simple: Roosevelt was paying. "He said he would guarantee us a share of anything made in the cattle business," Sewall recalled later. "And if anything was lost, he would lose it and pay our wages. ... told him I thought that was very one-sided but if he thought he could stand it then we could too."[2]

Roosevelt went further than that; he wrote checks to cover existing mortgages and personally assured the men's wives all would be fine in a year or so. Such was the power of money at a time when banks did not lend freely and companies did not pay for people to move anywhere. Would someone today pick up and move to an unsettled area in the West for such an opportunity? Perhaps some would; most would not. But the difference was in the psychology of the late nineteenth century. Without a "corporate state" to fall back on, working class citizens were quite used to "making it up" as they went along. The psychology of "try and fail, try and fail," was very real. The country depended on entrepreneurs to build it up. So when a potential employer guaranteed a living and took care of existing debts to boot...where was the downside?

On his way back from Maine, Roosevelt was interviewed by a reporter for the *Pioneer* in Mandan while the train changed engines. "Theodore Roosevelt, the New York reformer, was on the west-bound train yesterday, en route to his ranch near Little Missouri. He was feeling at his best, dressed in the careless style of the country gentleman of leisure and spoke freely on his pleasant Dakota experience.... Mr. Roosevelt believes that the young men of our country should assume a spirit of independence in politics...."

To the papers, Roosevelt was a man enjoying his time out West. In reality, he was a man who had left one world for another and his "independence in politics" had closed the door behind him for the present. When Dow and Sewall arrived in the Badlands in August 1884, Roosevelt asked Sewall what he thought of the country on his first night. The woodsman from Maine, who was nearing forty with powerful shoulders, stared at the desolation of the Badlands. "I like it well enough," said Sewall, "but I don't believe that it's much of a cattle country."[3]

"You don't know anything about it," Roosevelt replied. "Everybody says that."

Sewall shrugged.

"It's the way it looks to me, like not much of a cattle country."

Roosevelt did not listen; he would soon be taking in a delivery of a thousand more cattle. Besides, they were loggers from Maine. What did they know about the Badlands and raising cattle? Sewall wrote his family his impression of the Badlands: "It is a dirty country and very dirty people on an average but I think it is healthy. The soil is sand or clay, all dust or all mud. The river is the meanest apology for a frog-pond that I ever saw. It is a queer country, you would like to see it, but you would not like to live here long....his is a good place for a man with plenty of money to make more, but if I had enough money to start here I never would come, think the country ought to have been left to the animals that have laid their bones here."

Roosevelt sent the two Maine men down to the new site to build his ranch house and learn about cattle with one hundred head. Merrifield, of course, was none too happy to see the men from Maine had moved in on his territory, but Roosevelt mollified him by telling him they would go on a hunting trip in Big Horn country or Wyoming to find grizzly. He wrote his sister, "You will probably not hear from me for a couple months...if our horses give out or run away, or we get caught in the snow, we may be out very much longer—till towards Christmas."[4] He wanted to leave in a couple weeks, but they needed more horses for the journey.

Roosevelt was still setting up his life, creating something out of the Badlands that would give him purpose. He kept busy with building a ranch and buying cattle and hiring men; and more than that, he explored this new alien world with long rides in the saddle. On one of these rides, he and Sewall came across a couple of sun-bleached elk skulls with horns locked together. Roosevelt saw it as a battle to the death and took the name Elkhorn for his ranch. There was a hunting shack already on the property that Roosevelt would use until the big ranch house was finished.

He wrote his sister Bamie about the long rides he took during these days—the solitary rider looking for something in the harsh unforgiving landscape:

> I grow very fond of this place and it certainly has a desolate, grim beauty of its own, that has a curious fascination for me. The grassy, scantily wooded bottoms through which the winding river flows are bounded by bare, jagged buttes; their fantastic shapes and sharp, steep edges throw the most curious shadows, under the cloudless, glaring sky; and at evening I love to sit out in front of the hut and see their hard, gray outlines gradually grow soft…while my days I spend generally alone, riding through the lonely rolling prairie and broken lands.[5]

During these days when Roosevelt divided his time between Sewall and Dow and Merrifield and Ferris, making sure all was going to plan, he found himself in a state of transformation and wrote to his sister again, "I now look like a regular cowboy dandy, with all my equipments finished in the most expensive style."[6] He was speaking, of course, about his buckskin tunic and his broad sombrero, which now was accompanied by a fringed buckskin shirt, boots, chaparajos, and silver spurs. Movies had not come along yet, but Theodore Roosevelt could have certainly played the part of the newly minted cowboy.

It was on one of his long solitary rides out into the Badlands that a famous confrontation took place. Roosevelt often went out looking for stray horses, and on one ride he had gone far out on the prairie and night fell. The stars appeared like silver pepper over the lone rider, with the moon a crescent over the far buttes. The cool night air made the town of Mingusville stand out sharply in the distance. The town consisted of a railroad station and a hotel with a false front, really no more than a saloon.

Roosevelt paused and stared at the yellow lights of the clustered buildings, then turned his horse toward the town. He was headed for a showdown with a Wild West bad man. Little Missouri was rated as one of the wildest towns on the Northern Pacific line, and to a large extent the Badlands itself was a thieves' paradise. "They were here, there, and everywhere, sinister, intangible shadows, weaving in and out of the bright-colored fabric of frontier life. They were in every saloon and in almost every ranch-house. They rode on the round-ups, they sat around the camp-fire with the cowpunchers."[7]

Out in the West, there was no real law, and men took advantage of that fact; the Badlands was the escape valve that allowed them to blow off steam. So gunplay was common, with many taking pot shots at the railroad cars passing through, some shooting through the cars, some even shooting though the bottom of the train cars. Shooting up the town was standard entertainment on many nights when young cowboys came in to get "oiled," and then bullets would go flying from the saloons. Roosevelt later told of a cowboy in Medora who "spurred his horse up the steps of a rickety 'hotel' piazza into the bar-room, where he began firing at the clock, the decanters, etc., the bartender meanwhile taking one shot at him, which missed. When he had emptied his revolver he threw down a roll of bank-notes on the counter, to pay for the damage he had done, and galloped his horse out through the door...."[8]

As Hermann Hagedorn writes in *Roosevelt in the Badlands*, "Western Dakota was a sanctuary, and from every direction of the compass knaves of varying degrees of iniquity and misguided ability came to enjoy it. There was no law in the Bad Lands but 'six shooter law.' The days were reasonably orderly, for there were 'jobs' for everyone; but the nights were wild....Butchers and cowboys, carpenters and laborers, adventurous young college graduates and younger sons of English noblemen, drank and gambled and shouted and 'shot up the town' together with 'horse rustlers'...and 'bad men' with notches on their guns."[9] Roosevelt related another story of two men who slinked around town, each trying to get the drop on the other. "At last one of the partners got a chance at his opponent as the latter was walking into a gambling hell, and broke his back near the hips; yet the crippled, mortally wounded man twisted around as he fell and shot his slayer dead....The victor did not live twenty minutes."[10]

It was almost inevitable that this dude from the East, this newly dressed buckskin cowboy with the thick glasses, would bang up against one of the bad men. As he entered the town two shots rang out from the inside the Nolan Hotel. Here the myth of the Wild West was playing out yet again, but Roosevelt was tired and wanted to sleep. Instead of passing on, he tied up his horse and walked in. A drunken man with two drawn guns wheeled and turned on him.

"Four-eyes!" He bellowed.

Roosevelt stared at the wild-eyed man facing the tenderfoot with the buckskin coat and glasses. Nervous laughter erupted from some sheep-herders nearby, and Teddy noticed the clock over the bar was pocked with bullet holes.

"Four-eyes is going to treat," the man shouted, waving his guns in the air.[11]

Roosevelt walked slowly and sat down in a chair behind the warm woodstove. The air was smoky and smelled of horses, sweat, and gun-powder. The man followed him, shouting profanities, waving his guns over him.

"Four-eyes is going to treat," he shouts again.

Roosevelt was silent, but he knew then he would have to stand up to the gunman. The man was not going to leave him alone. He was too delicious a target for the drunken cowboy—a well-to-do "dude" out on a lark. Roosevelt later gave his own account of events:

> I heard one or two shots in the bar-room as I came up, and I disliked going in. But there was nowhere else to go, and it was a cold night. Inside the room were several men, who, including the bartender, were wearing the kind of smile worn by men who are making to believe to like what they don't like. A shabby individual in a broad hat with a cocked gun in each hand was walking up and down the floor talking with strident

profanity. He had evidently been shooting at the clock, which had two or three holes in its face....As soon as he saw me he hailed me as "Four-eyes" in reference to my spectacles and said, "Four-eyes is going to treat."[12]

Perhaps in this moment Roosevelt recalled his time as a boy at Moosehead Lake when he found himself the victim of two bullies who "teased him mercilessly" and then beat him up when he tried to fight them. This well-dressed cowboy with glasses was the classic bully's victim. No doubt many such had come West and adopted the garb, but not the code, only to find themselves humiliated by men with nothing to lose. Roosevelt continued:

I joined in the laugh and got behind the stove and sat down, thinking to escape notice. He followed me, however, and though I tried to pass it off as a jest this merely made him more offensive, and he stood leaning over me, a gun in each hand, using very foul language.... [I]n response to his reiterated command that I should set up the drinks, I said, "Well if I've got to, I've got to," and rose, looking past him. As I rose, I struck quick and hard and with a right just to one side of the point of his jaw, hitting with my left as I straightened out, and then again with my right. He fired the guns, but I do not know whether this was merely a convulsive action of his hands or whether he was trying to shoot at me. When he went down he struck the corner of the bar with his head...if he had moved I was about to drop on his ribs with my knees; but he was senseless. I took away his guns and the other people in the room, who were now loud in their denunciation of him, hustled him out and put him in a shed.[13]

The man who had entered the saloon had bested a wild, drunken cowboy who might have killed him. Roosevelt saw the man as a bully, but in the Wild West men could be shot for looking at someone funny, or for perceived offences. They were shot over a bottle of whiskey. They were shot for nothing. And Roosevelt had gone into the Western town alone, looking like a man who had just stepped off the train from the East with his glasses and new buckskin coat. He was a ripe target.

Roosevelt then sat and ate his dinner, keeping a watchful eye out for the bully's return. But he never did return and was hustled out on a freight train later. What better christening than this for the greenhorn? Roosevelt really couldn't have had it turn out any better, as news spread through the Badlands that "Four-Eyes" had something other than just money and a fancy buckskin coat.

When Roosevelt left the next day, he must have known that he too had passed into the myth of the Wild West. The news of the lone rider from the East facing down the gunman in the saloon made the rounds. Buffalo Bill riding in to save the day had nothing on Theodore Roosevelt at that moment. The West was a small community where lore and fact were mixed frequently into a potent mythology. The story of Roosevelt's showdown took on more drama as it circulated, until he was no less a hero than Gary Cooper in *High Noon*.

"Roosevelt was regarded by the cowboys as a good deal of a joke until after the saloon incident," Frank Green, a local official of the Northern Pacific, said many years later. "After that it was different."[14] Of course it was different. Courage counted for more than anything else on the frontier, and a man who had been discounted as nothing more than a rich greenhorn from the East had just shown he had grit. Clearly, Roosevelt had proven to the rough and tumble citizenry that he was not just a cowboy poser; and what is more, he had proven it to himself.

This was an important building block in the reconstruction of Theodore Roosevelt. Take a sickly young man devastated by the death of his wife and mother and put him out in the Wild West, where he turns into a rancher. Then add a showdown with a gunslinger and it is another plank, another brick, in the edifice that would be on display years later. Travail begets hardship begets character. Roosevelt must have grinned as he galloped back home.

In a larger sense, this incident proved the Wild West was not a myth. Teddy Roosevelt had stumbled into this vanishing frontier where bad men were sometimes bested by men with right on their side. Truly, Roosevelt could have been shot right there in the little scrub town of the Badlands and the course of American history would have changed forever. Ironically, the sickly boy who started boxing simply so he could breathe would one day use those same skills to knock out a murderous bully in a Wild West town. But in doing so, Teddy Roosevelt entered into myth and would be forever wed to this evanescent moment in the history of the American West.

13

THE BIG HORN HUNT

The storm had come up quickly and the hunters had to try to find shelter in the rock formations and washed-out gullies. The clouds struck down with bolts of blue fire as the wagon and the two men on horseback galloped to escape the mushroom cloud dropping lightning all around them. They were just a few days out on the hunt, and the sultry, heavy air had become violent with rain, wind, and electricity. Roosevelt dug his spurs into Nell and rode close to her mane, thinking of the month past that had seen him in New York.

The baby with blue eyes and curls had come to him in his dreams. But she was alien now as he saw her in his sister's parlor. The trip back East was to tie up loose ends now that he had started his new life as a rancher. Roosevelt had found Henry Cabot Lodge depressed at the state of his political fortune, which mirrored Roosevelt's own. He saw nothing back East and hurried for his train. The reform wing of his party had disowned him, as had the mainstream Republicans. Many saw Roosevelt as a traitor to his class. The Dakotas beckoned, and he returned after a final interview with the *New-York Tribune*.

"I like the West and I like the ranching life..." he told them. "It would electrify some of my friends who have accused me of representing the kid-glove element in politics if they could see me galloping over the plains day in and day out, clad in a buckskin shirt and leather chaparajos, with a big sombrero on my head. For good healthy exercise I would strongly recommend some of our gilded youth to go West and try a short course of riding bucking ponies, and assist at the branding of a lot of Texas steers."[1]

The real life out West was all that mattered. The *Mandan Pioneer* jumped on this bandwagon, writing, "If the New York politicians only knew it, they might find it a great advantage to come once or twice a year to West Dakota, to blow the cobwebs from their eyes, and get new ambitions, new aspirations, and new ideas. Mr. Roosevelt, although young, can teach wisdom to the sophisticated machine politicians..."[2]

Roosevelt was in mid-transformation and bore little resemblance to that young Albany reformer who left after so much disaster. The new cowboy believed the strenuous life in the Badlands was superior to the soft life of politics and intrigue. He must have fairly run to catch the train West.

On August 18, he headed out for the big hunt, but not before the Marquis reared his head. The "Wild" part of the Wild West was also due to land and the vagaries of ownership; claims upon land were many times verbal and when filed were barely worth the paper they were printed on. It had led to not a few confrontations. Land was plentiful but only became valuable once someone laid claim to it. So it was with Roosevelt's claim to the land surrounding his new ranch home.

The Marquis had let his 12,000 sheep graze on that land at one time, but they did not survive and had left only skeletons. Roosevelt did not regard this as a valid claim—and in truth it wasn't—but the Marquis was a man who wanted it all. He must have seen Roosevelt as the only real competition, a man of his class laying hold of a land where no one had much money. He sent Roosevelt a letter claiming the land for his own.

Theodore sent a return letter saying he saw no claim at all, but told Sewall and Dow to be on the lookout for trouble. There had been a lot of self-appointed vigilantes in the Badlands who had taken it upon themselves to string up horse thieves. Many who ended their existence on the long end of a hangman's noose were *in fact* horse thieves, but some were not. The law belonged to those who made it and who had the guns or the drop on their opponent. The Marquis had already murdered one man over a claim dispute. Roosevelt had been so warned and left matters as they stood, letting time take its course.

The hunt was further delayed by the wait for extra horses, and Roosevelt wrote to his sister. He was clearly becoming the cowboy in his own mind. "Tomorrow morning early we start out. Merrifield and I go on horseback, each taking a square pony...I wear a sombrero, silk neckerchief, fringed buckskin shirt, sealskin chaparajos, alligator hide boots and with my pearl-hilted revolver and my beautifully finished Winchester rifle, I shall be able to face anything."[3]

The old tactic of action after despair was at work again when an unwelcome duty associated with his past life pushed in. Roosevelt had to round up condolences and newspaper articles and compose a "Memorial for Alice" before he departed to hunt grizzly in the mountains.

"She was beautiful in face and form," he wrote, "and lovelier still in spirit; as a flower she grew, and as a fair young flower she died. Her life had always been in the sunshine. ... Fair, pure, and joyous as a maiden; loving, tender, and happy as a new wife; when she had just become a mother, when her life seemed to be but just begun, and when the years seemed so bright before her—then, by a strange and terrible fate, death came to her. And when my heart's dearest died, the light went from my life forever."[4]

Roosevelt, who fought melancholia at times, must have traveled back to that dark night in Manhattan. Staring across the Badlands, he remarked to Bill Sewall that "he had nothing to live for" and that his dreams all lay buried in the East, and his daughter "would be just as well off without me."[5] Bill Sewall, the lumberjack from Maine, shut one eye and nodded. "You won't always feel as you do now," he said, "and you won't always be willing to stay here and drive cattle."

And with that Roosevelt dove once again into action to prevent "overthought," as he called it. One can almost hear him muttering, "It is the action taken that counts," as he headed for Big Horn country with Merrifield behind the prairie schooner and a French Canadian, Norman Lebo, who would drive the wagon and cook for the hunters. Lebo was a short and stocky Western nomad, who said to Roosevelt, "If I had the money, no two nights would ever see me in the same bed."

Roosevelt had come heavily armed for the seven-week trip. "My battery consists of a long .45 Colt revolver, 150 cartridges, a no. 10 choke bore, 300 cartridge shotgun; a 45–75 Winchester repeater, with 1000 cartridges; a 40–90 Sharps, 150 cartridges; a 50–150 double barreled Webley express, 150 cartridges."[6]

Clearly he was ready for the hunt.

"How long I will be gone I cannot say; we will go in all nearly a thousand miles. If game is plenty and my success is good, I may return in six weeks; more probably I shall be out a couple of months, and if game is so scarce that we have to travel very far to get it...we may be out very much longer," he wrote to his sister.[7]

The hunters immediately ran into the kind of weather the Badlands was famous for. Another mushroom cloud of darkness moved in and the men galloped to seek shelter in a land that had none. They headed for a dry creek bed, but the storm broke before they could reach it. Roosevelt picks up the account here: "The first gust caught us a few hundred yards from the creek, almost taking us from the saddle, and driving the rain and hail in stinging level sheets against us. We galloped to the edge of a deep wash-out, scrambled into it at the risk of our necks, and huddle up with our horses underneath the windward bank. Although it was August, the air became very cold. ... Where the center of the whirlwind struck, it did great damage, sheets of hailstones as large as pigeons' eggs striking the earth with the velocity of bullets..."[8]

They camped on the edge of the gulley while the rain continued, and struggled through the muck of red gumbo, catching rain with their slickers to make coffee and spending the next night in the wagon under cover, huddled around a cracker barrel. When the weather cleared they headed to the southeast at a snail's pace, as Lebo moved the wagon along and Merrifield and Roosevelt rode along both sides, picking off game where they could find it. Roosevelt saw some chickens and rode toward them when Merrifield called out.

"Don't shoot!"

Roosevelt, being Roosevelt, went on anyway, when a mountain lion sprang out of some brush and bounded away. It was too late for either man to get a shot off.

"Now whenever I hold up my hand," Merrifield chastised his boss, "You stop, understand?"[9]

Roosevelt agreed, knowing he had been in the wrong. This solidified his view that in the wild all men were equals and merit trumped all. They traveled farther and farther, and one can imagine Roosevelt relishing the isolation as they saw no other humans. The days in the saddle when he first reached the Badlands, the search for something pure and primitive as opposed to the messiness of the "civilized world"—all were evident in another letter.

> I am writing this on an upturned water keg, by our canvas-covered wagon. ... I am going to trust it to the tender mercies of a stray cowboy whom we have just met. We left the Little Missouri a week ago, and have been traveling steadily some twenty or thirty miles a day ever since, through a desolate, barren-looking, and yet picturesque country, part of the time rolling prairie and part of the time broken jagged Bad Lands. ... Every morning we get up at dawn, and start off by six o'clock or thereabouts, Merrifield and I riding off among the hills or ravines after game, while the battered "prairie schooner," with the two spare ponies led behind is driven slowly along by old Lebo, who is a perfect character.[10]

This picturesque image of cowboys on the hunt with wagon train in tow is rounded out by Roosevelt's description of sleeping in the open when a rainstorm found them and "we shivered in our wet blankets until dawn."[11] He was still a man with acute asthma and chronic digestive problems that flared up periodically, but the West itself seemed to be the antidote.

"We go into camp a little before sunset, tethering two or three of the horses, and letting the others range. One night we camped in a most beautiful natural park; it was a large, grassy hill, studded thickly with small, pine-crowned chalk buttes, with very steep sides, worn into the most outlandish and fantastic shapes. All that night the wolves kept up a weird concert around our camp—they are most harmless beasts."[12]

Roosevelt finished with the image of primordial life under the moonlit beauty of the jagged rocks of the Badlands, and a man who found in it the tonic for the great despair of his life. "I heartily enjoy this life with its perfect freedom...there are very few sensations I prefer to that of galloping over these rolling limitless prairies, rifle in hand, or winding my way among the barren, fantastic, and grimly picturesque deserts of the so-called Bad Lands."[13]

They came upon three blacktail deer and Roosevelt took a running shot from two hundred yards out. He missed and then adjusted his rifle for a four hundred yard shot and waited. The bucks appeared with their head in line and he fired, both deer flipping over with a shot through their skulls.

"Bully! By God, that was a shot," Roosevelt proclaimed.

And then came a near disaster. Roosevelt and Merrifield rode into a sandy washout and began to clamber up the other side. It was so steep they had to dismount and lead their horses up, and then it turned into a perpendicular bluff. Merrifield was in the lead when his pony suddenly reared back and lost its balance, its weight shifting to its hind legs with its front legs pawing the air. The pony went over backwards in a cartwheel toward Roosevelt who just managed to dive out of the way as it went down in two somersaults and crashed to the river bottom.

Merrifield's horse managed to struggle to its feet and seemed none the worse for wear, but clearly Roosevelt would have been crushed if he did not dive out of the way. The everyday hazards in the Badlands could be more dangerous than the Indians. But of course there were the Indians too. Roosevelt and Merrifield came upon a band while galloping up to the Clear Fork of the Powder. They were just a little way from where they had pitched camp for the night. But let us pause now to get a fix on the historical period.

In the year 1885, it was eighteen years until the Wright Brothers would fly their plane; in eleven years a twenty-two-year-old Italian named Marconi would send sparks through the air and usher in the age of wireless communication; and in that same year Henry Ford would put the finishing touches on a car in a shed behind his home. But there was Teddy Roosevelt, staring at Indians in a scene as atavistic as Lewis and Clark's expedition. What is even more fascinating to consider is that in 1885, Sitting Bull, the man who killed Custer, joined Buffalo Bill's Wild West show. The show, started by William Cody (a.k.a. Buffalo Bill) in 1883, would keep the Wild West alive right up to 1913. At the very time the West was being exported by a man who was essentially a circus promoter, Roosevelt was stumbling on the last vestiges of the real thing in the Badlands.

The last real skirmish between cowboys and the Cheyenne happened in 1883, with bloodshed on both sides. "About the same time a band of Sioux plundered a party of buffalo hunters of everything they owned and some Crows attempted the same feat," Roosevelt would later write. "There is always danger in meeting a band of young bucks in lonely uninhabited country.... A man meeting such a party runs great risk of losing his horse, his rifle, and all else he has.... and in at least once such instance...the unfortunate individual lost his life..."[14]

This had to be on Roosevelt's mind when Merrifield stood up from the campfire.

"I'm going over to see the Indians," he announced.

We can picture Roosevelt's glasses in the campfire light, the incredulity spreading over his face. He was familiar with dark stories of men cut up and left for the wolves, or tied down and left to bake in the sun. He did not carry the poison that some men did in case of capture. As

Hermann Hagedorn writes in *Roosevelt in the Badlands*: "In the region between the Little Missouri and the Yellowstone, in the years 1884 and 1885, the wounds left by the wars, which had culminated in the death of Custer at the Little Big Horn, were still open and sore…many white men shot whatever Indians they came upon like coyotes, on sight, others captured them, when they could and stripping off their clothes, whipped them until they bled. The Indians retaliated horribly, delivering their white captives to their squaws, who tortured them in every conceivable fashion, driving slivers up under their nails or burning them alive."

This had to be in the mind of the man from Manhattan as he stared into the darkness, imagining Indians sneaking up on them. These might even be the Indians who murdered Custer and his men, the Indians who had scalped and hacked up men and left them to die in the sun.

"What do you want to go over there for?"

"Out in this country," Merrifield replied, standing up, "you always want to know who your neighbors are."[15]

Roosevelt and Merrifield rode over together and found the Indians were Cheyenne. Merrifield knew from experience that you had to prove to the Indians you were a worthy opponent. He suggested a shooting contest, and to Roosevelt's amazement he saw that the Indians were very bad marksmen. The two men outshot the Indians and rode back to their camp with Merrifield later saying, "Indians are the best judges of human nature in the world. When an Indian finds out that you are a good shot, he will leave you absolutely alone to go and come as you like. Indians are just like white men. They are not going to start something when they know you can out-shoot them."[16]

Surely Roosevelt stowed this away for future encounters with Indians. As they rode up on the Indians, perhaps he felt a thrill of fear as the archetypes came to life: the iconic stories in the papers of the East, the romantic Western landscapes painted by his father's friend Albert Bierstadt, or William Cody's Wild West show with its Indians whooping into the circus tent, guns blazing and war bonnets flying.

The encounter was another brick in the edifice of Teddy Roosevelt; the weak man was being remade into the man of action who faced down outlaws and now Indians. This new man would eventually return East with all these experiences etched in his soul, but his real confrontation with the Indians lay in the future and will be much more dangerous. For now, he was riding over the great arc of the Wild West and doing just fine.

14

THE CRAZY MAN
1877

The ice was rough and the wind blew cold as misery. Richard Welling was going ice skating on Fresh Pond with Teddy Roosevelt. The snow and wind blew harder as the two young men from Harvard, who could barely skate, made their way across the lake. Welling, who was dubious about crossing the ice at all, became cold and wanted to turn back. But Roosevelt continued on, gathering strength, at one point exclaiming, "Isn't it bully!" Welling later wrote, "Never in college was my own grit so put to the test and yet I would not be the first to suggest home."[1] They stayed out on the ice for three hours, and only when it became dark did Roosevelt concede they should go back. His was the crazy will of a man never daunted or of someone perhaps a little unbalanced.

Another story of Roosevelt concerns a boxing match that went badly for him in the Harvard gym. Teddy was being bested by a senior, C. S. Hanks, when the referee called time and Roosevelt dropped his guard. Just then Hanks delivered a right hook that smashed Roosevelt's nose, and blood exploded. The crowd demanded retribution, but Teddy held up his glove and said, "It's all right, he didn't hear him."[2]

Fact or legend, this story has followed Roosevelt as proof of his inviolable code: A man must stand for something and so must other men. No Harvard man would take advantage of a referee's whistle. Although he was never a good boxer or much of an athlete, Roosevelt believed he could be the best, as his cousin Maud Elliott observed, "Teddy always thought he could do things better than anyone else."[3] Why not? He had been homeschooled his whole life until he went to Harvard. The boy with the asthma, glasses, and chronic diarrhea became the young man entering the land of spires and gargoyles.

Harvard was the logical place for a rich man's son. Roosevelt was now seventeen years old and five-foot-eight and would grow no further. He was small at 125 pounds, and his glasses were moons that continually slid down when he laughed, which his mother said sounded like "an ungreased squeak."[4] He had a weird accent. In later years, in the Albany Legislature, he would cry out, "*Mr. Speakar, Mr. Speakar,*" a strange amalgam of upper class New York and maybe something to do with his asthma, where he seemed to be biting the words in half with his prominent teeth. Pinned to his head were small ears and he had absurdly small feet. He often wore his mother's slippers. A classmate at Harvard described him as "a youth in in the kindergarten stage of physical development."[5]

His health had improved, but of course there was only one direction it *could* go. The asthma had dried up and his diarrhea had come under control. He had been homeschooled by Arthur Cutler, who was rigorous in his approach to subjects, especially math. So Roosevelt had never faced a professor or had to socialize before going to Harvard, but he found the students friendly and he excelled in making acquaintances of a sort. Teddy was too eccentric for close friendships, however.

Hermann Hagedorn, in *Roosevelt in the Badlands*, was more brutal in his assessment of Roosevelt's relations with his Harvard classmates: "I have discovered no one who was intimate with him and few who were sympathetic...most of his classmates simply did not like him."[6] One classmate thought back on Roosevelt and wondered "whether he is the real thing or the bundle of eccentricities which he appears."[7] Another Harvard man, John Woodbury, thought Teddy might amount to a history professor, but added, "Some thought he was crazy." Martha Cowdin, a Boston debutante, summed up the toothy, short man as "not the sort to appeal at first."

Roosevelt had become depressed at Harvard after the death of his father. It had been a horrible death from stomach cancer, as his brother Elliott testified: "suddenly his face became distorted with pain and he called out for ether. ... he never said anything but 'Oh My!' but the agony in his face was awful. Ether and sedatives were of no avail...pretty soon father began to vomit...he turned sharp to the left and throwing up his arms around, he gave one mighty clasp...his eyelids fluttered, he gave three long breaths...thirteen and quarter hours it took to kill a man broken down by three months of sickness."[8]

Teddy was distraught. It was all a "hideous dream." He wrote to Henry Minot, "It was best that Father's terrible sufferings should end."[9] He later described in his diary the "bitter agony when I kissed the dear, dead face and realized he would never again on this earth speak to me.... He was the most wise and loving father that ever lived; I owe everything to him."

Then there were a series of diary entries at Harvard:

"Have been thinking about father all evening, have had a good square breakdown, and feel much better for it."

"Every now and then there are bitter moments; if I had very much time to think I believe I should go crazy."

"It is just one month since the blackest day of my life."[10]

In church in Oyster Bay, Long Island, he saw his father beside him in the pew "as distinctly as if he were alive." For a time he did not care about his grades or anything else. The memory of his father knocked him down as he compared himself to the man: "[H]ow little use I am or ever shall be...I am as much inferior to Father morally and mentally as physically.... He did everything for me and I nothing for him. I remember so well how, years ago, when I was a very weak, asthmatic child, he used to walk up and down with me in his arms...and oh, how my heart pains me when I think I was never able to do anything for him during his illness!"[11]

Roosevelt then eerily wrote, "Sometimes, when I fully realize my loss, I feel as if I should go mad."[12] He would cite the same feelings when his wife and mother left him on the same day. But then the physical therapy began. Great tragedy evoked physical exertion from Roosevelt. He began rowing the Sound in Oyster Bay like a demon. A man in a boat on sweltering days in July rowing until his arms ached and he screamed with the effort. Then he would run or hike in the rain with his rifle, blasting away at anything that moved. He ran his horse Lightfoot into the ground with grueling, punishing rides that bordered on animal cruelty.

One time he was out all day in the woods and on the return trip spied a neighbor's dog. He pulled out his revolver and shot the dog dead, "rolling it over with my revolver very neatly as it ran alongside the horse."[13] The horse was lame after these rides, and meanwhile a friendship with an old family friend, Edith Carow, went on the rocks after a blowup. His cruel temperament seemed to be in the ascendant. Roosevelt escaped to the wilds of Maine to hunt and hike, and he lost himself in the exertion of man against the elements. "Look out for Roosevelt," a doctor named Thompson said, who accompanied him into the woods in Maine. "He's not strong, but he's all grit. He'll kill himself before he'll even say he's tired."[14]

One thing was for certain: Roosevelt was a killer. He would hunt at the drop of a hat and would prove himself over and over as a man who had dominance over his world. In later years on the safari, he would kill so many animals the Smithsonian could take in only a quarter of his "scientific motherlode." He would turn on his old friend and successor William Howard Taft and hunt him the way he had hunted bears, lions, or humans in the Spanish American War. He destroyed his enemies and was really at his best in the fight, even when he destroyed himself in the process.

Of course, during his time at Harvard, all this was in the future. After Harvard, he became a man of means and inherited 125,000 dollars from his father, which gave him a dividend of 8,000 a year to live on. This is more than adequate for a young man unsure of his future, but what if he just plunked down 14,000 dollars on a log and bought a ranch out West? It is a crazy move for a normal person, and there were those who thought Teddy Roosevelt was crazy. But not every crazy man becomes a cowboy who can lasso the presidency of the United States.

15

RIGHT BETWEEN
THE EYES
1886

The Bighorn Mountains stretch from southern Montana to northern Wyoming. This sister range of the Rockies has sheer mountainsides, grasslands, and glacier-cut valleys. The lakes of crystalline blue and the soaring peaks inspired mountain men to name parts of the mountains Cloud Peak and Black Tooth Peak. The Sioux hid from General Crook's Army in 1876 in the spruce forests of the Big Horn. The peaks were rounded on top and temperatures during winter could plummet to forty below zero in just a few hours. The weather was unpredictable, and those who believed a fire could survive a wind-driven snowstorm disappeared.

Roosevelt and the hunters pushed on, and after three weeks of burning prairie they reached the mountains. Green pines and gurgling brooks surrounded them in their new camp up in the cold, clear air. It was excellent country for hunting and, compared to the hell they had passed through, a paradise of ice-skimmed water and pine-scented campfires with Lebo serving up food from the schooner. Sitting around the camp-fire, Roosevelt was impressed by the majesty of the mountains.

"If I listened long enough, it would almost seem that I heard thunder-ous voices laughing and calling to one another," he wrote, "and as if at any moment some shape might stalk out of the darkness into the dim light of the embers."[1]

"We've come to a land at last," said Lebo," where the leaves grow on trees."[2]

But it was eight thousand feet elevation and temperatures below freezing. The first order of business was grizzly, but it was an elk Roos-evelt killed first. The man from the East still had severe asthma, but even in thin air he acted like a man born to the mountains, as he recounted:

> We had been running briskly up-hill through the soft, heavy loam in which our feet made no noise but slipped and sank deeply; as a consequence, I was all out of breath and my hand so unsteady that I missed my first shot. ... We raced after them [elk] at full speed, opening fire; I wounded all three, but none of the wounds were immediately disabling. They trotted on and we panted afterwards, slipping on the wet earth, pitch-ing headlong over charred stumps, leaping on dead logs that broke beneath our weight, more than once measuring our full-length on the ground, halting and firing whenever we got a chance. At last one bull fell; we passed him by after the oth-ers, which were still running up-hill. The sweat streamed into my eyes and made furrows in the sooty mud that covered my face, from having fallen full length down on the burnt earth; I sobbed for breath as I toiled at a shambling trot after them, as nearly done out as well could be.[3]

Roosevelt was not totally "done out" as he did kill the second elk and went after the third. Of course, this sort of fatiguing, all-consuming activity gave him the necessary "too tired to think" remedy he prescribed for himself to keep thoughts of his dead wife and mother at bay. But even high up on the mountain he found himself pulled back into the darkness he had left in the East. Around the campfire that night with the mournful cry of the bull elks in the distance, he told Merrifield of the awful night in Manhattan. Roosevelt stared into the fire and told the rancher his pain was "beyond any healing" and he would never be consoled. Merrifield, who had also lost his wife, paused and gave back the usual "this too will pass." TR dismissed him, saying, "Now don't talk to me about time will make a difference…time will never change me in that respect."[4]

Roosevelt wanted a grizzly on this trip, but the king of the Rockies proved elusive their first week in the mountains. An amazing sense of smell and acute hearing made them very hard to hunt, but like Roosevelt, the grizzly had terrible eyesight. Stumbling upon this bear could be lethal, as they would lunge without warning. If they did not catch one by October, it would be all over as the thousand-pound grizzlies went to their dens to hibernate. Now, in September, was their chance to bag the monster bear, if only they could find one.

The hunter's luck changed when Merrifield rode into camp one evening shouting he had found some grizzly bear signs ten miles on the other side of the mountain. They moved their camp. At sunset, Roosevelt came upon bear tracks and followed them from tree to tree until dark. He knew they were close. The next afternoon, Roosevelt perched himself on a crag over a ravine and killed a great bull elk. "Now," he said "we'll go out tonight and get a bear."[5] But they found nothing, and it was not until the next day they discovered the bear had been feasting on Roosevelt's elk.

The next time out, they wore moccasins to quiet their steps and positioned themselves around the elk carcass, making sure they had clear shots once the grizzly returned for his meal. They stayed all night, listening to the wolves and hoot owls. And with each break of a branch, each snap in the dark woods, they anticipated the approach of the bear. Grizzlies are not black bears; they can maul and eat a man in minutes, and some people who have made the mistake of not respecting a grizzly have paid the ultimate price.

Roosevelt and Merrifield spent the long night with fingers on their rifle triggers, but the bear did not come back. The next morning Merrifield picked up the bear's trail over the pine needles and moss and led them through the woods. The hunters breathed in the cold, clean scent of pine needles as they crept forward. Roosevelt was following Merrifield "when in the middle of the thicket we crossed a breastwork of fallen logs, and Merrifield, who was leading, passed by the upright stem of a great pine," Roosevelt wrote later.[6] "As soon as he was by it, he sank suddenly on one knee, turning half around, his face fairly aflame with excitement; and as I strode past him, with my rifle at the ready, there, not ten steps off, was the great bear, slowly rising from his bed among the young spruces."[7]

To Merrifield's surprise, Roosevelt walked past him briskly. The nine-foot, twelve-hundred-pound grizzly had already heard them and was back on his haunches, baring his needle-sharp teeth. "He had heard us but apparently hardly knew exactly where or what we were," Roosevelt continued, "for he reared up on his haunches sideways to us, then he saw us and dropped down again on all fours, the shaggy hair on his neck and shoulders seeming to bristle as he turned toward us. As he sank down to his forefeet, I had raised the rifle."[8]

Roosevelt's heart was pounding and his mouth was dry as he faced down the fiercest creature in the West. He lifted his rifle, feeling his heart, telling himself that this was the moment; this was where the man confronted himself. If he missed, he would be dead. Roosevelt aimed between the fierce gleaming eyes and fired. "Doubtless my face was pretty white," he later wrote his sister, "but the blue barrel was as steady as a rock as I glanced along it until I could see the top of the bead fairly between his two sinister-looking eyes..."[9]

The grizzly would have mauled Roosevelt, and his only real shot was a kill shot to the head. This twelve-hundred-pound bear did not like to be surprised, and Roosevelt would have been torn to pieces if he missed, as Merrifield would not have had time to stop the razor claws and crushing jaw. Roosevelt relayed the moment: "As I pulled the trigger I jumped aside out of the smoke, to be ready if he charged, but it was needless, for the great brute was struggling in his death agony, and as you will see when I bring home his skin, the bullet hole was as exactly between his eyes as if I had measured with a carpenter's rule."[10]

Roosevelt had his grizzly bear. The adrenaline thrill-ride was complete. The man walking past Merrifield to take the shot and kill or be killed was the fruition of the boy who developed the policy of "forcing the spirit to ignore the weakness of the flesh" who believed that "man does in fact become fearless by sheer dint of practicing fearlessness."[11] Roosevelt must have been scared to death.

Today people have "bucket lists." Theodore Roosevelt's would have read like this: Go West. Check. Hunt Buffalo. Check. Buy a ranch. Check. Confront a bad man. Check. Confront Indians. Soon. Shoot a grizzly. Check. Survive. Check. And this tally of exhilarating experiences had the added benefit of distracting him from the black past. He had confronted the myth of the West once again and had exacted his pound of flesh... actually, about twelve hundred pounds.

The snow had begun to fall on the feathery pines when they packed up camp and went down the mountain single file. Roosevelt returned from the mountains with the pack ponies heavy with the carcasses of the hunt. He felt very accomplished as he rode the three hundred miles back home. Then the return trip turned into an ordeal. The horses began to falter across the burnt, desolate prairie, and in some sand hills on the east side of the Little Beaver one of the train horses gave out.

They swapped out the horse with their strongest pony and pushed on, coming by nightfall to the weird country of the Medicine Buttes. These teepee-like rock formations looked like a congregation of ancient dwellings or something even more fantastic. "Some of them rose as sharp peaks or ridges as connected chains... the sides were perpendicular and were cut and channeled by the weather into most curious caves and columns and battlements and spires,"[12] Roosevelt would later write.

They pitched camp among the curious formations under a full moon and built a large fire against a cliff face. The pines and the Medicine Buttes under the lunar light took on a weird, otherworldly character, reminding Roosevelt again that he was far from civilization. The fire flickered out into the still night, the silver formations glowing like a small city. Roosevelt stared at the pines lifting their branches to the heartless moon, as he drank his coffee in the cold night air.

In the morning the rain came with gale force winds and fog, and the three men moved from shelter to shelter with no fire and little food. Roosevelt would later say, "Fortunately, we had all learned that, no matter how bad things were, grumbling and bad temper can always be depended upon to make them worse, and so bore our ill-fortune, if not with stoical indifference, at least in perfect quiet."[13]

The next day the weather broke and they were still forty miles from Lang's.

"I think I'd like to ride in and wake the boys up for breakfast," Merrifield said.

"Good...I'll do it with you," Roosevelt replied.[14]

He had had enough. At nine o'clock in the evening the two men took off on their horses across the moon-drenched prairie. Riding at night across the wide open expanse of the Badlands at breakneck speed was probably the closest thing to a thrill ride in 1885. They hunched down close to the necks of their horses with the silvered ground rolling underneath. Cool October air blew across the open land as they galloped across the prairie in a scene from every boy's dream of the time. Roosevelt's description gives us his night ride across the West in all its romantic glory:

> The hoofbeats for our horses rang out in steady rhythm through the silence of the night, otherwise unbroken save now and then by the wailing cry of a coyote. The rolling plains stretched out on all sides of us, shimmering in the clear moonlight; and occasionally a band of spectral-looking antelope swept silently away from before our path. Once we went by a drove of Texan cattle, who stared wildly at the intruders; as we passed they charged down by us, the ground rumbling beneath their tread, while their long horns knocked against each with a sound like the clattering of castanets. We could

see clearly enough to keep our general course over the track-less plain, steering by the stars where the prairie was perfectly level and without landmarks; and our ride was timed well, for as we galloped down into the valley of the Little Missouri, the sky above the line of the level bluffs in our front was crimson with the glow of the unrisen sun.[15]

Could the myth be any brighter than right at that moment? Could there be any more fun than being a young man blazing across a moon-drenched prairie with its Indians and cattle and bad men, galloping across the vanishing history of the Wild West? The hooves pounding the hard earth and the wind in his face as they gallop through the darkness will stay with Roosevelt to his dying day. Teddy Roosevelt surely was at his zenith in living the cowboy dream.

Roosevelt had covered almost a thousand miles on horseback and risked his life several times. In relaying to his sister the highlights of the hunt, he displayed the Roosevelt swagger. "I...fully realized that we were hunting dangerous game, still I never made steadier shooting than at the grizzlies. I had grand sport with the elk, too, and the woods fairly rang with my shouting when I brought down my first lordly bull...but after I had begun bear-killing, other sport seemed tame. So I have good sport; and enough excitement and fatigue to prevent overmuch thought; and moreover, I have at last been able to sleep well at night."[16]

"Overmuch thought" was of course the code word for stress, neurosis, or depression. Roosevelt ranked experience according to its ability to obliterate recursive thinking on the past and the despair that came with it. And this was not the first time he had spoken of sleeping well. He was an insomniac, but the salutary effect of the West once again banished the cares of the East. Self-realization nipped at the close of his letter to Bamie. "But unless I was bear hunting all the time, I am afraid I should soon get as restless with this life as with the life at home."[17]

All drugs have a shelf life, and Roosevelt's prescription had to be constantly renewed. Fortunately for him, the West was still an open apothecary.

16

THE WINTER OF DISCONTENT

1886

While Roosevelt was busy confronting grizzly bears, the Marquis had been busy consolidating his hold on the Badlands. He was organizing a stagecoach line along with his slaughterhouse and refrigerated car line and part of his consolidation involved laying claim to Roosevelt's Elkhorn Ranch, through his henchman Joe Paddock. Paddock took a little ride and a confrontation with Merrifield followed that devolved into a drunken lunch and then threats against the owner of the Elkhorn ranch if he didn't pay up in blood or money.

The Frenchman Marquis De Mores was a sort of entitled nightmare. But he was dangerous. When he first arrived and started laying claim to land across the Little Missouri, he ran across frontiersmen gunslingers Frank O'Donnell, Riley Luffsey, and Dutch Wannegan. To make matters worse, O'Donnell had been an enemy of Paddock's long before Paddock worked for the Marquis. The trouble began when O'Donnell galloped home and found his hunting trail blocked by a fence built by the Marquis, who had apparently bought the land with a Valentine scrip.

O'Donnell tore the fence down and ignored the Marquis' claim. This was the West and claim jumping occurred all the time; besides, no one really knew where one line began and another ended. The Marquis had the fence rebuilt and of course O'Donnell and his riders destroyed it again. This went on for a while—a small storm steadily gathering strength. The tornado was unleashed when Paddock delivered the news that the Marquis was about to jump claim to his hunting shack and the surrounding land.

"Whoever jumps us," O'Donnell said to whomever wanted to listen, "jumps from there right into his grave."[1]

The stage was set. June 21 the three men whooped it up in Little Missouri and shot up the town. They drank Forty-Mile Red Eye and let everyone know that they would shoot the Marquis on sight. Paddock, ever the vigilant watchdog, reported to his boss the threats against his life. The Marquis headed to Mandan 150 miles away and gave the particulars to a justice of the peace. He finished up with a question.

"What should I do?"

The J.P., a man of the West, who saw the answer plainly, replied, "Why, shoot."

The Marquis had already dispatched two men in duels in France, so there was no lack of nerve. He took the train back to Little Missouri and found O'Donnell and company hung over and waiting for him. They let him pass, but a bullet cracked past him while he was chatting with Paddock outside his bungalow. The Marquis telegraphed for a sheriff, who would come on the next train. He then posted men along exit points of the town to make sure the sheriff would have someone to arrest when he arrived.

O'Donnell, Luffsey, and Wannegan passed the time until the train arrived and the sheriff found himself facing three men with three guns. He announced he had a warrant for their arrest. O'Donnell spat back in perfect cowboy fashion, "I've done nothing to be arrested for, and I won't be taken."[2]

Then, like in some Clint Eastwood movie, the three men rode out of town and left the sheriff staring at their backs. But the Marquis was waiting, and the men galloped from the showdown to the ambush. A crossfire knocked down all three horses and Riley Luffsey fell dead with a bullet in his neck after screaming "Wannegan, Oh Wannegan!"; another bullet struck O'Donnell's thigh, and Wannegan's clothes were tattered by flying lead. They gave up quickly.

In the quiet and the dust and the blood, the Marquis and Paddock and two others came out of their hiding spots. All were arrested by the sheriff except Paddock who somehow slipped out by saying he didn't take part in the shooting. They were all found not guilty, and Riley Luffsey was buried in Graveyard Butte with many swearing the Marquis was a dead man if he ever showed his face in Little Missouri again. He showed his face the next day and nothing happened.

Beyond these local disputes, the truth is the West was being consolidated by the large ranchers. A vigilante squad had come of age in Montana and the Dakotas. They were supposed to be after horse thieves but in fact they were running off "nesters" or independent ranchers on the edges of the Badlands. This would become a classic motif in later movies and novels: the early corporatization of the West against the independent rancher or lone frontiersman. In the grand scheme of American history, it was an ongoing theme.

A Western correspondent for New York's *The Sun* summed it up this way: "The cowmen here are opposed, not only to the Indians, but also to the white settlers. They want the land these white and red settlers are taking up. Vast tracts—uncultivated ranges, not settlements—are what they desire. The small holder—the man with a little bunch of cattle—is not wanted. They freeze him out. Somehow he loses cattle, or they are killed by parties unknown."

The Wild West was wild also because the open land created a void where powerful interests could move in and dominate with little consequence. Men were lynched for simply being suspected of horse thievery when in fact their real crime was taking land from the big ranching interests. This was the background of the men who had decided the Elkhorn ranch would be easy pickings, belonging as it did to "Four-Eyes" from the East.

Paddock must have believed he could extort money from Roosevelt with the Marquis' backing. After all, they had managed to kill a man who went against them and nothing had happened; surely, "The Dude" from the East did not have the sand to fight back against the powerful Marquis. Dow and Sewall were at the ranch when men galloped up. Sewall was writing a letter when he heard the horses and then shots. He went outside and found six rough-looking men led by Paddock with smoking rifles in their hands. They had all been drinking and Sewall offered them food. He served them beans, with his gun in easy reach. He had heard the stories of men being hung after being accused of being horse thieves.

"I thought I would do everything I could to make them comfortable," he said later. "And then if they cooked up any racket, we should have to see what the end would be. I knew that if they were well filled, it would have a tendency to make them good-natured, and besides that it puts a man in a rather awkward position, when he's got well tread, to start a rumpus."[3]

Sewall then showed the men around the cabin and eventually they left, but without a doubt he knew the men wanted to drive them off the land. When Sewall told him of the threats, Roosevelt merely nodded and murmured, "Is that so?" He then mounted his horse and rode over to Paddock's house near the railroad. The code of the West had asserted itself. Roosevelt knew of course that if he didn't make Paddock and the Marquis back down, he would never be respected and his ranch never safe. He arrived in town and tied off his horse and then walked onto the plank porch with his spurs clinking. The buck-skinned man with glasses knocked on the door of the shack just a few hundred yards from the Pyramid Hotel. It was High Noon for Roosevelt, and he was ready to confront another bad man of the West.

The gunman answered.

"Paddock," Roosevelt declared. "I understand that you have threatened to kill me on sight. I have come over to see when you want to begin the killing and to let you know that if you have anything against me, now is the time for you to say it."[4]

Paddock apparently was taken by surprise and declared he had been misquoted. Roosevelt of course was well-armed in his confrontation and fresh off the hunt for elk. He had his blood up and Paddock must have realized he was dealing with more than a just a drunken cowboy whom he could ambush. At any rate he backed down and so did the Marquis. For now.

Roosevelt parted, leaving Paddock to build up the Roosevelt legend. First there had been the bully in the saloon, and now he was known as the man willing to fight for his land and face down a land baron like the Marquis. In a land where legend is built from personal courage and initiative, Theodore Roosevelt had taken the field by storm. He was like the Marquis in that both men came from wealth and had come seeking their destiny in the West, but they were different men. Respect followed Theodore Roosevelt and proved once again that people might envy wealth, but they admire courage.

17

THE DARKEST OF MOMENTS

1886

In 1886, Roosevelt did a curious thing and briefly returned to New York. It was as if he were measuring the new man against the old with this visit back to his old political stomping grounds. He gave several speeches and checked the direction of prevailing winds, allowing that he had probably done the right thing by vacating to the West when he did. One can almost see him holding his finger up to see which way the winds of destiny were blowing. He returned west on the sixteenth of November and faced a winter he would not forget.

Roosevelt arrived on the train and visited with Sylvane and Merrifield at the old ranch before heading for the new one with Dow and Sewall. He started late for the long ride to Elkhorn. The "white weather" was already upon the Badlands, with the temperature plummeting to zero, and it was getting dark. In the Badlands men habitually froze to death when caught in the open during a winter storm. Roosevelt would later write of the winters in *Hunting Trips of a Ranchman*, "When the days have dwindled to their shortest, and the nights seem never-ending,

117

then all the great northern plains are changed into an abode of iron desolation. Sometimes furious gales blow down from the north, driving before them the clouds of blinding snow-dust, wrapping the mantle of death round every unsheltered being that faces their unshackled anger."

The trail Roosevelt was following turned into the Badlands and did the usual gyrations through ravines and gullies and over buttes, then breaking into open plateaus. The wind blew fierce and turned the snow into ice needles. The lone rider trudged on, disbelieving that he had just been in the heart of the world in New York. But Teddy Roosevelt was all about extremes. The burning mines threw up weird shafts of smoke. "A strong smell of sulphur hangs round them," Roosevelt later wrote of the mines around his ranch, "the heated earth crumbles and cracks, and through the long clefts that form in it we can see the lurid glow of the subterranean fires with here and there tongues of blue or cherry colored flame dancing up to the surface."[1]

He tried to cross the Little Missouri in several places, but the ice was too thin, soaking horse and rider. Now Roosevelt was in danger of freezing to death and there was no way for him to make it to Elkhorn with the snow and wind steadily increasing and the darkness coming down like a veil from the dark side of the moon. He knew he was in trouble. "The great white country wrapped in the powdery snow-drift seems like another land and the familiar landmarks are so changed that a man must be careful lest he lose his way..."[2]

There was a hunting shack belonging to a Captain Robins that was closer, and Roosevelt determined he could spend the night there. The problem was he couldn't see his hand in front of his face in the snowy darkness. There was, of course, no technology to swoop in and save Roosevelt. He was virtually alone, and if he became lost and froze to death he could very well not turn up until the spring. The bodies of many men were found after long, hard winters, their clothes torn off from the last spasms of freezing to death. The Badlands were littered with the skulls of cattle who had met similar deaths, when the cold-smitten plains seemed far from the sun.

The only sound in the silence of the snow-blown landscape was the muffled hoofbeats of his horse. Roosevelt tried to follow the trail, huddled against the snow blast freezing his cheeks, his streaked glasses making things even worse. He heard "the long drawn melancholy howling of a wolf, a quarter mile off." This huddled rider encased in snow and ice in the lonely night of the Badlands would one day be president of the United States. From the perspective of that moment, it is an incredible thought.

Roosevelt had once before become lost with a cowboy from Texas. "We started home together across the open parries but were caught in a very heavy snowstorm...we were suddenly turned around, the great soft flakes almost blinding us, and we had to travel entirely by compass."[3] After nine hours they came across an empty hut and stayed the night, with Roosevelt reading *Hamlet* to the cowboy.

Robins's shack was hidden among some cottonwoods, which made it hard to find on a clear day, much less on a snowy dark night. Roosevelt found it empty and cold. The place had been gutted and had no food. But it was shelter and he would not freeze to death in the open. Roosevelt went down to the river and brought back some water and built a fire. He took some tea he had in his pocket and brewed a cup. "I should have liked something to eat, but as I did not have it, the tea did not prove such a bad substitute for a cold and tired man."[4]

He slept then in the shack with the wind howling outside. The next morning, Roosevelt headed out with his rifle and found some sharp-tails in the trees. He shot five and returned to the cabin. "It was not long before two of the birds, plucked and cleaned, were split open and roasted before the fire. And to me they seemed most delicious food."[5]

It is the action taken that matters.

Roosevelt rode on and later reached the Elkhorn and found Sewall and Dow had made good progress on the ranch house and were already working on the walls. His ranch house would be large and spacious compared to other ranches in the Badlands. Teddy joined in and helped with the building of his new home for two days as winter cold again plunged down to zero and below. At night, fifty below temperatures split trees wide open.

The Elkhorn became the ranch in winter with white frosting on the backs of cattle and the cluttering of hard hooves against the glass of frozen ground. The coyotes' yipping became spectral sounds of the grave in the dead cold of night and the wolves haunted the working men with their long, mournful howls. The men hurried to build the shelter with blue hands and frozen cheeks.

During these days of toil in the bone-aching cold, Roosevelt brooded over his future. In a letter to his friend Henry Cabot Lodge, he wrote, "The statesman of the past has been merged, alas, I fear for good, in the cowboy of the present."[6] Sewall would become a sounding board for Roosevelt while they labored. He told the woodsman he did not care what became of him and reiterated he had nothing to live for.

"You ought not to allow yourself to feel that way," Sewall insisted. "You have your child to live for."[7]

"Her aunt can take care of her a good deal better than I can," Roosevelt replied. "She never would know anything about me, anyway. She would be just as well off without me."

Then Sewall prophetically described the future for the young man who saw none.

"You won't always feel that way. You will get over this after a while. I know how such things are; but time heals them over. You won't always feel as you do now, and you won't always be willing to stay here…because, when you get to feeling differently, you will want to get back among your friends where you can do more and be more benefit to the world than you can driving cattle. If you can't think of anything else to do, you can go home and start a reform. You would make a good reformer. You always want to make things better instead of worse."[8]

In the winter Roosevelt was probably most at home. Alone. Isolated from the world he once knew. He could reform himself while the world slept. His writings here are such a benefit to the historian. Roosevelt loved the land he wrote about, and this is most evident in the passage that describes the Badlands in the pale of winter's glow. It is the view of the civilized man looking at the West before it too would become settled; a glimpse of a moment, written in the flower of Victorian prose.

> When the days have dwindled to their shortest, and the nights seem never-ending, then all the great northern plains are changed into an abode of iron desolation. Sometimes furious gales blow down from the north, driving before them clouds of blinding snow-dust.... They roar in a thunderous bass as they sweep across the prairie or whirl through the naked canyons; they shiver the great brittle cottonwoods, and beneath their rough touch the icy limbs of the pines that cluster in the gorges sing like the chords of an æolian harp. Again, in the coldest midwinter weather, not a breath of wind may stir; and then the still, merciless, terrible cold that broods over the earth like the shadow of silent death seems even more dreadful in its gloomy rigor than is the lawless madness of the storms. All the land is like granite; the great rivers stand still in their beds, as if turned to frosted steel. In the long nights there is no sound to break the lifeless silence. Under the ceaseless, shifting play of the Northern Lights, or lighted only by the wintry brilliance of the stars, the snow-clad plains stretch out into dead and endless wastes of glimmering white."[9]

And in these darkest of moments, as he closed his eyes, we can imagine the bride Teddy Roosevelt had buried came back to him like a phantasm of the coldest night. Alice Lee was still surely there in the unguarded moments of his winter dreams.

18

SUCH GOOD FORTUNE
1873

Teddy Roosevelt fell in love at first sight on October 18, 1873. There could be no other way for the man, who was making his way through Harvard, and who took a buggy ride on a fall day of Bostonian red, yellow, and gold. The leaves heralded the arrival of his true love as they met on a path between mansions. Alice Lee was the daughter of George Lee, who lived in a mansion resembling the Roosevelt mansion in Oyster Bay. Dick Saltonstall was the Cupid who drove Roosevelt out to the family home, which was next to the Lee mansion, after classes had ended. Alice Lee was seventeen to Roosevelt's nineteen.

They were buds of the same privileged rose, and Teddy immediately was taken with the rather tall honey-blond with her stunning blue eyes—the tip of her nose slightly uptilted and the water curls giving her the appearance of a goddess to the man with the funny voice, clapping teeth, and brisk walk. They went for a walk in the woods and Roosevelt began immediately his Victorian courtship of buggy rides, poetry-laden picnics, parlor sits, letters, and dinners.

"We spent the evening dancing and singing, driving back around 11 o'clock," [1] he wrote afterwards in his diary. Then after church the couple went "chestnutting." Roosevelt returned three weeks later to lay siege, and was invited over for Thanksgiving dinner. Triumphantly he wrote, "They call me by my first name now." [2]

Alice played tennis and played it well. She probably beat Roosevelt or let him win—her proper role in those times. There are more dinners and dances and poetry and sits on the many porches of the Lee mansion and moments by the fire. "Snowed heavily all day long!" he wrote in his diary again. "But in spite of the weather I took a long walk with pretty Alice. I spent most of the remainder of the day in teaching the girls the five step and a new dance, the knickerbocker. In the evening we played whist and read ghost stories." [3]

All was going to plan. Teddy sealed the deal by having a rug made from a lynx he shot. She gave him a pair of slippers to replace the ones his mother had given him for Harvard. Teddy had his horse shipped to Cambridge so the young squire could attack at will and go to Chestnut Hill as much as desired. His letters home talk about many girls, but Alice Lee begins to stand out. "The more I see of Rose Saltonstall and Alice Lee the more I like them, especially Alice Lee." [4]

Somewhere he proposed, and Alice Lee did the proper thing and gave him no answer. A lady never accepted a first proposal. But this was Teddy Roosevelt, and he began to slowly go crazy waiting for her decision. The best guesses place his proposal around June 20. He and Alice sit in a window at Hollis Hall after some parties at Harvard, "looking at the Yard, brilliantly lighted, and listening to the Glee Club." It was a perfect setting to ask a beautiful girl of the upper crust to marry him. But now he must wait, and everything at Harvard, indeed his life, was put on hold while Alice Lee considered her options and other suitors.

"See that girl," he told an acquaintance at a Hasty Pudding function. "I am going to marry her. She won't have me, but I am going to have her." [5]

Roosevelt brought in the big guns and had Alice's parents over to visit his mother in Manhattan. Then he had his sisters come out to

Chestnut Hill. Then he had a lunch for the Lees at the Porcellian Club with thirty-four guests. Teddy was a hunter of the heart and he would use every weapon he had. But he was also losing his mind as the other suitors turned up the heat. Alice Lee was a hot catch and Roosevelt started strange nocturnal wanderings in the woods near Harvard. In the middle of the night, he would wander through the trees among the owls and the whippoorwills and not come back until the morning.

Friends became concerned and began to say he was becoming unhinged; Teddy heard of other suitors and ordered French dueling pistols that were delivered to him. Roosevelt would challenge anyone who tried to take Alice Lee from him. He continued his nighttime wanderings in the frozen snowy woods until somebody let his family know all was not well. Cousin West came up to check on the distraught Romeo. Things were quickly getting out of hand. Here was the Roosevelt temper, but also something else: a maniacal abandonment where all sense of proportion was lost.

Alice Lee gave him relief and returned at Christmas, and soon after, Roosevelt wrote in his diary, "I drove over to the Lees determined to make an end of things...and after much pleading my own sweet, pretty darling consented to be my wife. Oh, how bewitchingly pretty she looked. If loving her with my whole heart and soul can make her happy, she shall be happy; a year ago last Thanksgiving I made a vow that win her I would if it were possible; and now that I have done so, the aim of my whole life shall be make her happy..."[6]

In February he let the family know and bought Alice a diamond ring. He was riding the wave and went to insane lengths to see her at every opportunity, despite snow and ice. He wrote, "Snowing heavily, but I drove over in my sleigh to Chestnut Hill, the horse plunging to his belly in the great drifts, and the wind cutting my face like a knife. My sweet wife was just as loveable and pretty as ever; it seems hardly possible I can kiss her and hold her in my arms; she is so pure and innocent and so very pretty. I have never done anything to deserve such good fortune. Coming home I was upset in a great drift and dragged about 300 yards holding on to the reins before I could stop the horse..."[7]

Dragged three hundred yards through snow and ice by horses was nothing for the Romeo warrior of the heart. Nothing could stop him now and to celebrate he went with his brother Elliott to the Middle West. They hunted in Illinois, Iowa, and then Minnesota. Before he left, though, the old *cholera morbus* (acute diarrhea) came back violently at Oyster Bay when he was with Mittie—"very embarrassing for a lover."[8]

But Roosevelt did keep one thing to himself. After a visit to a physician in March, a Dr. Dudley Sargent let the young man know that he had a heart ailment (possible a result of rheumatic fever) and prescribed the only treatment of the time; a rest cure. Theodore Roosevelt must not lead a strenuous life, the doctor insisted. He must lead a *sedentary* life and avoid strenuous exertion at all costs. Roosevelt never told anyone, but he told the doctor he would continue to push himself and die in the process if need be; so much for the admonitions of Dr. Dudley Sargent.

In Minnesota his old friend asthma came back and he suffered a violent attack. Then the diarrhea hit him again and he could not walk. But a few days later, he and his brother returned to Chicago where he was the picture of health again and "as brown and well as can be," as Elliott would write his sister.[9] The trip never went as far as the real West, but it was a warm-up of sorts; they shot grouse, geese, snipe, ducks—about anything that moved.

Alice Lee and Roosevelt were married on a beautiful fall day on October 27, 1880. "I cannot take my eyes off her," he wrote in his diary. "She is so pure and holy...and yet when we are alone I cannot bear for her to be a minute out of my hands."[10] The smitten groom and his bride went to Oyster Bay for a honeymoon of two weeks, and later there would be the proper European honeymoon. They began living in a "perfect dream of delight." They played tennis and went for walks and long, winding buggy rides in the autumn hills. "There is hardly an hour out of the twenty-four we are not together," he wrotes. "I am living in a dream land, how I wish it could last forever."[11]

19

THE REFORMER AND THE RANCHER

1886

Theodore's father had been done in by Tammany Hall bosses when he became the Collector of Customs for the port of New York. President Hayes had made the appointment, but Boss Conklin decided his fate and deemed he would never be confirmed. The "collectorship row" went on for months and months, and Teddy made a connection between the stomach cancer that killed his father and the corruption that was Tammany Hall. In Albany, young assemblyman Roosevelt was a staunch reformer who ultimately found himself on the wrong side of things when he went against his own party and became a pariah. But when Roosevelt saw injustice, he became magnetized to the iron bar of right. What better place to bring out this sword anew than in the West where the cattle industry, while bustling, was also hopelessly disorganized and unruly.

Raising cattle depended upon cooperation. It was customary for a rancher's cattle to range freely and feed on other people's land, including that of other ranchers. It was only through a community "roundup" that all the cattle were brought in and sorted out according to brand. Big ranchers could and did take advantage of small ranchers and were perfectly capable of having a "private roundup" and shipping other ranchers' cattle to market as their own, and there was nothing anyone could do.

Enter Theodore Roosevelt. After working on his house for several days, he set out for the Maltese Cross ranch with Dow and Sewall. Of course, he did it in a blinding snowstorm, as he later related to his sister: "It was late at night when we reached the Merrifield's and the thermometer was twenty degrees below zero. As you may imagine, my fur coat and buffalo bag have come in very handily. I am now trying to get up a stockman's association, and in a day or two, unless weather is too bad, I shall start up the river with Sewall to see about it."[1]

Roosevelt quickly became the mounted politician of the West, stopping along the way at various ranches to convince fifteen or twenty men to join the new organization he proposed. Sewall and Dow accompanied "the boss" as they crossed the plains. Apparently, it worked. An editorial appeared in the *Bismarck Weekly Tribune* on December 12. "Theodore Roosevelt, who used to be a great reformer in the New York Legislature but who is now a cowboy, pure and simple, calls a meeting of the stockmen of the West Dakota region to meet at Medora, December 19th, to discuss topics of interest, become better acquainted, and provide for a more efficient organization. Mr. Roosevelt likes the West."[2]

Roosevelt slowly brought parts of his old life into the new, almost as if he were renovating himself, keeping some parts but discarding others. Certainly, the new life of the cowboy rancher was the core of the new man, and now he was hanging the ornaments he chooses; a personage but not yet a personality. Meanwhile he was building up to another hunting trip, but there was ranching still to be done in winter. Wood had to be chopped and coal brought in by the wagonload from a nearby lignite mine on his property, and most importantly the cattle had to be watched. Someone had to be in the saddle every day to make sure cattle didn't "rustle themselves."

But the winter was still brutal. As Hermann Hagedorn writes in *Roosevelt in the Badlands*, "in spite of heavy underclothing and flannel-lined boots, it was not often that one or the other of them, returning from a ride, did not have a touch of the frost somewhere about him. When the wind was at his back, Roosevelt found it was not bad to gallop along through the white weather, but when he had to face it, riding over a plain or a plateau, it was a different matter, for the blast cut through him like a keen knife, and the thickest furs seemed only so much paper."[3]

But the work had to get done, and breaking horses was part of that work. Sylvane Ferris had returned with fifty-two head in December, and this was a main part of a cowboy's job, to make sure wild ponies would be rideable. Some never were and continued to buck. Even the new stage-coach started by the Marquis had trouble with bucking ponies who refused to be tethered to the stage and literally kicked their way out of their place on "the tree." But it had to be done.

So in the days when temperatures stayed below zero, Roosevelt joined the experienced cowboys. As he later wrote, "It partook of the nature of adventure to rise at five...and ride under the starlight to bring in the saddle-band; and it gave a sense of quiet satisfaction to manly pride later to crowd around the fire where the cowboys were stamping and beating their numbed hands together and know that you had borne yourself as well as they."[4]

Roosevelt loved the nights in the cabin that was small but "storm-proof and homelike," sharing it with the other men and passing the time reading or playing checkers and chess or Old Sedge; he even wrote his friend Lodge saying, "Did I tell you about my cowboys reading and in large part comprehending your 'Studies in Literature?'"[5] It was important to bridge the gap between these men, many of whom, although function-ally illiterate, were men he truly venerated. He wanted to bring all things under one roof if possible.

And now with the work finished, he wanted to go hunting again with Merrifield after mountain sheep. They had waited for Sylvane to get back with more horses but now they could depart. It was the middle of December with George Meyers in the buckboard this time and Roo-sevelt and Merrifield following. As with the elk hunt, they passed through savage country and it became a sort of a Rooseveltian *Heart of Darkness* journey. Roosevelt's descriptions speak of a fascinating, alien land. "There were tracts of varying size, each covered with a tangled mass of chains and peaks, the buttes in places reaching a height that would in the East entitle them to be called mountains. Every such tract was riven in all directions by deep chasms and narrow ravines, whose sides sometimes rolled off in gentle slopes, but far more often rose as sheer cliffs, with narrow ledges along their fronts.... Indeed, it is difficult in looking at such formations, to get rid of the feeling that their curiously twisted and contorted forms are due to some vast volcanic upheavals...yet they are merely caused by the action of the various weathering forces of the dry climate..."[6]

They hunted across the terra cotta landscape on foot and worked their way up ice-covered buttes or inched along narrow ledges. But there were no sheep and the temperature had plummeted once again. The cabin that was to be their headquarters provided little warmth. George Meyers (a ranch hand) could not keep a fire going for the wind blowing between the cracks in the logs. In the morning, with the stars still shining, they set out on foot. They hunted the outlying foothills and again there were no sheep.

The next morning they were up again before dawn and continued hunting as the sky grew heavy and the scent of snow was in the air. The temperature again started downward as dark, bulbous thunderheads moved toward them. Ice made every step dangerous, and they had to stop several times to catch their breath in the thin air—and Roosevelt's asthma would likely have been acting up at this point. They continued on and crawled up a steep ridge as the first flakes began to float down.

The hunters stuck their heads over the ridge and saw two mountain rams. Roosevelt dropped to his knee and fired. The larger of the two rams pitched forward but managed to gallop over another ridge. The hunters followed and two hundred yards beyond the ridge their ram was dead. They took the head and started back toward the cabin as the sky grew more ominous. Packing up quickly, the hunting party took off for home; but, with Roosevelt riding ahead at a full gallop, the impending blizzard hit. Snow blew so hard it even pushed its way into their teeth.

Roosevelt summarized the trip to his sister Bamie this way: "I have just returned from a three days' trip in the Bad Lands after mountain sheep and after tramping over the most awful country that can be imagined, I finally shot one ram with a fine head. I have now killed every kind of plains game. I have to stay here till after next Friday to attend a meeting of the Little Missouri Stockmen . . . "[7]

The ranchers, who had been dealing with problems in the Badlands for much longer than the bespectacled man from New York, listened attentively and then voted to form an Association of the Stockmen along the Little Missouri and elected Theodore Roosevelt chairman. Amazingly, a man who had only been at their game a few years was now running the show. Even Marquis De Mores was present and worked to procure legislation from the Territorial Legislature of Dakota favorable to ranchers.

Why did the ranchers listen to Theodore Roosevelt? Because cattlemen as well as cowboys held up the virtues of the West, and the man in front of them was "direct, fearless, a good talker, sure of his ground, and in the language of the Bad Lands, 'he didn't take backwater from any one.'"[8] In short, Roosevelt had shown he had grit in a land that valued grit above all else. He couldn't help himself. Sneaking out of that buckskin cowboy was a man who was born to lead other men. And they saw it. Roosevelt's Little Missouri Stockmen codified unwritten rules of the free range cattle ranches. In doing so, the new cowboy took a big step toward settling down the Wild West he so loved, unwittingly hastening its demise. It would no longer be a place of lawless, unbounded freedom. Such was the price of progress.

20

THAT PHOTOGRAPH
1886

There is that photograph. Roosevelt in full buckskin regalia with his hat and his gun and his knife with an expression that a boy might think a frontiersman should have. Of course, the studio fixtures make the picture cheesy, with the painted backdrop and the carpet of fake grass and vegetation. But for our purposes, it serves to show how Roosevelt was viewing himself at that time. Edmund Morris describes the photograph this way in *The Rise of Theodore Roosevelt*:

> Bristling with cartridges, a silver dagger in his belt, Roosevelt stands with Winchester at the ready, against a studio backdrop of flowers and ferns. His moccasins are firmly planted on a mat of artificial grass. For some reason his spectacles have been allowed to dangle: although his finger is on the trigger, one doubts if he could so much as hit the photographer, let alone a distant grizzly. His expression combines

pugnacity, intelligence, and a certain adolescent vulnerability, which touched Henry Cabot Lodge, at least, very tenderly.[1]

Historians dismiss the photograph largely as Rooseveltian bravado or the boy coming through in the man. It might be argued that the staged man with the rifle is the new person rising from the ashes of the old: a fierce cowboy of the Wild West who would take on anyone, anywhere. Drugstore psychology aside, the photograph shows a man staring into the distance with eyes firmly set, a man of the past and the future.

And the photograph sold books. We forget about Roosevelt the writer during his sojourn in the West, but, in fact, that writer informs the "romance of his life." F. Scott Fitzgerald could easily have been speaking of Roosevelt when he said, "A sentimentalist is someone who hopes things will last, the romantic is someone with the desperate conviction they won't." Cleary, the poignancy of Roosevelt's romance with the West was that it was evanescent. The frontier was winding down and the clock would mark only a few more years before it was all over. And Roosevelt knew this, and before the confectionary of Western experiences closes he would take as much as he could.

We should also not forget that this was still the age of the explorer. The year Teddy Roosevelt was born, John Speke and Richard Burton discovered the source of the White Nile; when Roosevelt left the White House in 1909, Americans Matthew Henson and Robert Peary won the race to the North Pole; and in 1911, the Norwegian Roald Amundsen reached the South Pole. So Roosevelt in 1885 was right in the middle of this romantic age of exploration, and it was in this vein he returned to New York and wrote.

The cowboy had trouble sitting down to write in the Badlands. As with any writer, experience did not become real until it was set down on paper. This was Roosevelt, who would carefully map out most of his biggest life experiences in books and biographies. He was a man of his time and a reader of Swinburne and Tolstoy, which he read in the Badlands out on the hunt and in the rocker on the porch of his ranch. At this point in his life, a literary career was still in the roundup of possible career choices.

Even as a cowboy, Roosevelt was influenced by the literary flower of Victorianism, which informed his view of the world and gave shape to his prose style. Nature is something we see on our computer screens or beyond our smartphones. Not so for the nineteenth-century man and woman. Theirs was largely a pantheistic point of view—simply put, nature was as alive as man, and direct experience of nature could inspire and invigorate as well as entertain. In his writings, Roosevelt tried to capture the life of the Badlands. A naturalist at heart, he saw himself in the great concoction of God's world, and felt the divine spirit even in the hell of the most desolate plains of the Dakotas.

He was not a natural poet. And he was not a fiction writer. That would require more dexterity and natural flow. Roosevelt's writing often resembles mechanical boxcars lined up with their information within. At other times, though, he soars with the poets, and this is most evident when he describes the romance of the West.

So of course he was going to take stock and catalog his experiences. He wrote a hundred thousand words in nine months. "I have just sent my last roll of manuscript to the printer," he wrote to Cabot Lodge on March 8.[2] In July, G. Putnam's Sons brought out *Hunting Trips of a Ranchman*. The book was well received and sold for a very high price at the time, fifteen dollars. It was really a collector's item, much like coffee table books of today.

Upon reading this book, one is struck by the "blog quality" of the prose. Roosevelt rambles along from one experience to another, but the love of the West and the self-exploration of the man in the middle of that experience is evident. Roosevelt extols the virtues of the cowboy: "There he passes his days, there he does his life-work, there, when he meets death, he faces it as he has faced many other evils, with quiet, uncomplaining fortitude. Brave, hospitable, hardy, and adventurous, he is the grim pioneer of our race; he prepares the way for the civilization from before whose face he must himself disappear. Hard and dangerous though his existence is, it has yet a wild attraction that strongly draws to it his bold, free spirit."[3]

Roosevelt, of course, is talking about the ideal cowboy, but we quickly see whom he is really talking about: the man he would like to be. And yet he prefaces it by saying this man will not last. That he must be sacrificed for the good of the country, to expand the nation into the territories and make them safe for those who follow. Out in the high heat and deadly cold of the Badlands, Roosevelt was acting out something of a credo: the sacrifice of the self for something higher. Surely, a man who has suffered devastation grabs onto this branch of immortality.

And yet his book was essentially about killing, though it was a luxurious book, physically. "It was printed on quarto-size sheets of thick, creamy, hand-woven paper, with two-and-a-half-inch margins and sumptuous engravings."[4] The book received positive reviews and sold well. Roosevelt's first book, *The Naval War of 1812*, had been for the academic crowd, while this was for general consumption and was not dry, but lyrical; a bit overwritten and filled with purple prose, but very readable.

The hunt was the main topic, and Roosevelt had killed thousands of animals. It is hard for twenty-first-century people to accept that a man who so loved nature could also willingly destroy it. Of course, Teddy Roosevelt saw nature through the lens of "dominion," and man was at the top, with the responsibility to hunt only for sport or food—never for crass corporate gain like the buffalo hunters who decimated the herds for their hide or their tongues or for whatever the market would purchase, nor like the people who would wantonly slaughter the standing beasts from the trains.

Roosevelt had only disdain for "the swinish game butchers who hunt for hides and not for sport or actual food, and who murder the gravid doe and the spotted fawn with as little hesitation as they would kill a buck of ten points."[5] He viewed the *true hunter* as a noble man. "The hunter is the arch-type of freedom. His well-being rests in no man's hand save his own." These thoughts were in keeping with his time and his class, and hunting provided the adventure he so craved. So we get his grand descriptions of hunting grizzly, elk, buffalo, and then that Victorian purple prose swoops in, leaving Swinburnian devotees blushing and bloggers longing for such sinuous riffs.

> He [the cowboy] lives in the lonely land where mighty rivers twist in long reaches between the barren bluffs; where the prairies stretch out into billowy plains of waving grass, girt only by the blue horizon—plains across whose endless breadth he can steer his course for days and weeks, and see neither man to speak to nor hill to break the level; where the glory and the burning splendor of the sunsets kindle the blue vault of heaven and the level brown earth till they merge together in an ocean of flaming fire.[6]

And that is what the man in the photograph is proposing. The purple warrior of Victorian prose is a warrior of experience and his education is but half over. His return to the East has led some historians to conclude that Roosevelt's time in the West was not dramatic and was nothing more than an early Outward Bound excursion and about as forgettable. The return to the "old life" is part of the transmogrification of Teddy Roosevelt. It is this welding together of old and new that produces the synthesis of the man who one day will become president.

21

THE WANDERING COWBOY

1886

After the hundred-thousand-word sprint, Roosevelt was socked once again with the *cholera morbus* that would afflict him all his life. Sufferers today from Crohn's disease could relate to the young man laid so low his sisters asked Bill Sewall to keep an eye on him. He had to delay his departure for the Badlands until March 14. Roosevelt returned and as one cowboy said about him, "You could have spanned his waist with your two thumbs and fingers." But he was ready to get back in the saddle and immediately put himself to the test.

The Little Missouri gave him his first adventure and an opportunity to prove once again he was healthy. The river was swollen with rain from thaw water. The only way to cross was between the tracks of a train trestle spanning the river or across the submerged dam farther down. The skinny man from the East took Manitou across the top of the dam, even though everyone told him it was crazy.

"Where does the dam start?"[1] asked Roosevelt.

"You surely won't try to cross on the dam," exclaimed Fisher (a hired hand), "when you can go and cross on the trestle the way the others do."

Roosevelt frowned and shook his head.

"If Manitou gets his feet on that dam, he'll keep them there and we can make it finely."

"Well, it's more than likely that there's not much of the dam left."

Roosevelt set his jaw and jabbed his spurs into the horse.

"It doesn't matter anyway. Manitou's a good swimmer and we're going across."

Here was something of the boy again, telling the world he can breathe just fine as he gasps for air and then runs up a mountain to prove it. Roosevelt and Manitou started across the dam. The rushing, swollen river of ice melt washed over the dam, spouting white around the legs of his horse. Roosevelt gently nudged him along and kept his eyes on the far shore. And then Manitou lost the dam and the world turned over and Roosevelt found himself in the cold Little Missouri.

People on shore were sure Roosevelt would drown. The shock of the ice-cold water stunned the horse and both horse and rider were utterly submerged, but Roosevelt clung to his horse's mane and allowed the river to take them downstream. Manitou swam furiously with Teddy pushing ice blocks out of the way and they made it to the opposite shore before being swept downriver. Manitou found the bottom and galloped up the opposite shore, steaming from the cold water running off with Roosevelt patting his neck. People on the opposite shore just shook their heads. "I suppose it might be considered reckless," Roosevelt admitted later, "but it was lots of fun."[2]

Then he did it again when there was no one to watch him, and later wrote his sister triumphantly, "I had to strike my own line for twenty miles over broken country before I reached home and could dry myself. However, it all makes me feel very healthy and strong."[3] "Healthy" and "strong" were two words people did not typically ascribe to Theodore Roosevelt. But he willed the substance of those words into his being through arduous tests, and in doing so became *healthy and strong*. And we must remember he was a man of his times. People routinely traveled to various parts of the country to cure what ailed them. Roosevelt and his mother had visited many places for various "rest cures," and he had found that putting himself to the test after illness precipitated his recovery. Teddy Roosevelt, if he didn't have a horse, probably would have dove into the river alone and tried to swim to the other side.

He then left for the Elkhorn ranch house that had been finished. Hagedorn in *Roosevelt in the Badlands* describes the house as "a one-story log structure, with a covered porch on the side facing the river; a spacious house of many rooms divided by a corridor running straight through from north to south. Roosevelt's bedroom, on the southeast corner, adjoined a large room containing a fireplace..."[4] From here the cabin was decorated with animal heads mounted on the walls and rifles propped in the corners. Ever the voracious reader, Roosevelt had shelves bulging with books by "Irving, Hawthorne, Cooper, Lowell, Cable, Craddock, Macon, Joe Chandler, and with pot boilers such as Ike Marvel, Burroughs, Sherwood Bonner." It was too early for any Jack London but certainly that writer of the Northland would have found a welcome home in this literary ranch of the West. A rocking chair on the porch beckoned, and Roosevelt remarked, "When one is in the Bad Lands, he feels as if they somehow look just exactly as Poe's tales and poems sound."[5]

The cattle looked so good that summer that Roosevelt purchased another 1500 head of cattle for 39,000 dollars, bringing his total investment to 85,000 dollars—or about two million in today's dollars. His family was nervous, and Bamie asked if the ranch would pay off. "I honestly think it will," he replied.[6] And then he became the wandering cowboy again. They had lost a lot of horses and Roosevelt went on long journeys to find them. One of these journeys found him far out as night fell and not far from the small town of Mingusville. It was here that myth and reality become one as Roosevelt clucked his horse toward the small, yellow buildings of his rendezvous with the Wild West Bad Man.

The lore of Theodore Roosevelt in the West centers around several incidents. One of these touchstones was the confrontation with the gun-slinging bad man. Another totem of the Roosevelt legend is found again in Mingusville. The town had become a mecca for the ranchers. Medora, while closer and more accessible to ranches, didn't have the big space to hold all the cattle. The freight records of the Northern Pacific show that Mingusville was the place with wide open spaces allowing a vast amount of cattle to congregate for shipping. Beyond that it was only a dismal little cow town with a rundown hotel.

A movie could have been shot in Mingusville. It was the quintessential Wild West town of every Western, in which the cowboys come with the cattle to raise hell and shoot up the town. The realism of these scenes is only partial, and the term *shooting up the town* is suspect. The Colt .45 Peacemaker was the gun of choice in the Wild West, but despite the movies with narrow shootouts and close-call draws, the truth was that most people in the West were terrible shots.

A big reason was economics. Bullets and powder were expensive, so people didn't practice, and shooting a man with a handheld pistol was difficult. Anyone who has tried to hit a target with a pistol will agree. The pistol has to be steady and sighted, and the trigger has to be pulled back. Bullets would often go nowhere near their intended victims. There were no gun ranges for people to hone their skills, and a lot of cowboys had poor sight and glasses were not an option. No self-respecting cowboy, except Teddy Roosevelt, would be caught dead with glasses, or they *would be caught dead* rather than wear them.

There were reports of a gunfight in a Texas saloon where ten men were involved and later a hundred bullets found, yet no one had been hit. So when the cowboys entered town and busted out of the saloon with six-guns blazing, it was anyone's guess where the bullets would end up. Mingusville was a perfect place to unleash lead into the old dried-out buildings and watch the citizenry dive for cover. Cowboys were young and a lot were from Texas and they had steam to blow off. Enter Teddy Roosevelt into this comical yet deadly diorama of drunk cowboys and uncertain shooting; a "dude from the East" just looking for somewhere to lay his head.

A boarding house run by a Mrs. Nolan was full and that left the hotel where he had knocked out the gun-toting drunk the year prior. Roosevelt procured a room and then climbed the creaking old stairs. He entered his room and shut the door, then lit a lantern and took out a book from his rucksack. Teddy lined up his boots by the bed and began reading the book he had in his saddlebag. The hell-raisers reached him distantly with the pop of .45 cartridges.

But then a cowboy louder than the rest entered the hotel, drunker than the rest. He pulled out his Colt and put it against the proprietor's stomach and began to dance with the man across the room. What Roosevelt heard was the appeals of a man facing a drunk with a six-shooter in his abdomen.

"Jim don't! Don't Jim! It'll go off! Jim, it will go off!"[7]

Roosevelt turned his page and adjusted his glasses. It was the West and just another night in the Badlands. Then came the drunkard Jim's response.

"Yes, damn you, it'll go off! I'll learn you! Who in hell cares if it does go off! Oh, I'll learn you!"

By now Roosevelt was likely having a flashback of the man in the bar. He moved his stocking feet and turned the page. The confrontation before could have gone either way if he had not knocked the man out. Guns did go off and people were killed. The drunken Jim then demanded a bed, and Roosevelt heard the heavy tread of boots on the stairs leading to his room. He lowered his book and turned to the locked door just as the knock came.

Roosevelt got out of the bed and opened the door a crack. A white-faced man appeared with a lantern.

"I'm sorry," said the proprietor, "but there's a man I'll have to put in with you for the night."

"You're not as sorry as I am," Roosevelt replied. "And I am not going to have him come in here."

The small man was sweating and his eyes imploring.

"He's drunk and he's on the shoot...and he's got to come in," the man persisted.

Roosevelt stared him down with the lantern light in his glasses.

"I'm going to lock my door and put out my light. And I'll shoot anybody who tries to break in."[8]

Roosevelt then locked the door and waited. He had his Winchester and Colt, but the man never returned. This moment was amazing in that the man could have returned and Roosevelt would have shot him. A man had to back up his words and he had proven he could before.

Then it happened again. He was out looking for horses when darkness came and there was Mingusville in the distance under a pearl-white moon. This time he avoided the hotel and went to the boarding house of one Mrs. Nolan, "a tough wiry woman...with a fighting jaw and a look in her eye that had been known to be as potent as a six-shooter in clearing the room of undesirable occupants."[9]

Roosevelt had put his horse in an outbuilding and asked if she had any beds available. Mrs. Nolan let the man with glasses and the funny accent know he could have a bed in a room already occupied. Tired and not wanting to go to the hotel, Roosevelt accepted and followed her down the creaking hallway to a room with two double beds and two men snoring fast asleep in one.

Roosevelt recognized Three-Seven Bill Jones, a cowman from the Three-Seven outfit "who had recently acquired fame by playfully holding up the Overland Express in order to make the conductor dance."[10] Teddy set his pants, guns, boots, chaps, and hat down beside the bed and turned in for what he thought was a good night's sleep. The usual pistol shots of drunken cowboys exploded outside in the darkness.

Two hours later, the door crashed in, and Roosevelt sat up into a lantern by his face and the long, smooth barrel of a Colt pointed at him. A man spoke behind the lantern. Roosevelt's heart pounded as he looked toward the gun.

"It ain't him," the voice said.[11]

The darkness returned as the lantern crossed the room and Roosevelt saw two guns pointed at Bill Jones.

"Now Bill," said a gruff voice. "Don't make a fuss, but come along quiet."

"All right, don't sweat yourself," responded Bill. "I'm not thinking of making a fuss."

"That's right," the man answered. "We're your friends. We don't want to hurt you; we just want you to come along. You know why."

Bill then pulled on his trousers, slipped into his boots, and walked out with the two armed men. Roosevelt had watched all this in stupefaction, and the other man had seemingly slept through the exchange. Then a match scratched across the darkness and a candle flared. The two men stared at each other.

"I wonder why they took Bill," Roosevelt wondered aloud.

The other man didn't reply, so Roosevelt said again, "I wonder why they took Bill."

"Well," said the man dryly. "I reckon they wanted him."

He then blew out the candle. Such was the logic of the West. There was another education going on here that was not to be taken lightly. Roosevelt wanted his ranch to make money and provide a livelihood, and he lived with the men who rounded up his cattle and did the heart's work of a ranch in the West. "Roosevelt liked them all immensely; they possessed to an extraordinary degree the qualities of manhood which he deemed fundamental, courage, integrity, hardiness, self-reliance."[12]

In the rugged isolated land of the West, people had to depend on each other as much as, say, later-day astronauts. A man simply had to have *the right stuff*, to borrow another phrase, and Roosevelt was getting to know the common man in a way that would color his political views for the rest of his life. Still, they did not call him Teddy or Roosevelt or Theodore. It was *Mr. Roosevelt*—amazing, perhaps, that men twice his age would address him with such formality, but the DNA of the patrician class of the late-nineteenth century allowed only so much egalitarianism.

Through all these experiences, Roosevelt was governed by a personal code that he would never compromise. He was out with one of his men when they came upon an unbranded steer. The steer was on Lang's property and therefore belonged to the man whose land the animal was found on. These were the type of unwritten rules that Roosevelt was trying to codify through his rancher organization. The cowboy roped the steer, and they built a fire and heated up the branding irons. The man started to brand the steer when Roosevelt saw something was wrong.

"It is Lang's brand...a thistle," he pointed out to the cowboy holding the red-hot iron.[13]

"That's alright boss," the cowboy replied. "I know my business."

"Hold on!" Roosevelt exclaimed. "You are putting on my brand."

The cowboy grinned, knowing full well the majority of men would follow the law of "what I find I take."

"That's all right," he assured Roosevelt. "I always put on the boss's brand."

Roosevelt stood up and stared down at the man.

"Drop that iron," he said quietly "and go to the ranch and get your time. I don't need you any longer."

The cowboy stared at him.

"Say, what have I done? Didn't I put on your brand?"

"Yes. But a man who will steal for me will steal from me. You're fired."

The man rode away, and this story spread over the Badlands. In a land where reputation was everything, Roosevelt's climbed a little higher.

22

THE MORNIN' GLORY
1881

Roosevelt would say it was duty and curiosity that got him into politics. "I intended to be one of the governing class," he would later write.[1] An argument could be made that he was of the governing class already. A scion of a patrician family of New York was hardly a disenfranchised member of society, and most of his ilk saw the levers of power pulled behind the curtain as preferable to the sweaty world of politics with its political bosses, hacks, graft, and corruption.

But enter the young reformer with the pretty wife on Fifty-Seventh Street who was bored with law and looking for his life's purpose. The Republican Party was his home, and when he ran for a seat representing his district, he easily won. But no one was happy, least of all his family. "We thought he was, to put it frankly, pretty fresh," recalled a cousin Emlen. "We felt that his own father would not have liked it...the Roosevelt circle as a whole had a profound distrust of public life."[2]

But Theodore was fascinated with the Tammany Hall wash of local politics. When he reported for duty in Albany a reporter thought to himself, "What on earth will New York send us next?"[3] It had sent a twenty-three-year-old young man who made quite a first impression, as Ike Hunt would later write: "We almost shouted with laughter.... he came in as if he had been ejected by a catapult. He had on an enormous great ulster...he was dressed in full dress, he had been to dinner some place...the New York dude had come to Chamber."[4] And then there was that odd way Roosevelt had of speaking. "He would open his mouth and run out his tongue and it was hard for him to speak."[5] New York's *The Sun* boiled it down to this: "rather relieved" was "rawtherrelieved."[6]

We can picture Teddy Roosevelt with his mutton-chop whiskers in his foppish clothes leaning over his desk, "Mr. Spee-kar! Mr Spee-kar!" delivered in a falsetto that had to be from not getting enough air. He would later explain his speaking voice to his sister this way, "I do not speak from the chest, so my voice is not as powerful as it should be."[7] And so the dude with his gold watch fob, gold-rimmed spectacles, the tight cut of his pants, the slicked-down hair parted high in the middle was patronized as "the Dandy," "Oscar Wilde," "his Lordship," "Jane-dandy."

Like the cowboys in the West, the papers and his fellow representatives underestimated the overdressed little man. The question was would Roosevelt be just another "Mornin' Glory," as George Washington Plunkett called him, a man with high principles "who looked lovely in the mornin' and withered up in a short time"?[8]

The withering heat could come on quickly. Teddy's first term in 1882 ran for five months, and Roosevelt would spend only nine months in Albany, but he was a changed man. William Hudson said he would begin his day with a stack of newspapers and "threw each paper as he finished it on the floor, unfolded, until at the end there was, on either side of him, a pile of loose papers as high as the table for the servants to clear away. And all this time he would be taking part in the running conversation of the table. Had anyone supposed that this inspection of the papers was superficial, he would have been sadly mistaken. Roosevelt saw everything and formed an opinion on everything."[9]

Ike Hunt later said of Roosevelt's early days in the legislature, "He made me think of a growing child. You know you take a child and in a day or two their whole character will change."[10] Roosevelt was a fast learner if nothing else. Hunt always knew when Roosevelt arrived at the boarding house he stayed at because he would be halfway up the stairs before the front door banged shut.

Teddy Roosevelt was in the vanguard of progressivism sweeping the country. There were so many things that needed to be addressed in the explosive growth that had occurred especially in places like New York. Immigrants were being exploited and children were working in factories. There were no child labor laws and corruption was a way of life, and many politicians in the Albany legislature were bought off by political bosses, whose tentacles reached into every district. Roosevelt's first trial by fire would be the Cigar Bill.

The Cigar-Makers' Union had passed a bill outlawing the manufacture of cigars in homes. The manufacturers had gone around the Union by employing people in tenements to roll the cigars and paying them pennies. Roosevelt's committee was charged with investigating the merit of the bill. The young assemblyman was against it as it violated his idea of *laissez faire* and he saw it as overly restrictive. But Roosevelt went on a tour of the places where the cigars were being rolled and like many of his class was shocked to find how the other half lived.

Forty years later he would write, "I have always remembered one room in which two families were living...there were several children, three men, and two women in this room. The tobacco was stowed about everywhere, alongside the foul bedding, and in a corner where there were scraps of food. The men, women, and children in this room worked by day and far into the evening, and they slept and ate there."[11]

From then on, he backed the bill, having seen firsthand the exploitation of the immigrants. He spoke on the floor in favor of the Cigar Bill only to have it squashed by a lobbyist for the manufacturer. Even though he was not successful, Roosevelt had seen the pain of exploited immigrants who had no voice. It would be a revelation he would not forget. Law had ceased to be of any interest, and while he had written a book on naval warfare, politics was still a diversion as he waited for his real life's work to kick in. For now, he had been elected to a third term and

Alice was pregnant. He was happy playing backgammon with his young wife by the fire in their home on Fifty-seventh Street.

Edmund Morris in *The Rise of Theodore Roosevelt* describes life in Manhattan for the young couple and one can sense the idyll before the darkness that would consume Roosevelt. "Apart from the daily six-mile walk, sleigh-driving was Theodore's only exercise that winter. He went about it with his usual energy, speeding around Manhattan in huge loops, up to thirty miles at a time, while the rest of society sedately circled Central Park. With his sweet darling warmly wrapped in buffalo robes beside him, and Lightfoot's hooves drumming up an exhilarating spray of snow, he would zigzag through the farms and shanties of the Upper West Side until the dark, ice-clogged waters of the Hudson opened out on their left. Spinning north along Riverside Drive, they would admire the snowy Palisades showing in fine relief against the gray winter skies, before curving east across the white fields of Harlem, and south past the great estates of the East River into the pine-forested freshness of Jones' Woods."[12]

This was the high of his young life. The world was opening before him, and Roosevelt took up boxing again in Albany while waiting for the legislative term to begin. "I feel much better for it," he wrote his wife from Albany, "but am awfully out of training. I feel much more at ease in my mind and better able to enjoy things since we have gotten under way; I feel now as though I had the reins in my hand."[13]

Alice had visited him in Albany, but had since returned home with her advancing pregnancy. In a letter soon after leaving her in New York, Roosevelt writes, "How did I hate to leave my bright sunny little love yesterday afternoon. I love you and long for you all the time, and oh so tenderly, doubly tenderly now, my sweetest little wife. I just long for Friday evening when I shall be with you again."[14] Alice's pregnancy was uneventful. Roosevelt's mother had commented that Alice was "very large," but so far so good.

Roosevelt was nervous about being a five-hour train ride from her, but he reminded himself he would be back for the weekend. When he did go back to New York, he found his mother had a cold and the weather had turned cold and gloomy with fog moving in. On Tuesday, he returned to Albany, and on the twelfth of February, Alice went into labor. The telegram that reached Roosevelt said all was fine with mother and child. Ike Hunt would remember him as "full of life and happiness."[15] The fog turned thicker and more widespread. *The New York Times* called it "suicide weather." Traffic on land and on the Hudson River slowed to a crawl under the gray blanket.

Then the second telegram reached Teddy Roosevelt and Ike Hunt said he became suddenly "worn." He ran for the train to New York that would lead to the abyss and eventually the West. The train ride back to New York was the agony of a man who knows the world is slipping through his fingers. When he reaches his dying wife and dying mother, all that Teddy Roosevelt had known was put into doubt. The man who sleighed around New York with his young wife with the wind in his hair was gone. Someone new would have to replace that man—and *he* would be forged in the hell of the Badlands.

23

THE ROUNDUP
1886

The new herd arrived with Sewall and company, and now Roosevelt had more than 3500 cattle. He was like a man who buys a very large and expensive sailboat only to realize he now has to sail it. Teddy had been learning on the job, but the curve was steep because rounding up cattle could easily kill you if they stampeded. Old Westerns may come to mind, where Clint Eastwood–type cowboys magically drive cattle, but the truth is it was a brutal business, difficult and grueling, especially for the cattle. Even preparing for a drive was unpleasant if you were one of the poor four-legged bovines.

Sewall wrote to his brother about the operation of branding.

> The cattle were driven in from the country and put in a yard. This was divided in the middle by a fence and on one side was a narrow lane where you could drive six to eight Cattle at a time. This narrowed so when you got to the fence in the middle only one could pass by the post, and beyond the post

there was a strong gate which swang off from the side fence at the top so to leave it wide enough to go through. Well, they would rush them into the shoot and when they came to the gate would let it swing off at the top. The animal would make a rush but it was so narrow at the bottom it would bother his feet and there was a rope went from the top of the gate over his back to a lever on the outside of the yard. While he was trying to get through, the fellow on the lever would catch him with the gate and then the frying began. They had two good big fires and about four irons in each and they would put an iron on each side. One is a Triangle about four inches on a side, the other an Elkhorn about six inches long with two prongs. It smelt around there as if Coolage was burning Parkman.... I kept thinking of that and Indians burning Prisoners at the stake.[1]

It was not a scene for the faint of heart. Roosevelt met his men at Medora, and they began the cattle drive north to his Elkhorn ranch. They began by staying away from the Little Missouri, still swollen from rain and with quicksand abounding. Roosevelt chose a path between the Little Missouri and the Beaver. It was a path that would take the cattle across the Badlands, and this would be the first of many errors. Immediately, the new rancher realized he did not have enough men. There were only five men to assist in driving the cattle, and only one had any real experience.

Like the man who buys a sailboat without any sailing knowledge, Roosevelt soon found that driving cattle was unforgiving for the novice. Basically, well over a thousand animals had to be coaxed to go in one direction. The animals, of course, have their own ideas, and it is up to the cowboys to make certain their side wins the dispute. Roosevelt placed an experienced man in charge and learned quickly that experience does not make a leader. The proverbial chuck wagon and the riders and the cattle frequently got all snarled up. *Rawhide* this was not.

Roosevelt then took over. The thousand-plus cattle had spread out, with the speedy ones in front and the laggards in the rear. Between these two poles were the followers, lowing away and sending up titanic dust clouds. TR put two men at the head of the column and two men at the back while he and another cowboy rode up and down the sides to coax stragglers back to the fold.

The big danger, of course, was a stampede, where the cattle would bolt and the cowboys must try to bring them back under control. "Anything may then start them," Roosevelt wrote later in *Ranch Life and the Hunting Trail*, "the plunge of a horse, the sudden approach of a coyote, or the arrival of some outside steers or cows that have smelt them and come up. Every animal in the herd will be on its feet in an instant, as if by an electric shock, and off with a rush, horns and tail up. Then, no matter how rough the ground nor how pitchy black the night, the cowboys must ride for all there is in them and spare neither their own nor their horses' necks."[2]

Roosevelt's teeming herd was thirsty—quite a problem in the Badlands with its wildly fluctuating temperatures. Snow had actually been falling when the drive began, and the wind had forced them to lead the cattle into a valley for shelter. Water pools were frozen. Then, in a quick about-face, the temperature began to soar and the cattle became hot and water was nonexistent. Enter the night.

The job of the night-patrol was to make sure the cattle stayed put. The men took turns on watch, usually two to a shift, riding around the herd making sure the animals did not wander off or stampede. But the cattle were thirsty, and they were still miles from the water pools—the perfect storm for a stampede in that hot dusty night of the Badlands. It *was* a storm, actually, that swooped down and probably spooked the cattle. But whatever the reason, the cattle decided they had had enough and rose as one to look for water. Roosevelt and his men jumped onto their horses and galloped though the darkness to stop the thirst-crazed cattle.

"The riding in these night stampedes is wild and dangerous to a degree, especially if the man gets caught in the rush of the beasts," Roosevelt would later write.[3] But now he was riding with his glasses jumping on his nose, pounding over the uneven land, and he could not even see his hand in front of his face. Riding in the darkness at full gallop along the shadowy outline of the stampeding cattle was like trying to corral a tornado. Roosevelt knew if the cattle dispersed the cowboys would never be able to get them all back. He would turn in some cattle only to have others break around him while he galloped across the dark ground of ravines and gullies. The inevitable happened, as he wrote later: "The only salvation was to keep them close together, as, if once they got scattered, we knew they could never be gathered; so I kept on one side, and the cowboy on the other, and never in my life did I ride so hard. In the darkness I could but dimly see the shadowy outlines of the herd, as with whip and spurs I ran the pony along its edge, turning back the beasts at one point barely in time to wheel and keep them in at another. The ground was cut up by numerous little gullies, and each of us got several falls, horses and riders turning complete somersaults. We were dripping with sweat, and our ponies quivering and trembling like quaking aspens, when, after more than an hour of the most violent exertion, we finally got the herd quieted again."[4]

Galloping hell for leather in the darkness and the dust, with the cattle thundering in his ears, Roosevelt's horse fell in a ravine and TR found himself flying through the air. He hit his shoulder and did a somersault, his horse landing beside him. It is hard to imagine having a horse flip under you in the darkness and not kill you when it fell, but it is harder to imagine getting back onto the horse and riding after charging cattle. It is remarkable that Roosevelt was not killed or at least paralyzed, but he had the uncanny ability to risk his life over and over and walk away virtually unscathed.

Writing to his friend Henry Cabot Lodge on the fifteenth of May, he relayed the cattle drive in characteristic understatement. "I have hard work and a good deal of fun since I came out here. Tomorrow I start for the round-up, and I've just come in from taking a thousand head of cattle up on the trail. The weather was very bad and I had my hands full, working night and day, and being able to take my clothes off but once during the week I was out."[5]

It was just like Roosevelt not to mention nearly breaking his neck in a stampede, but rather noting the fact he could not change his clothes. He did, however, describe the exciting night stampede later in *Ranch Life and the Hunting Trail*. "Suddenly the wind began to come in quick, sharp gusts, and soon a regular blizzard was blowing, driving the rain in stinging level sheets before it…darkness had set in, but each flash of lightning shows us a dense array of tossing horns and staring eyes…I saw that the cattle had begun to drift before the storm, the night guards being unable to cope with them…we made quick work of saddling; and the second each man was ready, away he loped through the dusk…"[6]

The Brahmin from Boston would have found this exciting reading. He would have found the roundup even more exciting. The iconic roundup was where Roosevelt got to be just a cowboy. Bringing in stray cattle in the Old West could be as dangerous as a shootout, and this made it perfect for Theodore Roosevelt.

He arrived at Box Elder Creek on May 19 for the spring roundup in the Badlands. If there was ever a place where the boy who wanted to be a cowboy could come out to play, it was here, where everyone participated in the general gathering and sorting of cattle. The *Mandan Pioneer* reported on May 22, "Theodore Roosevelt is now at Medora and has been there for some time past. He is preparing his outfit for the round-up, and will take an active part in the business itself."[7]

The roundup would cover two-hundred miles, rolling down the Little Missouri Valley, and fan out east and west just as far. Sixty men would coax four thousand head of cattle from ravines and gullies and coulees and from just about anywhere the cattle could hide in the Badlands, and then sort them out into the proper owner's herd, branding strays and calves along the way. Theodore Roosevelt would spend thirty-two days rounding up cattle and ride at least a thousand miles.

The first thing a man must do was choose a string of ponies he would use during the roundup. Roosevelt felt he didn't have the right to pick the best ponies out of the saddle band, even if he was the owner of the Maltese Cross. So he picked his ten ponies and he picked badly. Four of the horses were broncos—untamed ponies that bucked their rider. But he was determined to be an "ordinary cowpuncher" and pulled no favors. The problem for Roosevelt was that he dreaded the idea of "breaking" a horse.

Lincoln Lang was there when Roosevelt mounted the worst of the broncos.

"Mr. Roosevelt mounted with the blind still on the horse, so that the horse stood still.... As soon as Mr. Roosevelt got himself fixed in the saddle, the men who were holding the horse pulled off the blind and turned him loose."[8] The horse at first did not buck, then went crazy—"he leapt in the air like a shot deer, and came down with all four feet buckled under him, jumped sideways and went in the air a second time, twisting ends," Bill Dantz would later recall.[9]

Roosevelt clung to the saddle pommel for dear life. More often than not, men thrown from bucking horses were seriously injured. Lincoln described Roosevelt's struggle this way: "he got the horn of the saddle in one hand and the cantle in the other, then swung his weight well into the inside and hung like a leech.... As it was, his glasses and six-shooter took the count within the first few jumps, but in one way or another he hung to it himself..."[10]

But there was one horse that got the best of Roosevelt, a certain Ben Butler whose tactic was to fall over backwards. He was a black-eyed horse about whom Bill Dantz declared, "That horse is a plumb outlaw." The other cowboys told Roosevelt not to take him, but of course he took him anyway. As he mounted, the horse jumped up and then fell over backwards and onto Roosevelt. He felt a sharp pain shoot through his shoulder where the point had broken. There was no doctor and Roosevelt just dusted himself off and remounted, stating later, "it was weeks before I could raise my arm freely."[11] His stock went up further.

Dutch Wannegan would later say about Roosevelt, "Some of these Easter punkin-lilies now, those goody-goody fellows, if they ever get throwed off you'd never hear the last of it. He didn't care a bit. By gollies, if he got throwed off, he'd get right on again. He was a dandy fellow."[12]

The dandy fellow was in his element. If there was ever a grand old time of cowboy life, it was during the roundup, when men worked together around the clock. The camaraderie of fellow cowboys working together to bring in the cattle was something out of the mythical West that would later be replicated in novels and then movies. Roosevelt would later write, "A round-up always had more than a little of the county fair. For though the work was hard, and practically continuous for sixteen hours out of twenty four, it was full of excitement."[13]

Since he neither had the skill of the other cowboys as a roper nor the eyesight to cut cattle out of larger herds, Roosevelt was on "day herd," which meant he basically rode round the herd and turned the cattle in. This went on at night as well when he would ride "night herd." Years later in his autobiography, Roosevelt would write of the experience, "When utterly tired, it was hard to have to get up for one's trick at night herd. Nevertheless, on ordinary nights the two hours round the cattle in the still darkness were pleasant. The loneliness, under the vast empty sky, and the silence, in which the breathing of the cattle sounded loud, and the alert readiness to meet any emergency which might arise out of the formless night... "[14]

Sometimes Roosevelt could not find the herd. On one occasion he wandered about in the darkness before locating the cattle. One can only imagine the young Roosevelt, sitting upon his horse in the darkness with the great pinwheel of the stars above and the lowing cattle crossing under the moonlight. He was all of twenty-five and he must have seen glimmers of his past and future way out there in the land of myth and magic and utter isolation.

It took some time, but Roosevelt earned the respect of the other cowboys. "As with all other forms of work, so on the round-up, a man of ordinary power, who nevertheless does not shirk things merely because they are disagreeable or irksome, soon earns his place."[15] Of course, the other cowboys stared at the skinny dude with the glasses and there were the usual taunts. Glasses held some sort of Eastern tenderfoot designation that nobody wanted. But here was this man with his toothbrush, and tightly-wound bedroll, looking not unlike a boy scout reporting for summer camp the first time.

Apparently the worst taunts were from the Texas cowboys: "When I went among strangers I always had to spend twenty-four hours in living down the fact that I wore spectacles, remaining as long as I could judiciously deaf to any side remarks about 'four eyes' until it became evident that my being quiet was misconstrued and that it was better to bring matters to a head at once."[16] One Texan finally got his goat, and Roosevelt told the man to "put up or shut up. Fight now or be friends!"

The Texan stared, his shoulders dropped a little, and he shifted his feet.

"I didn't mean no harm. Make it friends."[17]

The active life on the roundup started with breakfast at three a.m. As Roosevelt later described it, "Each man, as he comes up, grasps a tin cup and plate from the mess-box, pours out his tea or coffee, with sugar, but, of course, no milk, helps himself to one or two of the biscuits that have been baked in a Dutch oven, and perhaps also to a slice of the fat pork swimming in the grease of the frying pan, ladles himself out some beans, then squats down on the ground to eat his breakfast."[18]

And then the men mounted up and went to their duties. For Roosevelt, it was riding to the herd while keeping an eye out for wandering cattle. These were the moments he would recall later in writing about his time in the West. "These long, swift rides in the glorious spring mornings. ... The sweet, fresh air, with a touch of sharpness... the rapid motion of the fiery little horse combine to make a man's blood thrill and leap with sheer buoyant lightheartedness and eager, exultant pleasure in the boldness and freedom of the life he is leading. ... Black care rarely sits behind a rider whose pace is fast enough..."[19]

The "black care" he referenced was only a few years past, but in the all-encompassing "new life" there was nothing to pull him back. After riding herd all day, dinner was at nine. Roosevelt came to enjoy the moment of rest around the campfire where cowboys would swap stories, smoke, and sing. Broad hats and large handkerchiefs around their necks, their guns and spurs gleaming, and their broad cartridge belts—they were men whom Roosevelt came to know and respect to the point that, years later, he would tell men whom he had ridden with on the roundup to come and visit him in the White House anytime.

The roundup continued and the rain moved in. The camp had moved to the base of the peak known as Chimney Butte. The lightning crashed down with a hard downpour. The cattle didn't like the fireworks of the Badlands and Roosevelt was out on night herd with Lincoln Lang. The call went for "all hands out" because of the risk of a stampede in the storm. The men watched the cattle nervously as the sky opened up with a tremendous crack. The lightning touched down somewhere within the herd and that was all it took.

The cattle stampeded through the rainy, flashing darkness, as all the men rode out, desperately trying to bring the terrified cattle under control. Roosevelt would later write, "the men were shouting and swaying in their saddles, darting to and fro with reckless speed, utterly heedless of danger...racing to the threatened point, checking and wheeling their horse so sharply as to bring them square on their haunches...the din of the thunder was terrific; peal following peal until they mingled in one continuous roar; and at every thunder clap louder than before the cattle would try and break away."[20]

Roosevelt was galloping full speed through the rainy darkness with the crazed cattle all around him. The stampeding cattle were like a dark river flowing by him, and then he heard splashing. Roosevelt's glasses were a mess and in the nighttime rain he was blind and only dimly aware he was close to the Little Missouri when his horse plunged through the air. Roosevelt had a sensation of falling through space as he splashed into water. The Little Missouri flowed around him and the cattle were white splashes as he hung onto the horse fighting the current. Manitou struggled to the shore only to become mired in quicksand. Roosevelt dug in his spurs, and they finally climbed the far bank. The stampede, like a crazed flowing torrent, was now up over the far side.

Roosevelt galloped over a terrain of gullies and washouts and pitfalls. He was bent over the neck of his horse and several times almost fell off as the horse lost its footing. A pitfall appeared and the horse somersaulted over again with Roosevelt thrown clear. But he got up and remounted and continued on, working with the other men to curb the stampeding cattle. This went on through the night, and at one point Roosevelt saw a cowboy riding beside him who then vanished like a phantom. Men and cattle were mixed up all over the Badlands. Lincoln Lang would later say, "The country was muddy and wet. We were having a heavy rain all night. I don't know how we ever got through. All we had was lightning flashes to go by. It was really one of the worst mix-ups I ever saw."[21]

When day came, Roosevelt was wet and exhausted and not even sure where he was. The cattle had been turned back toward the camp, and he came upon the cowboy who had appeared the night before with his saddle in hand. Apparently his horse had hit a tree and died. Roosevelt finally reached the camp and grabbed a quick breakfast and a fresh horse and then was out again to find the cattle still missing from the stampede. It was another ten hours in the saddle before he would return again and then it was just to grab some grub and another horse.

By the end, Roosevelt was in the saddle over forty hours. He crawled under his wet sodden blankets and slept like a dead man. The new cowboy would later write of the dangers in that night of the stampede, "no matter how rough the ground or how pitchy black the night, the cowboys must ride for all there is in them and spare neither their own nor their horses' necks…the riding in these night stampedes is wild and dangerous to a degree, especially if a man gets caught in the rush of beasts."[22]

Again, here was Roosevelt the daredevil cheating death. Maybe it was because he was a small man and very young. Maybe it was just his destiny to have these adventures and emerge unscathed. But no matter what the reason he survived, the dangers were real, as evidenced by his next adventure, just days after the stampede.

Because of the storm, the river had risen to the point where the log bridge that cowboys used to cross was underwater. Roosevelt was riding with a young Englishman who had come to sample the life of the West but was not faring well. They crossed the submerged bridge, which promptly fell apart, and the riders were tossed into the swirling, rushing water. Roosevelt clung to his horse and made his way to the shore but the Englishman panicked.

"I'm drowning! I'm drowning!" he called.

It was a scene straight out of a Western. Roosevelt took his lasso and, even though he wasn't very good with the rope, managed to lasso the Englishman around the shoulders and haul him in like a lost steer. Roosevelt later remarked, "He did not seem very thankful."

Here was the courageous, resourceful, self-reliant cowboy saving the son of a lord (apparently) from drowning. Roosevelt was no longer the lily-livered four-eyes from the East, but the man with the sun in his face and the dead-eye lasso. In writing to Henry Cabot Lodge about his adventures on the roundup, he summed it up this way: "I have been three weeks on the round-up and have worked as hard as any of the cowboys; but I have enjoyed it greatly. Yesterday I was eighteen hours in the saddle—from 4 a.m. to 10 p.m.—having a half-hour each for dinner and tea. I can now do cowboy work pretty well.... I have had some fine circuses with them [horses]. One of them had never been saddled...besides bucking, kept falling over backwards with me; finally he caught me, giving me an awful slat, from which my left arm has by no means recovered. Another bucked me off going downhill.... Twice one of my old horses turned somersault while galloping after cattle..."[23]

If there is a corner turned in Roosevelt's adventure in the West, it is here. The skinny, sickly young man who had come West has been transformed, and a later reporter would remark "[he] was rugged, bronzed and in the prime of health."[24] Even his speech habits had changed. "There was very little of the whilom dude in his rough and easy costume, with a large handkerchief tied about his neck.... the slow exasperating drawl and the unique accent that the New Yorker feels he must use when visiting a less blessed portion of civilization has disappeared and in their place is a nervous, energetic manner of talking with the flat accent of the West."

In his diary, Roosevelt refers very little from here on to his asthma or his *cholera morbus*. The man whom we would know as "Teddy Roosevelt" had been given a new mold and it was now filling in rapidly. Bill

Sewall would say he "was as husky as almost any man I have ever seen who wasn't dependent on his arms for his livelihood."[25] Or even later, William Roscoe Thayer, who had not seen Roosevelt for several years, was amazed, "to find him with the neck of a Titan and with broad shoulders and stalwart chest."

Theodore Roosevelt was remaking himself. The physical tests of the West had built him up physically but even more so psychologically. There was a new personality rising from the ashes of that devastated young man who had come west on the train. The open frontier of the West had fortified him and he would carry it as his secret strength against future adversity. Teddy Roosevelt was now defined by the West, a place where only the strong survived and more than that *thrived*. The rough and tumble existence where what a man *does* was more important than what a man *says* cemented Teddy Roosevelt into a man of action. The *action taken* was pre-eminent and *the vigorous life* was actualized. The open country was there for the taking, and the United States was busy taking and flexing her young muscles and so was Teddy Roosevelt. A man who could ride hell for leather after stampeding cattle in a lightning storm in the Badlands, face down armed men in lawless towns, tame bucking horses, lasso a drowning man in a river, certainly had within him the tough coal that would in time become a diamond.

The West was working its magic, creating the man who would become a political dynamo, one who could match the energy of a nation on the cusp of the American Century. All that was left for Roosevelt was to confront some Indians and arrest some bad men.

24

THE RETURN OF THE COWBOY
1885

B y June 21, Roosevelt had returned to the East. This time he had come back as the changed man, the cowboy. A journalist from St. Paul remarked, "Theodore Roosevelt passed through St. Paul yesterday, returning from his Dakota ranch to New York and civilization...Roosevelt is changed from the New York club man to the thorough Westerner."[1]

This gives us the temperature of the man, and it is interesting that Roosevelt made a point of talking to these journalists. What better way to understand the change from within than to have it reflected back to you in the media? As Hagedorn relates in *Roosevelt in the Badlands*, a reporter from the *Dispatch* interviewed Roosevelt:

"I'm just in from my ranch. Haven't had my dinner yet, but I think a short talk with a newspaper fellow will give me a whetted appetite. Yes, I am a regular cowboy, dress and all—" and his garb went far to prove his assertion, woolen shirt, big neck handkerchief tied loosely around his neck, etc. "I am as much of a cowboy as any of them and can hold my own with the best of them. I can shoot, ride, and drive in the round-up with the best of them. Oh, they are a jolly set of fellows, those cowboys; tiptop good fellows, too, when you know them, but they don't want any plug hat or pointed shoes foolishness around them. I get along the best way with them.

"We have just finished the spring round-up. You know what that means. The round-up covered about two hundred miles of grass territory along the river and thousands of cattle were brought in. It is a rare sport, but hard work after all. Do I like ranch life? Honestly I would not go back to New York if I had no interests there. Yes. I enjoy ranch life far more than city life. I like the hunt, the drive of cattle, and everything that is comprehended in frontier life. Make no mistake; on the frontier you find the noblest of fellows. How many cattle have I? Let's see, well, not less than 3500 at present. I will have more another year."[2]

Interestingly, here Roosevelt showed that he had completed his break with his former life. He found the Western cowboy far superior to his brethren New Yorkers, turning his back on his own class, but really on everyone from his own heath. He was rebelling against the neurasthenia of his age, the stress of the white male, and he saw a better existence in the "vigorous life." There was a superiority in the self-reliance of the cowboy or frontiersman. Roosevelt faulted the East for corruption in deed and life and linked that with the death of his wife and mother. The old life was nothing but devastation and heartache.

Even the land was suspect—congestion versus the wide-open space of the last frontier where freedom abounded. Roosevelt went on to describe how he had become this new person, this cowboy, and how the man of politics was dead. "Don't ask me to talk politics," he said, when the reporter pressed him. "I am out of politics. I know that this is often said by men in public life, but in this case it is true. I really am. There is more excitement in the round-up than in politics. And it is far more respectable. I prefer my ranch and the excitement it brings to New York life."[3]

The twenty-six-year-old Roosevelt was thumbing his nose at politics and saying, essentially, this is no longer who I am. The ranch is far more pleasurable, and of course the ranch is far more exciting than political life. We can be sure that in this there was a bit of getting back at the system that had turned on him. But still, his comments reveal the mind and spirit of Roosevelt mid-swim in the Western adventure. He had proven himself in the new world and could walk the walk and talk the talk. As of now, the husky man who was "nut brown" and who even had a different manner of speaking could not have cared less about his former life.

He visited his recently-completed home at Oyster Bay and played with his daughter for the first time. Then Roosevelt marched in the funeral procession for President Grant. Beyond this, there was not much that was noteworthy in his New York visit. It was almost as if he had gone back simply to announce the new man he had become. His exploits became larger and more real when related to the people back East. We can imagine many nights where he held court and told of the roundup or facing down bad men or hunting grizzly or galloping across the Badlands in the dead of night.

These were adventures that for someone in New York in 1885 had the ring of fiction. People didn't do things like lasso men in raging rivers or get thrown off bucking horses or get caught in deadly snowstorms or fall into rivers with their horse. This was adventure, if not exploration, on a heroic scale, and through the telling the adventure took on mythical stature. So, there really was a Wild West, and it still existed? The man with the flat accent and barrel chest and wildly flailing arms proclaimed it was.

There were experiences, though, that Roosevelt couldn't convey to his New York brethren. The transformation of Teddy Roosevelt was something he couldn't fully articulate. Hagedorn does a good job of summing up what had become imprinted in the young man's soul.

The wild riding, the mishaps, the feverish activity, the smell of the cattle, the dust, the tumult, the physical weariness, the comradeship, the closeness to life and death.... He loved the crisp morning air, the fantastic landscape, the limitless spaces, half blue and half gold. His spirit was sensitive to beauty, especially the beauty that lay open for all in the warm light of dawn and dusk under the wide vault of heaven; and the experiences that were merely the day's work to his companions to him were edged with the shimmer of spiritual adventure.[4]

Thirty years later Roosevelt would write of his experiences, and of the West that no longer existed, and try to capture what had happened to him. "We knew toil and hardship and hunger and thirst and we saw men die violent deaths as they worked among the horses and cattle, or fought in evil feuds with one another; but we felt the beat of hardy life in our veins and ours was the glory of work and the joy of living."[5]

Dr. Stickney, of the Dakota Territory, said years later with prescient insight: "It was a wonderful thing for Roosevelt. He himself realized what a splendid thing it was for him to have been there at that time and had sufficient strength in his character to absorb it. He started out to get the fundamental truths as they were in this country and he never lost sight of that purpose all the time he was here."[6] After two months, the visiting cowboy boarded the Chicago Limited on August 22 and headed west once more.

25

DOMESTIC RANCH LIFE AND BAD MEN
1886

If Roosevelt really did mean what he said to the reporters in Minnesota and New York—that he was done with his old life—then what he was returning to in the West was a hoped-for future life on his ranch. He was not going to be forever the adventuring cowboy, and now he had a thirty-five hundred spread of cattle and essentially two ranches. This required a lot of work and maintenance, and the "womenfolk" had arrived from Maine to the Elkhorn ranch. In a sense, the pioneering early days had ended.

Mrs. Sewall had brought her three-year-old daughter, and Roosevelt really returned to a "home" rather than the rude ranch of men. Like the home life Roosevelt had briefly known with Alice Lee, the Elkhorn entered a halcyon era where men, women, and children led a "Little House on the Prairie" existence. If there was a golden age of the Elkhorn ranch, this was surely it. The women cooked meals complete with cakes and homemade jam and there was even a cow for milking.

"Eating was sort of a happy go lucky business at the Maltese Cross [before the women]" remarked Bill Sewall subsequently. "You were happy if you got something and you were lucky too." Now the men returned to a feast, "a table on the clean cloth of which are spread platters of smoked elk meat, loaves of good bread, jugs and bowls of milk, saddles of venison or broiled antelope steaks, perhaps roast and fried prairie chickens, with eggs, butter, wild plums, and tea or coffee."[1]

Roosevelt was the head of this extended family, but beyond his title all were equal and shared in the work. He saddled his own horse and washed his own clothes. The women by choice did all the cooking, and Roosevelt gained even more weight and became "husky."

When the work was done, he would sit on the porch and watch the cattle "while the vultures wheeled overhead, their black shadows gliding across the glaring white of the dry river bed."[2] Roosevelt sat in his rocking chair, still sweaty and dust-streaked from the day, with his boot crossed over his knee, and read Keats or Swinburne while the sun burned down across the tall buttes and the early mist settled over his herd. All he was really missing was a woman, and one can imagine this eating at him as he observed the happy domestic life of his hired men. Roosevelt might have begun to think back to Alice Lee and his life before. Somewhere in the cooling dusk, with the creak of his rocker the only sound, he knew that one day he would leave the West for good.

But the cattle business was doing well for now. Roosevelt had sunk 85,000 dollars into the ranch, and what had probably seemed like a crazy hobby to his family had stabilized. This was important for the spinning wheel of Roosevelts' future. Bill Sewall was still pessimistic and doubted the Badlands would ever be good cattle country. He later wrote to his brother an evaluation of the cattle business as he saw it. "I don't think we shall lose many of our cattle this winter. I think they have got past the worst now. Next year is the one that will try them. It is the cows that perish mostly and we had but few that had calves last spring, but this spring there will be quite a lot of them.... It is too cold here to raise cattle that way. Don't believe there is any money in she cattle here and am afraid there is not much in any, unless it is the largest herds, and they are crowding in cattle all the time and I think they will eat us out in a few years."[3]

What Bill Sewall predicted would come to pass. The days of "free range," where cattle were able to roam and feed at will, would end with the coming of the large corporate ranches. It is a funny word to use at this juncture in the West, but with the railroad came the corporations, and there would be more than a few range wars as the flames of the independent rancher were stamped out by the men who were cornering the market.

Sewall further wrote to his brother, "I think the cattle business has seen its best days and I gave my opinion to Mr. R last fall. I hope he may not lose but he stands a chance."[4] Roosevelt would stand more than a chance to fail at a business contingent on weather and the availability of grass for feeding. More than a few men had failed already, but for now all seemed bright and sunny. Medora was growing. The West was growing.

The *Mandan Pioneer* wrote, "Medora is distinctively a cattle town and is ambitious to be the cattle market of the Northwest. In two years it has grown from absolutely nothing to be a town which possesses a number of fine buildings and represents a great many dollars of capitol. The Black Hills freight depot is a well-built substantial building. A number of brick houses have been built during the last year, including a very neat and attractive Catholic church and a large hotel."[5]

Roosevelt had, to some degree, helped bring this about. He had financed Joe Ferris in erecting a store and a bank in direct competition with the Marquis' company store. Medora was the Marquis' town and his hand was in just about everything. But Roosevelt, while not having the means of the Marquis, was able to finance rival institutions, and in the credit vacuum of the West he was as good as a bank. Of course, Medora's real booming industry was drinking.

The saloons prospered and Bill Williams, the notorious bad man, maintained the classic saloon of bullets and bad men. The Marquis financed him and the place never closed day or night. There were rumors of robbery and murder in Williams's past, and many times he would shoot out of the swinging doors of his saloon just to attract business. What he *did* attract was newspapers, who wanted to cash in on the mythology of the Wild West; and to that end the Dickinson *Press* reprinted an article from the Estelline *Bell* on the basic nomenclature of being a bad man:

> The "gun" is still worn on the right hip, slightly lower than formerly. This makes it more convenient to get in a discussion with a friend. The regular "forty-five" still remains a favorite. Some affect a smaller caliber, but it is looked upon as slightly dudish. A "forty," for instance, may induce a more artistic opening in an adversary, but the general effect and mortality is impaired. The plug of tobacco is still worn in the pocket on the opposite side from the shooter, so when reaching for the former, friends will not misinterpret the move and subsequently be present at your funeral. It is no longer considered necessary to wait for introductions before proceeding to get the drop. There will be time enough for the mere outward formalities of politeness at the inquest. The trimming of the "iron" is still classic and severe, only a row of six cartridges grouped around the central barrel being admissible. Self-cockers are now the only style seen in the best circles. Much of the effectiveness of the gun was formerly destroyed by having to thumb up the hammer, especially when the person with whom you were conversing with wore the self-cocking variety. It has been found that on such occasions the old-style gun was but little used except in the way of circumstantial evidence at the inquest. Shooting from the belt without drawing is considered hardly the thing among gentlemen who do not wish to be considered as attempting to attract notice.... As regards the number of guns which it is admissible to wear, great latitude is allowed, from one up to four being noted on the street and at social gatherings. One or two is generally considered enough, except where a sheriff with a reputation

of usually getting his man and a Winchester rifle is after you, when we cannot too strongly impress upon the mind of the reader the absolute necessity for going well heeled.[6]

It is a tongue-in-cheek article, but it gives the basics of the Wild West customs concerning guns and protocol. Medora was a shoot-'em-up town and Roosevelt's Little Missouri River Stockman's Association, which he created and chaired, felt something had to be done. All the ranchers contributed a cowboy for a posse to "clean up" the country north of the railroad between the Little Missouri and the Missouri. Bill Sewall went for the Elkhorn ranch.

The Association also hired a stock inspector for all cattle for brands shipped to the stockyards in Chicago. This would certainly be the first line of defense against cattle thieves. But of course the man behind the scenes in Medora was languishing in jail for the ambush murder of Riley Luffsey. The Marquis was the other side of the Roosevelt coin. Both men came from aristocracy and wealth, but the Marquis believed in privilege ultimately and wanted to own just about everyone, while Roosevelt believed in equality of opportunity.

"When it came to a show-down, the Marquis was always there," said Dr. Stickney, "but he had no judgment. You couldn't expect it. He was brought up in the army. He was brought up in social circles that didn't develop judgment. He didn't know how to mix with the cowboys. When he did mix with them, it was always with the worst element. Now, when Roosevelt came to the Bad Lands he naturally attracted the better element among the cowboys, such men as Ferrises and Merrifield, men of high character whose principles were good."[7]

And Arthur Packard, the publisher of *The Bad Land Cow Boy*, added, "Roosevelt was the embodiment of the belief of obedience to the law and the right of the majority to change it. The Marquis was equally honest in his belief that he himself was the law and he had a divine right to change the law as he wished."[8]

Roosevelt was a better man, morally, and believed in progress, whereas the Marquis believed in hegemonic rule. The Marquis' grand plan to slaughter beef on site and ship it to Chicago in refrigerated cars backfired when the slaughterhouses would not accept the inferior quality. His stagecoach operation had also failed quickly and now he was planning to buy up all the hops on the Pacific coast and sell them to brewers in Milwaukee. His real problem was that he had the European view of class and saw his men as servants, while Roosevelt honestly liked the cowboys of the West. The Marquis and Theodore Roosevelt were bound to clash eventually.

26

HIGH NOON FOR THE MARQUIS

1886

The Marquis had made the mistake of assuming that money and title equaled influence. He was finding that in America this was not so. He had hoped to bully his way into the cattle business with the novel idea of slaughtering cattle on the spot and shipping them east to Chicago. But he was getting a lesson that his very royal French upbringing had not taught him: no one likes an upstart, and business is for the savvy—and the Marquis had no savvy.

So when his meat was refused by wholesale dealers, and yardmen delayed his cars, he suspected a conspiracy of powerful interests in Chicago. He was probably not far wrong, but his "noble blood" also prevented him from digging down to find whose toes he was stepping on and why he was not being allowed to play the game. He assumed money bought power, but he was up against men with money who already had the power.

Enter Roosevelt. The Marquis had his suspicions, as Roosevelt hailed from New York and belonged to the same moneyed class the Marquis suspected of thwarting his ambitions. He was a bit like a petulant child who continues flinging his cereal even though the parents hold all the power. Roosevelt was an easy target for this child, and a cattle transaction was the Marquis' first spoonful of mush to throw.

Roosevelt had agreed to sell a hundred head of cattle to the Marquis. The price on cattle was always agreed upon before the cattle were delivered regardless of market conditions. Like a stock or an interest rate, sometimes the market went for the seller and sometimes the buyer. But the swings were usually minimal from the time the price was set to delivery. Roosevelt delivered his cattle into the holding pen of the Northern Pacific Refrigerator Car Company. The cattle were weighed and Roosevelt went to the Marquis to be paid.

The Frenchman looked up at the dust-covered Roosevelt.

"I am sorry I cannot pay you as much as I agreed for those cattle," said the Marquis.[1]

Roosevelt frowned.

"But you bought the cattle," he protested. "The sale was complete with the delivery."

The Marquis shook his head.

"I am sorry. The Chicago price is down half a cent. I will pay you a half cent less than we agreed."

The tension was palpable. Arthur Packard told about it afterwards. "It was a ticklish situation. We all knew the price had been agreed on the day before; the sale being completed with the delivery of the cattle. Fluctuations in the market cut no figure. Roosevelt would have made delivery at the agreed price even if the Chicago price had gone up."[2]

Roosevelt then turned to the Marquis.

"Did you agree to pay six cents for these cattle?"

"Yes," The Marquis admitted. "But the Chicago price—"

"Are you going to pay six cents for them?" Roosevelt interrupted, cutting him off.

The Marquis shook his head, smoothing his waxed mustache.

"No. I will pay five and a half."

Roosevelt pushed his glasses up on his nose, then turned to the cowboys he came with.

"Drive 'em out boys."

The cattle were driven out. A deal was a deal as far as Roosevelt was concerned. And a man's word was his bond. These were ironclad principles from which he would not deviate. The Marquis acknowledged no such principles; he did what he wanted. The *Pioneer Press* gives this version of the story. "About a year ago the Marquis made a verbal contract with Theodore Roosevelt, the New York politician, who owns an immense ranch near Medora, agreeing to purchase a number of head of cattle. Roosevelt had his stock driven down to the point agreed upon, when the Marquis declined to receive them, and declared that he had made no such contract. Roosevelt stormed a little, but finally subsided and gave orders to his men not to sell any cattle to the Marquis or transact any business with him. The relations between the Marquis and Roosevelt have been somewhat strained."[3]

The strain would grow worse quickly. The natural antipathy between the two men, cloaked by dinner and lunches as well as Roosevelt entertaining the Marquis and his wife in New York, came into the open quickly. The Marquis was the murderer of Riley Luffsey, and a grand jury in Mandan indicted him for murder in the first degree. The Marquis viewed this as a nuisance, but also further evidence of a nefarious conspiracy against him, and behind this conspiracy he saw Theodore Roosevelt.

"I think the charge has been kept hanging over me," he later said, "for the purpose of breaking up my business. It was known that I intended to kill and ship beef to Chicago and other Eastern cities, and had expended much money in preparations. If I could have been arrested and put in jail some months ago, it might have injured my business and perhaps put an end to my career."[4]

So it is with the paranoid. The Marquis conveniently dismissed the fact he had organized the ambush of three men and one was buried up in the graveyard of Little Missouri. More than that, he had drawn a straight line to Roosevelt through Joe Ferris, whom he believed had paid off several witnesses against him. Roosevelt had financed Ferris in his bank and store, and so to the Marquis this was the smoking gun that led to the great Roosevelt conspiracy against him, with tentacles reaching all the way back to the packinghouses of Chicago and Wall Street.

So from his jail cell in Mandan, he stewed while a mob gathered outside and stoned the courthouse. He had been told that for fifteen hundred dollars the whole matter might just go away. But the veering top that was the Marquis drew up haughtily and proclaimed to the *New York Times*, "I have plenty of money for defense but not one dollar for blackmail."[5]

The truth was he didn't like the fifteen-hundred-dollar deal because they couldn't guarantee he wouldn't be charged again. Roosevelt had visited the Marquis in his cell and found him there with his valet and his secretary. The Marquis smoked a cigarette calmly while the valet hid under the bed. A crowd had recently gathered and threatened vigilante justice. The Frenchman merely yawned. But now he was not yawning. Sometime after Roosevelt's visit, the Marquis wrote a letter openly challenged him to satisfy his complaint that Roosevelt was in fact conspiring against him. It was an ominous letter, given that the Marquis was a crack shot and had killed another man in a duel.

> My Dear Roosevelt, My principle is to take the bull by the horns. Joe Ferris is very active against me and has been instrumental in getting me indicted by furnishing money to witnesses and hunting them up. The papers also publish very stupid accounts of our quarreling.... Is this done by your orders? I thought you my friend. If you are my enemy I want to know it. I am always on hand as you know, and between gentlemen it is easy to settle matters of that sort directly.[6]

Roosevelt was at the Elkhorn ranch when he received the letter. One could not blame him if he felt real fear. He was an average shot and the Marquis was noted for being a marksman. Also, the Marquis was a murderer with a dilettante's disregard for law. Shooting down a man with myopic vision would not keep him up at night. He read the letter aloud to Bill Sewall.

"That's a threat," Roosevelt exclaimed. "He is trying to bully me. He can't bully me. I am going to write him a letter myself, Bill." He went on, "I don't want to disgrace my family by fighting a duel. I don't believe in fighting duels. My friends don't any of them believe in it. They would be very much opposed to anything of the kind, but I won't be bullied by a Frenchman. Now, as I am a challenged party, I have the privilege of naming the weapons. I am no swordsman and pistols are too uncertain and Frenchie for me. So what do you say if I make it rifles?"[7]

Roosevelt had resigned himself to a duel at this point. And he knew the odds were bad. Still, he could not back down. In the West, this was not an option. And in those times, the Marquis would have stood for imperial Europe, from which America had broken a scant one hundred and ten years before. This type of bullying by the landed smacked of everything Westerners and Americans detested. The Frenchman would have his duel.

Roosevelt sat down on a log, and on the back of the letter scrawled his reply.

"Most emphatically I am not your enemy; if I were you would know it, for I would be an open one, and would not have asked you to my house nor gone to yours. As your final words, however, seems to imply a threat, it is due to myself to say that the statement is not made through any fear of possible consequences to me; I too, as you know, am always on hand, and ever ready to hold myself accountable in any way for anything I have said or done."[8]

Sewall said he would be Roosevelt's second but doubted anything would come of it. One has to wonder also at this point if the Marquis was a bit insane. Why pick a fight with a friend like Roosevelt, a man who had always been his supporter? But of course there was that gap that would undo the Marquis in one entrepreneurial venture after another: a rich man's son who just didn't get it. The reply came by courier. Roosevelt showed it to Sewall and remarked, "You were right, Bill."[9] The Marquis had in fact backed down. He said Roosevelt had misunderstood his letter and what he meant was "There was always a way to settle misunderstandings between gentlemen—without trouble."

So what did the Marquis really want? Like a bully, he was bluffing to find out if Roosevelt would fight or back down. He didn't understand why he was in jail and probably there was some jealousy. Teddy Roosevelt was a famous man in the West with a reputation to back him up, while the Marquis was a strange novelty. This whole incident could be seen as a precursor to Roosevelt's taking on the big trusts twenty-five years later. John D. Rockefeller was like the Marquis in many ways: wealthy beyond belief, delusional in his belief that his interests came first, and always looking to see what he could acquire. Of course, Rockefeller was a brilliant banker, but the imperial prerogative of *might makes right* was the bottom line.

Roosevelt summed up, years later, what he took to be the Marquis' motives at the time: "The Marquis had a streak of intelligent acceptance of the facts, and as long as he did not *publicly* lose caste or incur ridicule by backing down, he did not intend to run risk without adequate object. He did not expect his bluff to be called; and when it was, he had to make up his mind to withdraw it."[10]

He had wrongly assumed Roosevelt would cower at the thought of a duel, allowing him to claim victory on the field. He was not the first man to misjudge Theodore Roosevelt and he clearly would not be the last. The two men would not meet again.

27

COWBOYS AND INDIANS

C owboys and Indians was arguably the most popular game for boys in the nineteenth and twentieth century. It might have had a falling off by the mid-twentieth century with the advent of board games, and then video games, but it had always been a staple. In the game, the Cowboys are out in the open or behind a barricade ready to shoot the stealthy savages. The Indians, on the other hand, are usually sneaking up in a most unfair way. The Cowboys spot them and shoot them dead. It's good guys versus bad guys, and the straight-and-narrow Cowboys are the good guys. This same scenario was spooled out a thousand times over in novels and movies; the savagery of the unscrupulous Indians was an obvious foil to pristine Cowboy virtue.

And of course Buffalo Bill would codify it in his show, and, as mentioned before, the climax of his Wild West extravaganza was the settler's house besieged by craven savages who, if successful, would kill or torture the men and rape the women. There was nothing less than "white womanhood" on the line, and so the cavalry came running. The "cavalry" did not have to be the army. It could easily be the cowboys with Buffalo Bill at the head on his white horse—the knights arriving to slay the dragon or the fiendish marauders.

And in 1885 this was the case. No one really bothered to think of the Indians as the indigenous people who had been stripped of their land and their way of life and then herded onto reservations. This was lost for a very long time under the rapacious land grab marked by the tombstone of Indian rights called Manifest Destiny. This philosophy said it was the destiny of white men to settle the continent. It would not be until the 1970s with the publication of *Bury My Heart at Wounded Knee* that a different narrative would punch holes in the cowboy-Indian myth, and the land grab and the genocide would be revealed.

When Theodore Roosevelt came out West in 1883, the Badlands had been largely emptied of its Indian problems, though there were still incidents. What started happening in 1885 was range fires. The fires were in "drive country," which meant they occurred on the cattle drive route toward the Northern Pacific railroad. This ensured the cattle would have no grass and would lose weight on their way to the train and end up as low quality beef. The Indians saw it as payback for depriving them of their ancient hunting grounds in the Badlands.

Roosevelt fought the fires with other cowboys. "The process we usually followed was to kill a steer, split it in two lengthwise, and then have two riders drag each half-steer, the rope of one running from his saddle horn to the front leg, and that of the other to the hind leg. One of the men would spur his horse over or through the line of fire, and the two would then ride forward, dragging the steer, bloody side downward, along the line of flame to beat out any flickering blaze."[1]

It was hot, fatiguing work and the men were covered with black soot at the end of the day. It turned out seventy-five Indians who had received hunting permits from an agent were the ones responsible. The raids and counterraids involved atrocities on both sides that few newspapers at the time would even report. These occurred mainly between Yellowstone and the Little Missouri with the big show at Little Big Horn when Custer died in a hail of arrows and bullets. Many times, robberies were committed by

Indians who simply did not have any food. The ranges they used to hunt no longer belonged to them and many corrupt agents on the reservations would not distribute the cattle and ponies.

During the worst times, ranchers saw the Indians as the enemy plain and simple, and many shot them on sight or captured them and stripped off their clothes and proceeded to whip them horribly. The Indians retaliated, and many men were shot, flayed with a knife, or simply beheaded on the spot; women were tied to stakes and raped repeatedly and then mutilated.

This was the background of the ongoing war that Roosevelt had stepped into. He was enlightened to a point, but in a lecture in New York in 1886, he revealed his Western view. "I suppose I should be ashamed to say that I take the Western view of the Indian. I don't go so far as to think that the only good Indians are dead Indians, but I believe nine out of ten are, and I shouldn't like to inquire too closely into the case of the tenth. The most vicious cowboy has more moral principle than the average Indian. Turn three hundred low families of New York into New Jersey, support them for fifty years in vicious idleness, and you will have some idea of what the Indians are. Reckless, revengeful, fiendishly cruel, they rob and murder, not the cowboys, who can take care of themselves, but the defenseless, lone settlers on the plains. As for the soldiers, an Indian chief once asked Sheridan for a cannon. 'What! Do you want to kill my soldiers with it?' asked the general. 'No,' replied the chief, 'want to kill the cowboy; kill soldier with a club.'"[2]

Complete with a joke at the end, this speech shows Roosevelt had little feeling for the people deprived of their land. There was bravado and a puffing up of the Rooseveltian chest for the audience. Soldier, Indian fighter, cowboy—Roosevelt was always posturing. Americans had been outraged when the British invaded America twice. There were the principles of liberty and freedom, but Americans also fought for "home." The Indians fought back for this same reason, but this was not recognized in the late 1800s. The country was expanding, and the Indians were simply in the way. America's destiny was to become a power from coast to coast. The message for the Indians then was: Adapt or die.

On his ranches, Roosevelt was very fair with the Indians who crossed his path. He allowed them the same rights as white people and would not put up with anyone mistreating them. In fact, he retrieved two stolen horses for an old Indian. "Um Um," the Indian muttered and then rode away without thanking Roosevelt. He thought that was the end of it, but the next day the Indian returned and silently put in his arms a buffalo hide with a painting of the battle of Little Big Horn on it.

In his book *Hunting Trips of a Ranchman*, Roosevelt did take on the notion that Americans took the Indians' land and they were merely fighting back.

> During the past century a good deal of sentimental nonsense has been talked about our taking the Indians land. Now, I do not mean to say for a moment that gross wrong has not been done the Indians both by government and individuals, again and again.... where brutal and reckless frontiersmen are brought into contact with a set of treacherous, vengeful, and fiendishly cruel savages a long series of outrages on both sides is sure to follow. But as regards taking the land, at least from the western Indians, the simple truth is that the latter never had a real ownership in it at all. Where the game was plenty they hunted, they followed it when they moved away to new hunting grounds, unless they were prevented by stronger rivals.... The Indians should be treated in just such a way that we treat white settlers. Give each his little claim; if, as would generally happen, he declined this, why then let him share the fate of the thousands of white hunters and trappers...who have lived on the game that the settlement of the country has exterminated...[3]

But now we must go back to the man of adventure. Truly, the Wild West adventure wasn't complete without facing down Indians. Boys and men harbored this fantasy of stopping the attacking Indian with courage and cunning, while the Indians were treated as buffoons who did not understand weaponry or tactics. But of course this was far from true. They understood the power of the repeating Winchester and made a point of getting them at every opportunity. They also understood guerilla warfare after the initial disasters of charging into the barrels of rifles. The Indians understood terror, so much so that men carried poison to commit suicide rather than be tortured when captured. But as for Roosevelt, besides one encounter in the mountains when hunting with Merrifield, he had yet to confront Indians in the classic cowboy style.

His buckskin coat with rifle on the ready in that famous photograph seemed to cry out for this encounter. The man in the photograph was not on the ready for buffalo or grizzly—no, the man holding the Winchester and looking menacingly ahead was holding off the *Indian* or at least he was ready to come to the rescue. He is the white version of the Indian in his buckskin coat—the Davy Crockett or mountain man or frontiersman who lives off the land and who savages the savage in his own world.

So it was, when Roosevelt was out on a ride looking for stray ponies, that the gods smiled on him once again. He had traveled to the territory to the north, where some of his cattle grazed, when he rode up a plateau and saw a group of five Indians directly in front of him. The day was bright and the wide-open sky seemed to go on forever. The Indians all had Winchesters, and they immediately pulled out their rifles and held them high and charged at a full gallop.

The whoops went right through him. Roosevelt knew it was foolish to try and outrun them as they were on light, fast horses. Was he scared, or was he excited, as he realized he was too far out and a man had been killed by Indians the week before? It is hard to say, but Roosevelt swung off Manitou and pulled his Winchester from the scabbard. The Indians were closing in and still whooping it up with rifles held high. He recalled later, "The instant they saw me they whipped out their guns and raced full speed at me, yelling and flogging their horses. I was on a favorite horse, Manitou, who was a wise old fellow, with nerves not to be shaken at anything. I at once leaped off and stood with my rifle ready."[4]

Now he was waiting for the moment. Roosevelt had crossed again into the mythology of the West and was now facing down the savages—like vintage Buffalo Bill and the Wild West show. Certainly this very scene was played out a hundred times under the great canvas circus tent while people watched in sawdust-scented fascination. Roosevelt was now the bulwark against the Red menace, and while protecting himself, he was also protecting his land, his cattle, his ranch, his way of life. Wasn't this all wrapped up in the mythology of the cowboy-Indian duel—progress versus chaos, and savagery versus morality? Of course, none of this was on Roosevelt's mind while he aimed at the center Indian and waited for them to reach him. He later wrote, "It was possible that the Indians were merely making a bluff and intended no mischief. But I did not like their actions, and I thought it likely that if I allowed them to get hold of me they would at least take my horse and rifle, and possibly kill me. So I waited until they were a hundred yards off and then drew a bead on the first. Indians—and for the matter of that, white men—do not like to ride in on a man who is cool and means shooting..."[5]

So here was Roosevelt with his Winchester in the Badlands with his sight pinned to the chest of an Indian. He was facing destruction—and we can only marvel that this same man who would one day ride in an airplane and drive a car is *here*, in the last glimmering twilight of the Wild West frontier, fighting off Indians. In less than twenty years, the Wright Brothers would fly their plane, and soon the frontier would be declared closed. Roosevelt really was a man with one boot in the primitive West and one in the modern East, straddling two very different worlds at once.

The hot breath of that overheated mesa was blowing against the rim of his hat. He could hear Manitou snorting and felt his finger curled into the rifle's trigger. His eye was on the far sight, and Roosevelt knows he would at least take one with him. He stood his ground, the sweat cooling under his hat band, his eye fixed to the sight. He was inside the mythology of the West and in that way he was immortal.

Roosevelt described the moment years later: "In a twinkling every man was lying over the side of his horse" and "all five turned and were galloping backwards, having altered their course as quickly as so many teal ducks."[6] Then the Indians drew back and circled and stopped. It seemed to Roosevelt they were conferring when one of them rode forward. He made a peace sign with his open hand, and Roosevelt let him proceed to about fifty yards. The Indian then waved a piece of paper, probably a reservation pass.

"How! Me good Injun," he called.

"How!" Roosevelt replied. "I'm glad you are but don't come any closer."

The Indian then asked for some sugar or tobacco.

"I have neither," Roosevelt replied.

He wrote later, "Another Indian began slowly drifting toward me in spite of my calling out to keep back, so I once more aimed with my rifle, whereupon both Indians slipped to the side of their horses and galloped off with oaths that did credit to at least one side of their acquaintance with English."[7]

Roosevelt then led Manitou back toward the prairie, with the Indians following for a few miles. They eventually vanished in the long haze of the twilight—much like this moment in history, a time that would only live on in books and movies. Teddy Roosevelt had once again cheated death and, more than that, he had been allowed to touch another bulwark of a vanishing ship. There is no doubt the Indians were capable of killing him, but in what seems like a Western to our sensibilities, he dispatched the menacing savages with his Winchester and plenty of grit. Buffalo Bill could do no better in his Wild West show touring Eastern cities, showing neurasthenic people a world where Indians were always cowards ... and cowboys always won.

28

COWBOY IN LOVE
1886

If we take Roosevelt at his word, then we would have to believe he was going to stay in the West and pursue ranching as his chosen profession. But there was often a difference between Roosevelt's public words and his private actions. What Roosevelt did on his trip back to New York in September 1885 was to become secretly engaged to Edith Carow, his childhood sweetheart. It had been one and a half years since Alice Lee passed away.

Edith Carow came from the same social stratum as Teddy Roosevelt, and she was always over at the Roosevelt house when he was a boy. They played together and shared a mutual interest in books. The assumption was that Edith and Theodore could very well end up together. But something happened. "It being Edith Carow's 17th birthday, I sent her a bomboniere."[1] On August 22 he went out for a "wild" ride with his horse, and then he and Edith went on a sailing trip, then "Edith and I went up to the summer house."

Then his diary stops mentioning her. Something happened, and we can probably assume from Roosevelt's silence that things did not go his way. Perhaps there was a promise offered and then withdrawn. Whatever happened, Edith was out, and Roosevelt met Alice Lee. "As long as I live, I shall never forget how sweetly she looked, and how prettily she greeted me."[2] Alice Hathaway Lee stole his heart with her "quick intelligence," her "singular loveliness," and her "unfailing sunny temperament." In a final reference to Edith, Roosevelt told a friend, "Tell her that I hope that when I see her at XMAS it will not be on what you might call one of her off days."[3] Clearly they had clashed, and Edith had lost out to Alice.

But now Roosevelt was back at 422 Madison, and on opening the door he bumped into Edith. Since the death of his wife and his subsequent sojourn in the West, he had managed to avoid her. Edith's family had fallen on hard times in the 1880s, and like many great families faced with genteel poverty, she now clung to the old social group for position. She and Roosevelt's sister Corinne were still very close. Her father had died and her mother and sister were vacationing in Europe.

And here was Theodore Roosevelt back from the West. Edith was twenty-four, and, while considered at the time "an old maid," she was physically very much at her peak and presented a very full figure and a very sharp mind to Roosevelt.[4] What *she* saw was almost unbelievable. Theodore had been the skinny, frail asthmatic who always looked as if he might jump out of his own skin. Now she saw a man tanned and burnt, with close-cropped hair and a drooping cowboy mustache above a barrel chest and strong arms, who moved and spoke with authority. It was a different man staring at her from the doorway of the New York home. It was a cowboy.

Edith must have been somewhat on guard, as this man had once hurt her and had very much left her for another woman. Years later, Edith would assert she had always been the rightful Mrs. Roosevelt. Edith had very direct blue eyes that didn't back down, and this had probably been a factor in the confrontation all those years before. Now after having made himself on the frontier, Teddy and Edith were equals.

No one really knows what happened, but that meeting led to others. They would not announce their engagement until November 17, 1886. No word was spoken publicly and this gives us added insight into Roosevelt's thinking at the time. It had been less than two years since the death of his wife and now he was engaged. This would not sit well with an electorate that saw him as a moralizing force. No mention would be made of his engagement for a year, but the meaning of the engagement was clear: Roosevelt's adventure in the West would now have a definite endpoint.

That the West had made a man who could love again is plausible, but it is even more obvious this roughhewn cowboy, who had physically changed and become a force within himself, was not the same man Edith had known. Roosevelt himself probably saw no connection, but he had moved on from the death of Alice and his mother. Somewhere in the hell of the sunbaked Badlands, a new man had been forged, capable of loving again, and what's more, capable of looking to the future.

Edith would not come to live in the Badlands. She was a Victorian woman who disapproved of excess in anything—drinking, swearing, sex (of course), actions; and the West was all about excess. She was an intensely private person who routinely burned letters, especially those that had anything to do with her and Roosevelt—a historian's nightmare. The cowboy would have to hang up his spurs eventually in the world of Edith Carow. Roosevelt must have known this, but he had no way of knowing the Badlands would make his decision for him.

29

HIGH NOON

1886

Gary Cooper in the movie *High Noon* made an unforgettable image—a man in the dusty street facing the men who outnumber him. He alone stands up for what is right. He alone is the sheriff. The iconic sheriff is as much a part of the mythology of the West as are the cowboys and Indians. The Wild West was *wild* because there was too much land and not enough law. There were towns with no law at all, like Little Missouri and Medora. The law was a good 150 miles away and had to be sent for; and by the time they arrived, the issue usually had been resolved one way or another.

So the only man of legal authority in the town was the sheriff—a one-man band of morality with his jail cell and his six-shooter and a couple of Winchesters. Usually there was a deputy, who typically had no credentials at all and could easily be the town blacksmith or the town drunk. The Barney Fife character, while exaggerated, was not a stretch in his fundamental lack of authority. Only the sheriff could set the law, and in the towns of the Wild West this required a lot of courage.

There was no back up. Sometimes a posse was rounded up to assist the sheriff in pursuit. Usually the posse consisted of men who worked for ranchers, those who had a vested interest in catching a horse thief or a cattle thief. Sometimes they were men just out for blood, and many times the wrong man was strung up. But the sheriff stood alone, and it was only through his moral fortitude that justice could prevail and he could get his man.

This type of figure appealed to Roosevelt immensely, for he was driven by a moral fervor to do the right thing. Even later in his Big Stick Diplomacy, there was the swagger of the lawman daring other nations to mess with the "new sheriff" in town. Roosevelt would see the United States as a sheriff in the community of nations, and he made sure that the sheriff was well-armed with his Great White Fleet sent around the world. *Speak softly and carry a big stick* could easily be the motto for a sheriff in the West. For Roosevelt to carry his big stick in the West, he would need to *become* the long arm of the law. It is ironic that in the era of the horse, it was a boat that made it all possible.

Roosevelt had arrived in the spring of 1886 and given his sister the lowdown on the Badlands. "I got out here all right, and was met at the station by my men; I was really heartily glad to see the great, stalwart bearded fellows again, and they were honestly pleased to see me. Joe Ferris is married and his wife made me most comfortable the night I spent in town. Next morning snow covered the ground; we pushed down …to this ranch, which we reached long after sunset, the full moon flooding the landscape with light. There has been an ice gorge right in front of the house, the swelling mass of broken fragments having been pushed almost to our doorstep…. No horse could by any chance get across; we men have a boat, and even thus it is most laborious carrying it out to the water; we work like artic explorers."[1]

Roosevelt felt he had to get out to his ranch to keep Sewall and Dow around. The winters were brutal and the men could easily terminate their contracts. So it was good for him to find the men in high spirits even if the winter was proving to be long. The Little Missouri was usually very low. Cowboys could ride across and barely get their boots wet or when frozen they could cross at will. But the spring thaw had brought about a high, growling ice-river that would likely have pushed aside Roosevelt's cabin if some cottonwoods had not blocked it.

The Elkhorn ranch possessed one of the few boats around. The middle passage of the river was flowing but no horse could cross. So the boat became invaluable. Roosevelt wanted to go hunt for some cougars, which would necessitate using the boat. Sewall had roped the skiff to a tree to keep the river from taking it, and the next morning he walked up to Roosevelt with a piece of rope and a mitten.

"I guess we won't go today," said Sewall.[2]

Roosevelt stared at the piece of rope cut with a knife and at the red mitten.

"Someone has gone off with the boat," Roosevelt proclaimed, and then became so angry he wanted to gallop after the thieves with Manitou.

Sewall pointed out the futility of such action with the frozen river. He would never catch the men floating down the river. The only thing to do was build a scow to follow the men. Roosevelt consented and sent for supplies. One might wonder at this point why he'd go after men in arctic conditions. It was only a boat, after all; but Roosevelt was an unofficial deputy sheriff by virtue of his chairmanships in the Stockmen's Association, which had morphed into a policing organization.

Besides his duty to the Stockmen's Association, the theft of the boat violated a deep moral code that Roosevelt and those in the West lived by. It was what gave men the authority to string up horse thieves or shoot to defend themselves. In later times one might have called it "the honor system," where men were expected to police themselves and live by a code. Preparatory schools used a system where students were on their honor not to cheat and to tell the truth if they did. Roosevelt saw the West like this. Men lived by a code and the code must be fiercely upheld. Besides, he knew who did it.

The leader of the three outlaws who had snagged Roosevelt's boat was "Redhead" Finnegan; a perfect name for the Wild West ruffian. He was assisted by misfits like those in the outlaw gangs of the movies—a half-breed named Burnsteed and a half-wit named Pfaffenbach. Finnegan, who sported long red hair, had long been suspected of stealing cattle and of other nefarious activities. The Stockmen's Association had wanted to get rid of him and some had talked about a necktie party. This was after Finnegan had woken up after a long drunk and shot up the town and nearly killed several people. Finnegan and company, in short, were the bad element Roosevelt saw as no longer having a place in the West.

After Roosevelt checked Finnegan's shack, he came to the conclusion that the three men had lit out under threat of imminent action by vigilantes. Roosevelt's boat was the perfect getaway vehicle. Unfortunately for the new deputy sheriff of Little Missouri, the weather had gotten worse. Roosevelt began writing a new book, a history of the senator Thomas Hart Benton, while waiting for Sewall and Dow to finish the boat.

"At present we are all snowed up by a blizzard," he wrote to his friend Henry Cabot Lodge. "As soon as it lightens up I shall start down the river with two of my men in a boat we have built while indoors, after some horse-thieves who took our boat the other night to get out of the country with; but they have such a start we have very little chance of catching them."[3]

Of course, the other reason for Roosevelt's pursuit of the bad men was that it was going to be the ultimate adventure. He had read novels and heard stories of desperados pursued by fearless men who brought them to justice. Even Buffalo Bill riffed on this fantasy with his white hat and white horse. He stood for justice, progress, and civilization. The Indians and desperados were the darkness of the untamed continent.

So while the blizzard raged outside, Roosevelt worked on his book and then fired off a letter to his sister. "In a day or two, when the weather gets a little milder, I expect to start down the river in a boat, to go to Mandan; the trip ought to take a week or ten days, more or less. It will be good fun. My life on the ranch this summer is not going to be an adventurous or exciting one; and my work will be mainly one of supervision."[4] A different tone from previous Roosevelt missives; he even wrote, "Life has settled down to its usual monotonous course here."[5] These are not words one would think Roosevelt would use regarding the Badlands; but there was someone else in his life now, and that can make all the difference. At the moment, however, there was still adventure, and the boat was soon finished.

On March 30 the blizzard let up, and Roosevelt, Sewall, and Dow set off to bring the outlaws to justice—or at least get their boat back. Mrs. Sewall and Mrs. Dow watched the men become small in their boat. They were worried. The temperature was dropping again and the North Country was full of Indians, and there was a good chance the men could freeze to death in the treeless, wind-blasted terrain of the Badlands in winter.

Roosevelt brought books along, including Tolstoy's *Anna Karenina*; he also brought a camera, with an eye to publishing his adventure. He did know, of course, that he was on a grand adventure, so the third eye of the writer was ever present. With Sewall steering and Dow on the bow keeping an eye out, Roosevelt dug himself down under some buffalo robes and watched the piles of ice pass by. The landscape took on the early, pristine look of some ice age, with the buttes rising above, ice-laced with black coal veins that ran through them and burned red in the gloom. The wind cut down the vein of the Little Missouri and caught them head on.

"We're like to have it in our faces all day," remarked Dow, pushing ice away from the bow.

"We can't," said Sewall, "unless it's the crookedest wind in Dakota."

They followed the river's course like a canoeist, staying as much in the center as possible and away from the ice pile-ups. The wind was brutal and immediately froze their noses and cheeks. "It is the crookedest wind in Dakota," muttered Sewall.

Meanwhile, Roosevelt read Tolstoy, determined "to have as good a time as possible."[6] Again here was a man determined to ride the Wild West adventure curve before it all ended. He watched the frozen, craggy landscape changing color, shading from vermillion to purple. He would later write, "The river twisted in every direction, winding to and fro across the alluvial valley bottom, only to be brought up by the rows of great barren buttes. ... [E]very now and then overhanging pieces would break off and slide into the stream with a loud sullen splash, like the plunge of some great water beast."[7] The temperature fell to zero and the wind never stopped. "In the afternoon a sharp-tailed prairie fowl flew across stream ahead of the boat. ... Shooting him, we landed and picked off two others that were perched high up in the leafless cottonwoods. ... These three birds served as supper; and shortly afterward, as the cold grew more and more biting, we rolled in under our furs and blankets and were soon asleep."[8]

The morning brought even lower temperatures. Roosevelt and his men hunted for some deer and then got underway. The ice was thick and progress slow. He later wrote, "It was colder than before and for some time we went along in chilly silence, nor was it until midday that sun warmed our blood in the least."[9] The men slipped past a group of abandoned teepees; the only sign of life they had seen on the desolate trip thus far. The Indians would not be far off.

They stopped for lunch on a frozen sand bar; "a simple enough meal, the tea being boiled over a fire of driftwood, that also fried the bacon." They shoved off again with the wind gusts buffeting the boat and torturing the men with frozen ice crystals. Even before the sun set, the ice had begun to freeze on their poles. They made camp and ate of the fowl again.

The next morning, the ice had become so thick they had to delay starting for a few hours. They tracked and killed a deer, then made a fire and ate. They were finally able to set off again. The outlaws had a six-day start, and Roosevelt began to wonder if they would ever catch up with them. He looked around and marveled at the landscape. "At times the cliffs rose close to us on either hand, and again the valley would widen into a sinuous oval a mile or two long, bounded on every side, as far as our eyes could see, by a bluff line without a break..."[10]

They had traveled a hundred miles from Elkhorn, and the frozen men had had enough. The outlaws could have made their way from the river a long time ago and pursued a different route of escape, though no one knew what that could be. The only logical course was to follow the river and float on down. They passed in silence with Roosevelt in the middle, sitting on top of the buffalo robes, his finger marking his place in the book. He had just looked down when they rounded a frozen bend in the river and Sewall cried out,

"There's your boat! Get your guns ready!"[11]

The boat was moored on the right side of the river, with blue smoke trailing up from the trees further back. Obviously, the three men were thinking they had not been followed (and who *would* bother to follow them in weather such as this?), so they had stopped to hunt and camp and would proceed at their leisure. Roosevelt and his men had closed the gap of the six-day lead, though surely the "boat thieves" assumed they were well away. Not so with Sheriff Roosevelt in hot pursuit, as he later writes: "[F]rom among the bushes some little way back, the smoke of a camp-fire curled up through the frosty air. ... Our overcoats were off in a second, and after exchanging a few muttered words, the boat was hastily and silently shoved toward the bank. As soon as it touched the shore ice I leaped out and ran up behind a clump of bushes, so as to cover the landing of the others, who had to make the boat fast. For a moment we felt the thrill of keen excitement, and our veins tingled as we crept cautiously toward the fire.... "[12]

It was dangerous. Finnegan was known to shoot first and ask questions later. Also, Roosevelt and his men were not technically the law, and men running up with guns could be met with the same. Sewall would later write to his brother, "It was rather funny business for one of the men was called a pretty hard ticket. He was also a shooting man. If he was in the bushes and saw us first he was liable to make it very unhealthy for us."[13]

Lucky for the sheriff and his deputies, the men weren't standing guard by the boat. They moved stealthily though the bushes and saw a man sitting by the campfire with his guns by his side. It was the half-witted German Pfaffenbach, whom Sewall would later describe as an "oldish man who drank so much poor whiskey that he had lost most of the manhood he ever possessed."[14] But Roosevelt didn't know this. He saw a man with his guns by his side, so he busted through the bushes with his rifle pinned to the man.

"Hands up!"[15]

Pfaffenbach's hands shot to the sky. They searched him and took his guns and knives and told him that if he did as he was told nothing would happen. But if not, they would kill him instantly. He did as he was told. Roosevelt would later recount it with much less drama. "We took them absolutely by surprise. The only one in the camp was the German whose weapons were on the ground, and who of course gave up at once, his companions being off hunting. We made him safe, delegating one of our number to look after him particularly and see that he made no noise, and then sat down and waited for the others."[16]

We pause here for a bit of a reality check. Yes, these men were "outlaws," in the sense that they had stolen Roosevelt's boat and were suspected of cattle rustling and of shooting up the town, but Roosevelt was playing a dangerous game, and the fact that everyone was armed made it a very deadly game. Roosevelt would doubtless have killed the German had he resisted. And if the man was a half-wit, as has been said, could he not have easily mistaken the motivations of men rushing at him with weapons?

But the myth of the West was pre-eminent here, and Theodore Roosevelt was in the heart of that mythology as the principled sheriff. Roosevelt and his men were now waiting for Finnegan, who truly was a dangerous man. They had gone hunting, indicating that the outlaws had believed themselves quite safe. Sewall guarded the captive, while Roosevelt and Dow crouched behind a cut bank and waited. Sewall later wrote his brother about how dangerous the situation had become.

> Will and I kept watch and listened—our eyes are better than Roosevelt's, Will on the right and I on the left. R. was to rise up and tell them to hands up, Will and I both with the double barrel guns loaded with Buck shot, and we are all going to shoot if they offered to raise a gun. It is rather savage work, but it don't do to fool with such fellows. If there was any killing to be done we meant to do it ourselves."[17]

An hour before sunset they heard the men approaching, but then it sounded like the men were heading up the river.

"We are going to lose them," Roosevelt whispered. "They are not coming to the camp."[18]

"I think," answered Sewall, "they are looking for the camp smoke."

The men broke through the sagebrush then and walked right toward Roosevelt and his men. Roosevelt's heart was beating in his ears as he stood up and pinned the rifle to Finnegan. He would later write, "We heard them a long way off and made ready, watching them for some minutes as they walked toward us, their rifles on their shoulders and the sunlight glittering on their steel barrels. When they were within twenty yards or so we straightened up from behind the bank, covering them with our cocked rifles, while I shouted them to hold up their hands…"[19]

The half-breed obeyed with his knees "trembling as if they had been made of whalebone," but Finnegan predictably had other ideas.[20] He didn't drop his gun as he tried to decide if the man with thick glasses would really shoot him. Roosevelt advanced then. "I walked up within a few paces, covering the center of his chest so as to avoid overshooting and repeating the command, he saw that he had no show and with an oath, let his rifle drop and held his hands up beside his head."[21]

Roosevelt's recitation of events here is interestingly much the same as his descriptions of his hunting adventures: the same calculation as to "overshooting," the same drama of shooting a grizzly, a buffalo, a man. He was an efficient killer of animals, and this skill surely would lend itself to killing a man as well. Finnegan was right to drop his gun.

They searched the men and relieved them of their weapons.

"If you keep quiet," Roosevelt told them, "and not try to get away, you'll be alright. If you try anything, we'll shoot you."[22]

Truer words were never spoken. Dow told Sewall the right barrel of the shotgun went off sometimes on its own, to which Sewall replied, "I'll be careful but if it happens to go off it will make more difference to them than me."[23]

The sheriff had gotten his man or men, but now the question was, what to do with them? If they tied them up, then their hands and feet would certainly freeze in the brutal cold. Roosevelt came up with the idea of taking their boots and gave them buffalo robes to keep warm. Now that they could not attempt an escape, he really had to decide how to bring them to justice. Upriver was out. Downriver was 150 miles to Mandan through the frozen river. And they had to be fed, and they had very few provisions. Better to shoot them or at least leave them without weapons or transportation, which would be the same as shooting them in the barren wastes of the Badlands.

Or Roosevelt the sheriff could take them downriver and fight his way through the ice and cold. Roosevelt being Roosevelt decided on that course of action. After all, the deputy sheriff's job was to bring in his man, and in this way the mythology of the West and the moral certitude of the enforcer of laws would be upheld. Roosevelt would bring Finnegan and company to justice by poling down river though the ice and hope for the best.

30

SHERIFF ROOSEVELT

1886

E ven sleeping was a problem now. Someone had to stay up all night and watch the prisoners. They could not be bound, so this meant a man with a gun had to sit in the freezing darkness and not fall asleep while standing guard over men who *were* sleeping. Roosevelt took the first watch. "We determined to watch in succession a half-night apiece, thus each getting a full rest every third night. I took first watch, my two companions, revolver under head, rolling up in their blankets on the side of the fire opposite that on which the three captives lay; while I, in fur cap, gantlets, and overcoat, took my station a little way back in the circle of firelight. ... For this night-watching we always used the double-barrel with buckshot, as a rifle is uncertain in the dark. ... The only danger lies in the extreme monotony of sitting still in the dark guarding men who make no motion."[1]

Then came eight days of freezing and unceasing toil. As Roosevelt would later write, "there is very little amusement in combining the functions of a sheriff with those of an arctic explorer."[2] They started off down the river, but immediately started to slow and then came to a halt behind an ice jam. They went ashore and climbed a hill and felt their spirits fall, for "as far as we could see the river was choked with black ice. The great Ox-Bow jam had stopped, and we had come to its tail."[3] They could not go upstream and they could not go overland. "We had nothing to do but pitch camp, after which we held consultation."[4]

The men decided they had no choice but to wait out the ice floe. It was thawing; it was just not thawing fast enough. Roosevelt and his captors would have to pick their way down through the ice and hope the river kept moving before they starved to death. The eight days of fighting ice blocks in the exposed small boat with six men was a real battle. "The weather kept as cold as ever. During the night the water in the pail would freeze solid. Ice formed all over the river, thickly along the banks; and the clear, frosty sun gave us so little warmth that the melting hardly began before noon."[5]

Each day the jam moved a little and the men picked their way with long poles, all the while keeping guard over Finnegan and company. And then the river would turn into a torrent where the ice at the edge of the jam had melted and the fast-moving current was sucked forcefully under the ice. This was very dangerous to the small boat. Roosevelt wrote later, "Once we came around a bend and got so near that we were in a good deal of danger of being sucked under. The current ran too fast to let us work back against it, and we could not pull the boats up over the steep banks of rotten ice. ... We could only land and snub the boat up with ropes, holding them there for two or three hours..."[6]

The stop and start momentum of their journey is recorded in Roosevelt's journal:

> April 1 Captured the three boat thieves
> April 2 Came on with our prisoners until hung up by ice jam
> April 3 Hung up by ice
> April 4 Hung up by ice

April 5 Worked down a couple of miles until hung up by
ice

April 6 Worked down a couple of miles to tail of ice jam[7]

And there were Indians to worry about as well. They had to camp and find game as best they could and this meant a campfire. Roosevelt wrote later, "We had to be additionally cautious on account of being in the Indian country, having worked down past Killdeer Mountains, where some of my cowboys had run across a band of Sioux—said to be Tetons—the year before."[8]

Then the food started to run out. Roosevelt and his men had packed food for three men, now there were six. To make matters worse, the Indians had recently staged a big hunt all down the river and driven off the game. They were soon reduced to unleavened bread made with muddy river water. Roosevelt through all this crashed through Tolstoy's *Anna Karenina* remarking, "my surroundings were quite grey enough to harmonize with Tolstoy."[9] Incongruity heaped upon incongruity. A man who had arrested three bad men in the Badlands was floating down in an ice floe in the Little Missouri in winter with the ever present danger of Indians, freezing, starving—a man who really was not even a Deputy Sherriff but a scion a patrician family from the East turned cowboy, now sailing along with sullen-eyed outlaws—all the while reading *Tolstoy*; if this was not adventure, what is?

Roosevelt even wrote a review of the book for his sister Corinne. "I hardly know whether to call it a very bad book or not...Tolstoy is a great writer. Do you notice how he never comments on the actions of his personages?"[10] Roosevelt's review was extensive and shows how he lived in two worlds that complemented each other; the world of action and the life of the mind. He was the Renaissance man complete, and if any Indians on the cliffs had observed the passage of the two boats, they would have seen three men huddled down with two men poling and standing guard while a third sat ensconced in the middle with his glasses and his book.

The other enemy was the tedium and monotony and fatigue. Every night someone had to be awake and stand guard. "So long as we kept awake and watchful there was not the least danger, as our three men knew us, and understood perfectly that the slightest attempt at a break would result in their being shot down."[11] But the nights and the days wore on the men. The rows of hills and valleys, "barren and naked, stretched along without a break. ... The discolored river, whose eddies boiled into yellow foam, flowed always between the same banks of frozen mud or of muddy ice."[12]

With their remaining flour almost gone, the men held a meeting.

"We can't shoot them," said Roosevelt, "and we can't feed them. It looks to me as though we'd have to let them go."[13]

Sewall disagreed. "The flour will last a day or two more...and it's something to know that if we're punishing ourselves, we're punishing the thieves also."

"Exactly!" cried Roosevelt. "Well, hold on to them."

As will happen between prisoners and their captors, the men started to become friends. So much so that Finnegan said to Roosevelt, "If I'd had any show at all, you'd have sure had to fight, Mr. Roosevelt; but there wasn't any use making a break when I'd only have got shot myself, with no chance of harming anyone else."[14]

Roosevelt just laughed. But their situation was not a laughing matter and something had to be done. The river would not get them where they were going before they could starve. They decided to try to find a ranch nearby. Sewall hiked out from the river the next day on one side of the river, and Roosevelt and Dow searched the other side. They finally found an outlying camp of the Diamond C Ranch where Roosevelt secured a horse and rode further onto a ranch at the edge of the Killdeer Mountains.

There he hired man with a prairie schooner to drive supplies to the camp by the river, where Sewall and Dow were waiting with the prisoners. "I was able to hire a large prairie schooner and two tough little bronco mares, driven by the settler himself, a rugged old plainsman, who evidently could hardly understand why I took so much bother with thieves instead of hanging them off-hand."[15]

It is worth commenting here on this logic. Stealing was a common crime in the East in the 1880s, yet men were not hung for the offence. They were fined or jailed. But in the West the thievery of just about anything meant a good certainty of hanging, whether horse thievery or cattle rustling or stealing a boat for that matter. One can only surmise that this was precisely because *there was no law* and the draconian consequence kept a lot of would-be thieves in check. Steal a horse and die. Also since survival was not dependent on any sort of social safety net at all—there were no soup kitchens or associations to help the poor—then the theft of a horse or some cattle or any implement that was necessary for survival could in itself be a death sentence. So while we may think a horse thief is a bad person, to the Westerner of 1880s that person was a potential murderer, and so all thievery fell under this general charge and consequence.

Roosevelt returned and it was determined then that Sewall and Dow would continue down the river with the boats and provisions while Roosevelt would take the thieves with him in the prairie schooner to the nearest jail, which was in Dickinson. Thus would begin the final trek of the Rooseveltian journey to fulfill justice, not unlike a polar explorer's final push for the prize—and it was just as brutal.

It was a two-day journey and Roosevelt had to walk behind the prairie schooner with his gun at the ready. "It was a most desolate drive. The prairie had been burned the fall before and was a mere bleak waste of blackened earth, and a cold rainy mist lasted through the two days."[16] Roosevelt trudged behind the wagon all day long through the ankle-deep mud while his prisoners rode in comfort. "It was a gloomy walk. Hour after hour went by always the same, while I plodded along through the dreary landscape—hunger, cold, and fatigue struggling with a sense of dogged, weary resolution. At night, when we put up at the squalid hut of a frontier granger, the only habitation on our road, it was even worse. I did not dare to go to sleep, but making my three men get into the upper bunk from which they could not get out only with difficulty, I sat with my back against the cabin door and kept watch over them all night long."[17]

After thirty-six hours of no sleep, they reached Dickinson, and Roosevelt handed over his bad men and received a fee for deputy sheriff as well as compensation for miles traveled; about fifty dollars. Roosevelt was relieved to turn over the men, but he was hurting and bumped into a man who was a doctor, a Victor H. Stickney. His impression of Roosevelt after his ordeal is illuminating.

> This stranger struck me as the queerest specimen of strangeness that had descended on Dickinson in the three years I have lived there.... He was all teeth and eyes. His clothes were in rags from forcing his way through the rosebushes that covered the river bottoms. He was scratched, bruised, and hungry, but gritty and determined as a bulldog...I remember he gave me the impression of being heavy and rather large. As I approached him he stopped me with a gesture, asking whether I could direct him to a doctor's office. I was struck by the way he bit off his words and showed his teeth. I told him I was the only practicing physician, not only in Dickinson, but in the whole surrounding county. "By George," he said emphatically, "then you're exactly the man I want to see....My feet are blistered so badly that I can hardly walk. I want you to fix me up."[18]

The doctor bandaged Roosevelt's feet while he told of his adventure.

> You could see he was thrilled by the adventures he had been though. He did not seem to think he had done anything particularly commendable, but he was, in his own phrase, "pleased as punch" at the idea of having participated in a real adventure. He was just like a boy....I told my wife that I had met the most peculiar, and at the same time the most wonderful man I had ever come to know.[19]

Yes, another adventure. Roosevelt had just experienced the apotheosis of the self-reliant cowboy. He had arrested bad men at risk to himself and brought them to justice and enforced the code of the old West. This was nothing short of a childhood fantasy spun out with hats and cap guns of the boy, now realized by the man. Relaxing in his hotel room, he wrote to his sister Corinne, "I was really glad to give them up to the sheriff this morning for I was pretty well done out with the work, the lack of sleep, and the constant watchfulness, but I am as brown and as tough as a pine knot and I feel equal to anything."[20]

In a strange postscript, the prisoner Finnegan wrote Roosevelt later from prison and explained his motivations for taking the boat and finished by saying, "I have read many of your sketches of ranch life in the papers since I have been here and they interested me deeply...should you drop over to Bismarck this fall make a call to the prison. I should be glad to meet you."[21]

31

A DARKENING CLOUD

1886

R oosevelt was something of a folk hero after his capture of the three boat thieves. He testified at their trial, and Redhead Finnegan and the half-breed each received three years in prison while the German was let off because of his impaired mental state. The man thanked Roosevelt for not prosecuting him, to which Roosevelt replied he was the only man to ever be thanked for calling a man a fool. He was the star at the meeting of the Montana Stock Grower's convention as they had all heard of his river pursuit of Redhead Finnegan. Even the papers back East got wind of the story. The *Newburyport Herald* in Massachusetts reported: "Theodore Roosevelt, who is quite prominent in New York politics and society, owns a ranch on the Little Missouri, about eighty miles northeast from here, and created quite a stir last Sunday by bringing to town three horse thieves whom he had captured with the help of his two cow men."

Many of the cowboys still had one question for Roosevelt: Why didn't he kill the three thieves? They could have killed him, they pointed out repeatedly. Roosevelt settled the matter once and for all. "I didn't come out here to kill anybody. All I wanted to do was defend myself and my property. There wasn't anyone to defend them for me, so I had to do it myself."[1]

But after this triumphant adventure, a dark cloud on the horizon was growing larger. Roosevelt, when it was all said and done, was no businessman. He was a man who was inspiring, who was inspired, a leader, a zealot, an adventurer, but he lacked the hard, God-given practical insight men must have to make money. He was not required to have this by his birth, but he had sunk a cool 85,000 dollars (a couple million today) into the ranch, and it was beginning to leak away.

And he didn't have the fortune he once did. The other Roosevelts were concerned, as they all had a vested interest in their brother not losing his shirt in the West. We can hear the first warning signal in a letter to his sister. "This winter has certainly been a marvelously good one for cattle. My loss has been so trifling as hardly to be worth taking into account; although there may be a number who have strayed off. I think my own expenses out here this summer will be very light indeed..."[2]

He even sent a clipping from a review of *Hunting Trips of a Ranchman* with the lines *as shrewd and enterprising in the conduct of business* underlined. This he directed to be sent to his sister's husband, Douglas, who was the businessman of the family. He didn't send the article to demonstrate he knew what he was doing; he sent it for the irony implied by this commendation.

Clearly he knew the good ship *Roosevelt's Cattle Adventure* was taking on water. Bill Sewall, ever the prophet of doom, was equally concerned and probably saw the end more clearly than Roosevelt at this juncture. "There was always a cloud over me," he said afterward. "I tried to make him see it. He was going to buy land. I urged him not to. I felt sure that what he was putting into those cattle he was going to lose."[3]

Even Roosevelt started to admit privately to Bill he might have been right about the long winters in the Badlands ultimately making it not good cattle country. They had just taken a long hard look at the herd, and Roosevelt turned to Sewall and said: "Bill...you're right about these cows. They're not looking well and I think some of them will die."[4]

The Roosevelt optimism returned when he wrote his sister later that things would work out. "While I do not see any great fortune ahead yet, if things go on as they are now going, and have gone on for the last three years, I think I will each year net enough money to pay a good interest on the capital, and yet be adding to my herd all the time."[5] Sewall of course was ringing the fire alarm meanwhile to his brother in Maine, writing, "As for hard times they are howling out here, and lots are leaving the country. Lots more would if they could."[6]

But the summer of 1886 was shaping up nicely. Roosevelt was doing what he did best—losing himself in his writing. He had been working on a history of Senator Benton and soon there would be the roundup. The Elkhorn ranch was a marvelous place to write. He could divide his days, as most writers dream about, between cerebral and physical work. "Some days," Sewall wrote, "he would write all day long, some days only a part of the day, just as he felt. He said sometimes he would get so he could not write. ... Then he would take his gun and sometimes saunter off... "[7]

Bill Ferris, who let Roosevelt use the upstairs of his store to write, reported hearing him pacing back and forth, sounding out sentences. One gets the sense that Roosevelt was not a natural writer, but a man who had to build his sentences one by one. Sometimes he read portions to Sewall to get his take, when his writing did not sound right to him.

What a relief the June roundup must have been; no more worries over the ranch or his writing, just pure cowboy fun. "The saddle-bands numbered about a hundred each; and the morning we started, sixty men in the saddle splashed across the shallow ford of the river that divided the plain where we had camped from the valley of the long winding creek up which we were first to work."[8]

It would seem the roundup and ranch work did the trick, and *Thomas Hart Benton* progressed very quickly. He wrote to his sister that he had "been on the round-up for a fortnight and really enjoy the work most greatly; in fact, I am having a most pleasant summer."[9] That he was. Roosevelt had probably found the right balance for the first time in his life between fulfilling literary work and a fulfilling physical regimen. "I was much at the ranch, where I had a good deal of writing to do; but every week or two I left to ride among the line camps or spend a few days on any round-up which happened to be in the neighborhood."[10]

The 1886 summer had the quality of a summer before college where everything was in perfect attention. Roosevelt's college would be his impending marriage and the resumption of his political life, though he had not formally made this decision. He did have angst over the guilt of marrying so quickly after Alice Lee. Once he was overheard saying, "I have no constancy...I have no constancy..."[11] One could almost guess what he was referring to. His cattle ranch, his marriage, his wavering between a political and literary career...like many men who came West, Roosevelt was running from something and the future was still an unknown.

And this summer, despite the steep learning curve, he had become a cowboy, a rancher, and a writer. It was his last summer of adventure and certainly his last roundup. "These days of vigorous work among the cattle were themselves full of pleasure. At dawn we were in the saddle, the morning air cool in our faces; the red sunrise saw us loping across the grassy reaches of prairie land, or climbing in single file among the rugged buttes. All forenoon we spent riding the long circle with the cowpunchers of the round-up, in the afternoon we worked the herd, cutting the cattle, with much breakneck galloping and dexterous halting and wheeling.... Soon after nightfall we lay down, in a log hut or tent, if at a line camp; under the open sky, if with the round-up wagon."[12]

Then Roosevelt, after a week or so, would return to his ranch and his writing. Even here was the sense of a man who knew his time was limited and was taking in every moment. "I stood on the low-roofed veranda, looking out under the line of murmuring, glossy-leaved cottonwoods, across the shallow river, to see the sun flame above the line of bluffs opposite."[13] Or he would head off by himself across the prairie in one his famous solitary rides among the buttes and return later with a buck across his saddle.

Then it was back to the roundup for another ten days or so. This time they were working around Andrews Creek, about a mile from Medora, and had gone to a saloon at the end of the day to blow off steam. Roosevelt, who had ridden to town to keep an eye on his cowpunchers, followed them. Dutch Wannegan was there and would later relate what happened. "The men were getting kind of noisy" when Roosevelt entered. "I don't know if he took a drink or not...I never saw him take one but he paid for the drinks of the crowd. 'One more drink boys,' he says and then just as soon as they had their drinks he says 'Come on,' and away they went. He just took the lead and they followed him home. By gollies, I never seen anything like it."[14]

Roosevelt was a natural leader and this came from respect. Men will follow a man they respect, and "the boss" had a reputation built on deeds and a willing capacity to do the work alongside his men. The roundup moved south and Roosevelt stayed with it, writing his sister, "I have been off on the round-up for five weeks, taking a holiday when we had a cold snap...I have never once had breakfast as late as four o'clock. I have been in the saddle all day and work like a beaver and am as happy and rugged as possible."[15]

Roosevelt's ritual as he finished *Thomas Hart Benton* was to rise before the sun, then stand on the piazza and watch the light cross the land, then write until the cabin became too hot. A heat wave had struck Dakota and the temperature soared to 125 degrees. But he did finish the book and went to Dickinson to speak at the Fourth of July celebration, celebrating the 110th anniversary of the Declaration of Independence. It was a classic celebration of the country's birthday. "At ten o'clock the parade got under way. So many spectators decided to join in that the sidewalks were soon deserted. The Declaration of Independence was read aloud in the public square, followed by a mass singing of 'My Country 'Tis of Thee.' The crowd then adjourned to Town Hall for a free lunch. When every cowboy had eaten his considerable fill, the master of ceremonies, Dr. Stickney, introduced the afternoon's speakers. 'The Honorable Theodore Roosevelt.'"[16]

His speech shows his meditation on the West as something in his past, for there is the nuance of a graduation in his words.

"Like all Americans, I like big things; big prairies, big forests and mountains, big wheat-fields, railroads—and herds of cattle, too,—big factories, steamboats, and everything else. But we must keep steadily in mind that no people were ever yet benefited by riches if their prosperity corrupted their virtue...each one must do his part if we wish to show that the nation is worthy of its good fortune. Here we are not ruled over by others, as in the case of Europe; we rule ourselves. ... In a new portion of the country, especially here in the Far West, it is particularly important to do so. ... I am myself at heart as much a Westerner as an Easterner; I am proud, indeed, to be considered one of yourselves... "[17]

Roosevelt then rode a freight train with Arthur Packard of the *Bad Lands Cow Boy* to Medora. In the quickening dusk, fireworks exploded in the sky behind them. He discussed his future with Packard and revealed he wanted to return to public life. Packard would later write, "It was during this talk, that I realized the potential bigness of the man. One could not help believing he was in deadly earnest in his consecration to the highest ideals of citizenship."[18] Roosevelt confided to Packard he believed he could do more in political service than anything else and let him know that a position as president of the Board of Health in New York was available to him. Packard's reply was surprising and prescient.

"Then you will become President of the United States."[19]

Roosevelt stared out into the passing darkness of the old West.

"If your prophecy comes true," he said slowly. "I will do my part to make a good one."

Packard's prophetic vision would not come true for fifteen more years.

32

THE ROOSEVELT GANG
1887

One thing Roosevelt had not done that was part of the iconic mythology of the West was to rob a train. How many times have we seen the outlaws riding up to a steaming, chugging train with guns blazing, forcing the iron horse to come to a stop, divesting all the passengers of their worldly possessions, and then riding off into the safety of the vast landscape? Of course, this would require Roosevelt to be an outlaw—which he was not. Then again, he was not really a sheriff or a gunslinger either, yet he had managed to play these roles. Why not rob a train?

Roosevelt went briefly back East to check on a job with the Board of Health that did not open up to him after all and to confirm a December wedding date with Edith in London. Clearly, he was making plans that would take him away from the West. He returned to a deteriorating situation for his ranches. A drought had been punishing the Badlands and was becoming worse.

The broiling August days rolled on, and Roosevelt felt frustrated and caged. When a possible war with Mexico failed to materialize, his plans to organize cowboys to fight fell apart. There were glimmers of the Rough Riders in Roosevelt's romantic idea of a fighting force culled from the frontier, but the twentieth century would put to bed the knight's errand of men organizing and fighting as heroic individuals. Roosevelt was really restless, itching to get on with his life, as several elements were coming together to make the cattle business untenable.

The *Mandan Pioneer* wrote in July, "[T]he losses this year are enormous owing to the drought and over-stocking. Between the drought, the grasshoppers, and the last frosts, ice forming as late as June 10th, there is not a green thing in all the region I have been over."[1] Sewall and Dow had seen the writing on the wall and they sold their beef to Chicago for ten dollars less than the cost of raising and transporting each animal. They felt at this point "they were throwing away his money" and informed Roosevelt they wanted to end their contracts.[2]

The "boss" had reached the same conclusion and figured he better start cutting his losses before his 85,000-dollar investment slipped away altogether. The herd from Elkhorn he would turn over to Bill Merrifield and Sylvane Ferris. His reply to Sewall was short and bittersweet: "How soon can you go?" Roosevelt was winding down his operation—and all the West had left to offer him was the great train robbery.

He was rounding up cattle twenty miles west of Medora when word came that a cowboy who used to work for him, George Frazier, had died from a lightning strike. His body had been taken to Medora. Roosevelt, knowing that many a cowboy's bones were left bleaching on the prairie, started making arrangements for the funeral.

"We will flag the train and go to Medora," he said.[3]

The next train was a Number 2 that was fast and probably wouldn't stop for a bunch of cowboys whom the crew would naturally assume to be outlaws. In this age, trains could be stopped for whatever lucre they were carrying with the added bonus of passenger booty for men who then vanished into the Badlands with little chance of anyone catching them. It had gotten so bad the railroads started employing armed Pinkertons to ride on the trains, with heavy iron safes and reinforced cars, but this did little to slow men who many times carried dynamite.

"They won't stop here for nuthin," one of the men insisted.

"By Godfrey, they'll have to stop," Roosevelt declared, and sent a man down to the track to flag the train.

Sure enough, the train came on and the Roosevelt gang waited patiently. The chugging, smoke-billowing creature grew louder and louder, as Roosevelt's man stood waiting and waving his hands. The engineer did begin to slow, but then decided better of it and maintained his speed. The Roosevelt gang sped into action and galloped alongside the train and began firing shots in the air. To the engineer and conductors, this seemed like a train robbery pure and simple, and the bandits might just turn their six-shooters on them with their next shot.

The train came to a halt with the passengers scrambling wildly to hide valuables. The known standard procedure for train robberies was for the desperados to walk up and down the train cars with a bag for watches, jewelry, silver, gold. The passengers were fully expecting to see bloodthirsty men spun out of pop culture in the East. What they got was a man with spectacles on a horse.

"I don't believe," remarked one of Roosevelt's cowboys, George Meyers, afterward, "Some of the passengers ever did find all the things that was hid away."

They left their horses, and Roosevelt, Sylvane, and Merrifield boarded the train and explained to the conductor what they were really looking for was a passage to arrange a funeral. The conductor apparently flew into a rage when he realized the train had been stopped not for a hold-up but to honor the dead.

"You be good," Roosevelt told the irate man, "Or you'll be the one to get off."[4]

They rode the train to Medora in style while the passengers eyed the dusty men in their chaps and sombreros.

"You'll hear from this," called the conductor when the Roosevelt gang departed.

Roosevelt covered the expenses of the cowpuncher's funeral. It was a story bandied about by cowboys up and down the line and added to the plus column of the Roosevelt reputation, soon to become the Roosevelt legend.

As domesticity beckoned on the horizon, Roosevelt seemed more determined than ever to kill himself. He chose the spot for his latest dance with death in the mountains of Northern Idaho, where one more hunt beckoned with a man named John Willis. He and Willis were to hunt the white goat. Willis immediately underestimated Roosevelt after assuming he was the pampered son of a wealthy brewer, and told him, "You can't stand a trip like this."[5]

"You take me on the trip and I'll show you. I can train myself to walk as far as you can," Roosevelt replied.

Willis was right, though. They hunted in the timber line and then they headed up into the mountains. Roosevelt had a hard time keeping up with the hunter as he climbed the craggy rock face. Their moccasins were shredded and briars tore at their hands and arms. The elusive white goat remained hidden until the moment Roosevelt was resting against a tree and a goat appeared a short distance away. Roosevelt took the shot but only broke his foreleg.

The chase was on. The goat scrambled up the mountain, and the men chased his bloody trail. Roosevelt was running along a ridge when his foot slipped on the rocks and he went headfirst over the precipice. He fell fifty feet and bounced down through a tall pine tree, breaking snow-covered branches in an avalanche of snow and pine boughs, and then ended up in another balsam. Finally, he hit the ground. John Willis called down, sure the man with glasses was paralyzed or dread.

"Are you hurt?"[6]

Roosevelt stood up feeling bruised and scratched, but the pine branches had broken his fall. Even his glasses had remained on. He yelled up the mountain.

"No!"

"Then come on!"

They continued their chase, scrambling up and down the mountain again. Roosevelt came upon the goat again and fired. He shot too high and the goat took off down the mountain with the winded, sweaty men behind him. Darkness came and they lost the trail.

"Now," said Willis, "I expect you are getting tired."

"By George," said Roosevelt, "How far have we gone?"

"About fifteen or twenty miles up and down the mountains."

"If we get that goat tomorrow, I will give you a hundred dollars."

"I don't want a hundred dollars," Willis replied. "But we'll get that goat."

Roosevelt got his goat the next day at noon and spent the next two weeks with Willis in the mountains. The two men talked around their campfires long into the night, and years later Willis said, "He was a revelation to me. He was so well-posted on everything. He was the first man I had ever met that really knew everything."[7]

Roosevelt returned to finish up his business with Sewall and Dow. Both men now had families who were packing up for the trip back East. "Three weeks from today," Roosevelt said after consulting with both men, "We go."[8] Essentially, by closing Elkhorn Ranch, he was concluding a very big chapter of his life. It was Bill Sewall who had told the distraught man years before, "you'll come to feel different...and then you won't want to stay here anymore." And Roosevelt was different now. He had a life to return to, a marriage coming up in London, and a slumbering political career that was beginning to stir.

He rode into the prairie with Sewall many times during the last three weeks, and he told the Maine woodsman he was considering going into law. "You'd be a good lawyer," Bill replied. "But I think you ought to go into politics. Good men like you ought to go into politics. If you do and if you live, I think you'll be President."[9]

Roosevelt just laughed. "That's looking a long way ahead."

"It may be a long way ahead to you, but it isn't as far ahead as it's been for some of the men who got there."

Roosevelt replied he was going East to see about a job and he wanted to write. Roosevelt was still spinning the roulette wheel of his life to see what occupation it would settle on. But he had a direction and it was to the East. As the two men sat on their horses with the long plains stretching out from them, a very bright part of their lives was ending.

In September a blue haze settled on the Badlands. Some men thought it was from the prairie fires, but the old-timers knew it to portend something else. They started to lay in supplies for a long winter, as the haze persisted even in the heat. There were rumors that the white Arctic owl had been seen in Montana, and to the original settlers, the Indians, this portended something ominous. As Hermann Hagedorn wrote in *Roosevelt in the Badlands*, "The beavers were working by day as well as by night, cutting the willow brush, and observant eyes noted that they were storing twice their usual winter's supply. The birds were acting strangely. The ducks and geese, which ordinarily flew south in October, that autumn had, a month earlier, already departed."[10]

Roosevelt did not wait around for what nature portended and left in October, leaving Sewall to close up the cabin. He did so, and as he closed the door to the cabin he must have paused. Men are allowed but a few adventures in their lives. He would later say he was shutting the door on "the happiest time that any of us have ever known."[11] The Elkhorn ranch fell silent, as an army of snowflakes descended from the sky.

33

THE WINTER OF BLUE SNOW

1887

W hat followed in 1886 and 1887 was the winter from hell. It was as if nature in the Badlands was participating in the Roosevelt saga, and now that it was winding down it was time for the deathblow. It struck in early October, with the snow coming down from the eerie haze that had persisted through autumn. The Winter of the Blue Snow, as pioneers would call it afterward, was the worst in history.

On the afternoon of November 13, the snow began to fall and slowly increased. Then the temperature hit zero and the super-fine snow was powered by a gale from Canada. By morning, there were six or seven-foot drifts and the cattle could not breathe, and the ones that faced north were asphyxiated as the snow clogged their nostrils and throats. "Upon getting up in the morning," said Lincoln Lang describing the storm, "the house was intensely cold and with everything that could freeze frozen solid. The light was cut off from the windows looking south. As we opened the front door we were confronted by a solid wall of snow reaching to the eaves of the house. There was no drift over the back door, looking north, but as I opened it I was blown almost from my feet by the swirl of snow, which literally filled the air, so that it was impossible to see any of the surrounding ranch-buildings or even the fence, less than fifty feet distant. It was like a tornado of pure white dust or very fine sand, icy cold, and stinging like a whip-lash."[1]

The snow continued through November—one blizzard after another with temperatures minus thirty-five degrees. The trees exploded from the cold, and by New Year's it was minus forty-one, and still the snows came on. The cattle froze in place with their hooves cemented into the ice, standing like frozen statues that wouldn't fall until spring. Ranches were buried with people asleep inside. Drifts piled up to a hundred feet and put a smooth blanket over the prairie. Thousands of cattle became entombed in the snow.

People went mad from the unceasing winter. They were stranded in their cabins, and children froze to death on trips to a barn. Men died and couldn't be buried in the iron-hard ground; their bodies were propped up outside of cabins, soon buried in snow and ice. The cattle died from starvation and cold and suffocating snow. The drought had killed what little grass there was, and overgrazing had taken the rest. The "perfect storm" of the "great die off" of free range herds had begun in the American West. The cattle took shelter in gulches or coulees only to be buried in snow. Then they started going into Medora and eating the tar paper off the sides of the buildings. People had to put boards over their windows so the cows wouldn't try to come through.

On January 28 the mother of all blizzards struck. One survivor wrote, "for seventy-two hours it seemed as if all the world's ice from Time's beginning had come on a wind which howled and screamed with the fury of demons."[2] The cattle stared at passing trains, huddled along the tracks, waiting for garbage. People in town listened to the low, agonizing moans of the cattle starving to death in the streets. The majority of cattle on the prairie simply blew over and died by the thousands and tens of thousands.

The unrelenting cold and snow continued until March. Then the great thaw began. "Within a day or so," said Lincoln Lang, "the snow had softened everywhere. Gullies and wash-outs started to run with constantly increasing force, until at length there was a steady roar of running water, with creeks out of bounds everywhere. Then, one day, we suddenly heard a roar above that of the rushing water, coming from the direction of the Little Missouri, and hurrying there saw a sight, once seen, never to be forgotten. The river was out of banks clear up into the cottonwoods and out on to the bottom, going down in a raging, muddy torrent literally full of huge, grinding ice cakes, up-ending and rolling over each other as they went, tearing down trees in their paths, ripping, smashing, tearing at each other... as we gazed we could see countless carcasses of cattle going down with the ice, rolling over and over as they went, so that at times all four of the stiffened legs of a carcass would point skyward. ... Continuously carcasses seemed to be going down while others kept bobbing up at one point or another to replace them."[3]

Dead cattle were everywhere. Images of battlefields come to mind. Cattle carcasses filled the gullies and were even found in trees where they had walked on packed snowdrifts to find some vegetation. All along the river they had died looking for shelter. "I got a saddle horse and rode over the country," said Merrifield later, "and I'm telling you, the first day out, I never saw a live animal."[4]

Ranchers lost more than half of their herds in the Winter of the Blue Snow. The Hash Knife outfit lost seventy-five thousand out of a hundred thousand. Lincoln Lang's father lost twenty-four hundred cattle out of three thousand. The skinny, emaciated cattle that remained were a poor testament to the teeming herds that once roamed the Badlands. The wagons of the dead trundled across the Badlands as the agents of fertilizer companies moved in for the thousands of skeletons and made a killing.

Roosevelt returned in April 1887 and was appalled. He had heard of the Dakota winter while in Europe and hoped it wouldn't be too bad for him. He rode from Medora and found out the worst. "You cannot imagine anything more dreary than the look of the Bad Lands," he wrote Sewall. "Everything was cropped as bare as a bone. The sagebrush was just fed out by the starving cattle. The snow lay so deep that nobody could get around; it was almost impossible to get a horse a mile. In almost every coulee there were dead cattle. There were nearly three hundred on Wadsworth bottom. ... In one of the Munro's draws I counted in a single patch of brushwood twenty-three dead cows and calves. You boys were lucky to get out when you did; if you had waited until spring, I guess it would have been a case of walking."[5]

Merrifield's assessment was bleak, "I don't know how many thousand we owned at Elkhorn and Maltese Cross in the autumn of 1886, but after that terrible winter there wasn't a cow left, only a few hundred sick-looking steer."[6] The roundup that spring was never held because there simply were not enough cattle left. There are no official numbers on the amount of cattle lost from the winter of 1886 to 1887, but estimates put it at seventy-five percent for most ranchers. Clearly, Roosevelt's investment was gone, and his days as a rancher were over.

"I am bluer than indigo about the cattle," he wrote to Corinne. "It is even worse than I feared; I wish I was sure I would lose no more than half the money I invested out here. I am planning to get out."[7]

But even getting out was impossible. Ranchers were dumping their remaining cattle on the market for whatever they could at low prices. Like any sort of sell-off, the market followed it down. For Roosevelt this was the final nail in the coffin, and for him the West had changed, as he wrote to his friend, Lodge: "The losses are crippling. For the first time I have been utterly unable to enjoy a visit to my ranch. I shall be glad to get home."[8]

Theodore Roosevelt's great Wild West Adventure was over.

34

THE ROMANCE
OF HIS LIFE

Theodore Roosevelt would return to the West over the years. But in 1889 he became a member of the Civil Service Commission in Washington and from there on he only went to the Badlands once a year. South Dakota was admitted to the Union as a state in 1890, and the frontier was declared closed when the census bureau realized the population line now extended to the West coast. The Wild West of Teddy Roosevelt's youth was now relegated to history and the movies.

It was after Roosevelt was Governor and nominated for the vice presidency that he returned to the Dakotas in 1900 and pulled into a way station across the border. Joe Ferris, the first man who had taken him on a buffalo hunt, was there to greet him.

"Joe, old boy!" Roosevelt cried out exuberantly. "Will you ever forget the first time we met?"

"You nearly murdered me. It seemed as if all the ill luck in the world pursued us."[1]

Roosevelt had Ferris ride with him to Medora. As the train approached, the Governor became misty-eyed and murmured, "The romance of my life began here."[2] Teddy Roosevelt came back from the West, a new man of vigor with a barrel chest. Many did not recognize the man who had disappeared in 1883. He was wider, with a tan, florid face, and a voice that no longer squeaked but reached the back of the room like a megaphone. Roosevelt now leaned forward when speaking, slamming one fist into his hand, pounding home point after point with his teeth clapping off each sentence. He had been transformed into a cowboy in a suit and walked with a swagger. All that was missing was the Colt on his hip.

The West had transformed him, and even though he lost the race for Mayor of New York, he would soon reach as high as the vice presidency. When President McKinley was assassinated, he became, in 1901, the youngest president in history at forty-two. This was after being a reform Civil Service Commissioner, police commissioner, and Assistant Secretary of the Navy, a post he quit to go lead a band of cowboys up San Juan Hill in the Spanish-American War of 1898. He would do all of these things fearlessly with the same reckless abandon he observed when hunting buffalo, confronting bad men, hunting grizzly, going on roundups, fighting Indians, herding cattle, and catching thieves on the Little Missouri.

He was that "damn cowboy" in the White House and forever left the door open to any old Western friends with a standing invitation to come see him anytime day or night. Theodore Roosevelt energized the White House and the country with his presence, embodying the vigorous life. "The outstanding incomparable symbol of vitality of his time," Mark Sullivan would write.[3] And to others he was "that damn cowboy" or "an excellent specimen of the genus Americanus egotisticus."[4] But he also was a man who could speak German and French and had a superb grasp of history and literature.

In 1901 the American Century was just beginning, and the bluster and pure unadulterated energy of Teddy Roosevelt mirrored the bristling country flexing her young muscles, ready to take on the world. Roosevelt had a Great White Fleet built and had it sail around the world to announce America's arrival and her power. He himself boasted of speaking softly and carrying a big stick. Then he joined the oceans by inaugurating the building of the Panama Canal. He sued corporations, busted up the trusts, took on J. P. Morgan, and settled the anthracite coal strike of 1902 by mediating the negotiations himself—the like of which no president had ever done before. He then received a Nobel Prize for settling the Russo-Japanese War.

The cowboy then turned around and by executive order set aside forty-million acres for future generations. The lands out West, which Teddy Roosevelt had seen as a young man, he wanted the unborn millions to be able to enjoy. There never was a conservationist president like Teddy Roosevelt, and in the end he had set aside land for five national parks, created sixteen national monuments including the Grand Canyon, and, more than all that, he made Americans aware of conservationism at a time when people barely knew what the word meant.

He was the cowboy when he became restless after naming William Howard Taft as his successor. The vigorous life demanded that he return to politics, and so he did in 1912 and created the Bull Moose Party when the Republicans would not give him the nomination. Taft and Roosevelt split the electorate and allowed a professor from Princeton to capture the election. The Republicans would never forgive Roosevelt for Woodrow Wilson's election.

The cowboy then headed down to the Amazon to explore the River of Doubt. The unexplored river in the Amazon rainforest nearly killed him. Roosevelt had gained weight and suffered from gout along with his hidden heart disease, asthma, and high blood pressure; the middle-aged explorer was so plagued with illness he urged his son to leave him by the river to die. Through sheer grit and determination he did manage to survive, but his health had been permanently fractured.

He and Edith had five children—Theodore, Kermit, Ethel, Archibald, and Quentin—but he rarely spoke of his first wife Alice Lee. Mention of her violated the Roosevelt code established firmly when he went West. There was the old world and the present world and the door to the old world was forever closed. Even in his autobiography in 1913, there is no mention of his first marriage. There was a permanent divide between life before Teddy Roosevelt went West and life after. The West had washed his old life away, much like the melting winter snow swept the Badlands of the frozen dead cattle. Death would be wiped away by the natural order of life. Roosevelt revealed this mindset in his correspondence with intimates. A letter to his sister about a tragedy that had befallen a mutual friend reveals the psychological tack he takes when dealing with personal loss: "I hate to think of her suffering, but the only thing to do now is to treat the past as past, the event is finished and to dwell on it, and above all to keep talking of it with anyone, would be both weak and morbid."[5]

Black care rarely plagues the fast rider, and Teddy Roosevelt rode hard and fast his entire life. He wrote twenty books on history, literature, politics, and natural history, as well as 150,000 letters before it was all said and done. He wrote all of his own speeches. And still he managed to ride, shoot, hike, row, play tennis, explore, and forever plot his return to the White House. Teddy Roosevelt read all the time in the Badlands,— even reading Tolstoy while on the trail of boat thieves. He was a great re-reader and read Cooper, Scott, Twain, and Lincoln many times over.

Roosevelt's vision and general health was always a problem. When he charged up San Juan Hill, he carried no less than a dozen extra pairs of glasses. His eyesight was forever damaged by a lucky punch when he was sparring in the White House.

He never recovered from his trip down the Amazon, and he was devastated by the death of his son Quentin in World War I. When thinking back on his time out West, he told Senator Albert Fall that if forced to pick one part of his life to remember, "I would take the memory of my life on the ranch with its experiences close to Nature and among the men who lived nearest her."[6]

It was truly, as he said, the romance of his life.

35

THE LAST COWBOY

The romance of Theodore Roosevelt's life began in 1883 when, as a distraught asthmatic young man, he stepped off a train in the middle of the night in the Dakota Territory. The West was still there—and it was still wild—and the individual was wed with his time there in mutual destiny. The West created Theodore Roosevelt because he *became* the West—individualistic, tough, fair, brash, self-reliant, courageous.

The West took a man at the end of his rope and rebuilt him from the ground up, physically and psychologically. Teddy Roosevelt became a cowboy and then became a rancher. He did what all young men long to do—to be part of an adventure bigger than oneself. He found that adventure in the West, and it was seared into his soul and became "the vigorous life." Teddy Roosevelt, as president, brought the West with him. Big Stick Diplomacy was nothing more than the swagger of the man in the West who had faced down armed men more than once.

The man who took on the trusts was the same man who faced down the Marquis when he tried to take his land. The pursuit of corporate criminals and all who were corrupt was Roosevelt chasing down the boat thieves and bringing them to justice. The very tough resiliency of a man who continued to give a speech while reeling from a would-be assassin's bullet was the same man who trudged across the Badlands in arctic cold and desert heat. And, of course, the man who would set aside millions of acres for future generations could only do so with a deep love of the land where he had become a man.

These were the lessons learned and they took. The self-reliant *cowboy* who was as big as the Wild West was in Roosevelt from the day he left the Badlands to the day he died. The *action taken* was always preeminent in everything he did, and Americans loved him for it. The *vigorous life* was the life of the cowboy, and the modern populace of America in the twentieth century craved that vanishing world. The West was unique in its open-spaced freedom and limitless opportunities, and Roosevelt brought this spirit with him to the White House. Even when he was president, he had standing orders that "The cowboy bunch could come in whenever they wanted."

Teddy Roosevelt went to live the last great adventure the Wild West could offer a young man. He realized every heroic role the myth of the West had to offer. It was an amazing intersection of opportunity, circumstance, and the individual. By leading a life in the West that was bigger than life, Teddy Roosevelt himself became bigger than life.

In 1903 Roosevelt returned to Medora as president of the United States. He stared off from the rear platform of his car and spoke to John Burroughs beside him. "I know all this country like a book. I have ridden over it, and hunted over it, and tramped over it, in all seasons and weather, and it looks like home to me." Roosevelt himself recognized what his experience in the West had done for him, saying after becoming president, "If it had not been for my years in North Dakota, I never would have become president of the United States."[1] The forging of a president began in the year 1883 in the hell of the Badlands in the last years of the frontier, when a sickly young man went to recover from the loss of his wife, his mother, and his career.

Theodore Roosevelt's communion with the West and his many adventures there had a lasting effect. Like good fiction, it was the journey and not the destination that mattered, and so here the man who led this life, a writer himself, can put the capstone on his years in the West in his own words. Roosevelt's glance back to his youth expresses the essence of what he lived:

It was still the Wild West in those days, the Far West, the West of Owen Wister's stories and Frederick Remington's drawings, the West of the Indian and the buffalo-hunter, the soldier, and the cow-puncher. That land of the West has gone now, "gone, gone with lost Atlantis," gone to the isle of ghosts and of strange dead memories. It was a land of vast silent spaces, of lonely rivers, and of plains where the wild game stared at the passing horseman. It was a land of scattered ranches, of herds of long-horned cattle, and of reckless riders who unmoved looked in the eyes of life or of death. In that land we led a free and hardy life, with horse and with rifle. We worked under the scorching midsummer sun, when the wide plains shimmered and wavered in the heat; and we knew the freezing misery of riding night guard round the cattle in the late fall round up. In the soft springtime, the stars were glorious in our eyes each night before we fell asleep; and in winter we rode through the blinding blizzards, when the driven snow-dust burnt our faces. They were monotonous days, as we guided the trail cattle or the beef herds, hour after hour, at the slowest of walks; and minutes or hours teeming with excitement as we stopped stampedes or swam the herds across rivers treacherous with quicksands or brimmed with running ice. We knew toil and hardship and hunger and thirst; and we saw men die violent deaths as they worked among the horses and the cattle, or fought in evil feuds with one another; but we felt the beat of hardy life in our veins, and ours was the glory of work and the joy of living.[2]

Teddy Roosevelt died in his sleep on January 6, 1919 after a blood clot moved into his lungs. He was sixty years old. His son Archie cabled to his brothers, "The Old Lion is dead." President Woodrow Wilson's vice president summed up Roosevelt's death this way: "Death had to take Roosevelt sleeping; if he had been awake, there would have been a fight."

It's true—the last cowboy would have fought to the death.

NOTES

PREFACE

1. Edmund Morris, *The Rise of Theodore Roosevelt* (New York: Random House, 1979), 466.
2. Theodore Roosevelt, *Ranch Life and the Hunting-Trail* (New York: The Century Company, 1899), 3.
3. Eric Foner and John A. Garraty, eds., *The Reader's Companion to American History* (New York: Houghton Mifflin Harcourt Publishing Company, 1991), s.v. "Cowboys."
4. Ibid., 6.
5. Frederick Jackson Turner, *The Frontier in American History* (New York: Henry Holt and Company, 1921), 38.
6. Roosevelt, *Ranch Life and the Hunting-Trail*, 7.

PROLOGUE

1. Candice Millard, *The River of Doubt* (New York: Anchor Books, 2005), 420.

CHAPTER 1

1. Edmund Morris, *The Rise of Theodore Roosevelt* (New York: Random House, 1979), 198.
2. Theodore Roosevelt, *The Strenuous Life* (New York: The Century Company, 1904), 11.
3. Theodore Roosevelt, *Ranch Life and the Hunting-Trail* (New York: The Century Company, 1899), 102.

CHAPTER 2

1. Edmund Morris, *The Rise of Theodore Roosevelt* (New York: Random House, 1979), 24.
2. David McCullough, *Mornings on Horseback* (New York: Simon and Schuster, 1981), 108.
3. Ibid., 95.
4. Ibid.
5. Ibid.
6. Ibid., 107.
7. Ibid., 108.
8. Ibid., 111.
9. Morris, *The Rise of Theodore Roosevelt*, 25.
10. McCullough, *Mornings on Horseback*, 111.
11. Kathleen Dalton, *Theodore Roosevelt: A Strenuous Life* (New York: Alfred A. Knopf, 2002), 50.
12. Theodore Roosevelt, *An Autobiography* (New York: Charles Scribner's Sons, 1921), 28.
13. McCullough, *Mornings on Horseback*, 115.
14. Ibid., 332.

15.   Morris, *The Rise of Theodore Roosevelt*, 32.

CHAPTER 3

1.   Edmund Morris, *The Rise of Theodore Roosevelt* (New York: Random House, 1979), 80.
2.   Ibid., 229.
3.   Ibid., 237.
4.   Ibid., 238.
5.   Ibid., 248.
6.   Ibid., 259.

CHAPTER 4

1.   Edmund Morris, *The Rise of Theodore Roosevelt* (New York: Random House, 1979), 186.
2.   David McCullough, *Mornings on Horseback* (New York: Simon and Schuster, 1981), 321.

CHAPTER 5

1.   Kathleen Dalton, *Theodore Roosevelt: A Strenuous Life* (New York: Knopf, 2002), 52.
2.   Ibid.
3.   Hermann Hagedorn, *Roosevelt in the Badlands* (New York: Houghton Mifflin Company, 1921), 17.

CHAPTER 6

1.   Edmund Morris, *The Rise of Theodore Roosevelt* (New York: Random House, 1979), 199–200.
2.   Ibid., 201.
3.   Ibid., 203.

CHAPTER 7

1. Hermann Hagedorn, *Roosevelt in the Badlands* (New York: Houghton Mifflin Company, 1921), 23.
2. Edmund Morris, *The Rise of Theodore Roosevelt* (New York: Random House, 1979), 203.
3. Ibid.
4. H. W. Brands, *T. R.: The Last Romantic* (New York: Basic Books, 1997), 155.
5. Kathleen Dalton, *Theodore Roosevelt: A Strenuous Life* (New York: Alfred A. Knopf, 2002), 45.
6. Morris, *The Rise of Theodore Roosevelt*, 204.
7. Ibid.
8. Ibid.
9. Hagedorn, *Roosevelt in the Badlands*, 28.
10. Ibid.
11. Theodore Roosevelt, *Hunting Trips of a Ranchman* (New York: G. P. Putnam's Sons, 1885), 259.
12. Ibid., 262–63.
13. Ibid., 263.
14. Morris, *The Rise of Theodore Roosevelt*, 207.
15. Hagedorn, *Roosevelt in the Badlands*, 36.
16. Ibid.
17. Ibid., 37.
18. Ibid.
19. Ibid., 38.

CHAPTER 8

1. Edmund Morris, *The Rise of Theodore Roosevelt* (New York: Random House, 1979), 208.
2. Ibid.

3. Hermann Hagedorn, *Roosevelt in the Badlands* (New York: Houghton Mifflin Company, 1921), 209.
4. Morris, *The Rise of Theodore Roosevelt*, 211.
5. Ibid.
6. Ibid., 212.
7. Theodore Roosevelt, *Hunting Trips of a Ranchman* (New York: G. P. Putnam's Sons, 1885) 106.
8. Hagedorn, *Roosevelt in the Badlands*, 46.

CHAPTER 9

1. Louis Warren, *Buffalo Bill's America* (New York: Knopf, 2005), 211.
2. Ibid., 212.
3. Ibid., 213.
4. Ibid.
5. Ibid., 215.
6. Kathleen Dalton, *Theodore Roosevelt: A Strenuous Life* (New York: Alfred A. Knopf, 2002), 98.
7. Warren, *Buffalo Bill's America*, 252.

CHAPTER 10

1. Theodore Roosevelt, *Ranch Life and the Hunting-Trail* (New York: The Century Company, 1899), 6; David McCullough, *Mornings on Horseback* (New York: Simon and Schuster, 1981), 328.
2. Theodore Roosevelt, *Hunting Trips of a Ranchman* (New York: G. P. Putnam's Sons, 1885), 33.
3. McCullough, *Mornings on Horseback*, 329.
4. Hermann Hagedorn, *Roosevelt in the Badlands* (New York: Houghton Mifflin Company, 1921), 48.

5.   Edmund Morris, *The Rise of Theodore Roosevelt* (New York: Random House, 1979), 259.
6.   Hagedorn, *Roosevelt in the Badlands*, 74.
7.   Ibid., 75.
8.   Ibid., 90.
9.   Ibid., 91.
10. Roosevelt, *Ranch Life and the Hunting-Trail*, 59.
11. Morris, *The Rise of Theodore Roosevelt*, 261.
12. Hagedorn, *Roosevelt in the Badlands*, 218.
13. Morris, *The Rise of Theodore Roosevelt*, 263.
14. Ibid., 264.
15. Ibid., 265.
16. Ibid.
17. Ibid.
18. Hagedorn, *Roosevelt in the Badlands*, 105.

CHAPTER 11

1.   David McCullough, *Mornings on Horseback* (New York: Simon and Schuster, 1981), 109.
2.   Hermann Hagedorn, *Roosevelt in the Badlands* (New York: Houghton Mifflin Company, 1921), 102.
3.   Ibid., 97.
4.   Henry F. Pringle, *Theodore Roosevelt* (New York: Harcourt, Brace and Company, 1931), 97.
5.   Roger L. Di Silvestro, *Theodore Roosevelt in the Badlands* (New york: Walker Publishing, 2012), 94.
6.   Theodore Roosevelt, *Ranch Life and the Hunting-Trail* (New York: The Century Company, 1899), 77.
7.   Dale L. Walker, *The Boys of '98* (New York: Forge Press, 1999), 66.

8. Eugene Thwing, *The Life and Meaning of Theodore Roosevelt* (New York: Current Literature Publishing Company, 1919), 70.

CHAPTER 12

1. Edmund Morris, *The Rise of Theodore Roosevelt* (New York: Random House, 1979), 268.
2. Jon Knokey, *Theodore Roosevelt and the Making of American Leadership* (New York: Skyhorse Publications, 2015), 30.
3. Frances Cavanah, *Adventure in Courage: The Story of Theodore Roosevelt* (Chicago: Rand McNally, 1961), 55.
4. Robert L. Wilson, *Theodore Roosevelt: Outdoorsman* (New York: Winchester Press, 1971), 43.
5. Hermann Hagedorn, "The Roosevelt Country," *The Outlook* 129 (September–December 1921): 259.
6. Morris, *The Rise of Theodore Roosevelt*, 275.
7. Hermann Hagedorn, *Roosevelt in the Badlands* (New York: Houghton Mifflin Company, 1921), 141.
8. Theodore Roosevelt, "Frontier Types," *The Century* 36 (May–October 1888): 838.
9. Hagedorn, *Roosevelt in the Badlands*, 126.
10. Theodore Roosevelt, *Ranch Life and the Hunting-Trail* (New York: The Century Co., 1899), 94.
11. Theodore Roosevelt, *An Autobiography* (New York: Charles Scribner's Sons, 1921), 122.
12. Ibid.
13. Ibid.
14. Hagedorn, *Roosevelt in the Badlands*, 154.

CHAPTER 13

1. Theodore Roosevelt, interview with the *New-York Tribune* in 1884, quoted in Edmund Morris, *The Rise of Theodore Roosevelt* (New York: Random House, 1979), 273.

2. Ibid.

3. Stefan Lorant, *The Life and Times of Theodore Roosevelt* (Garden City, NY: Doubleday, 1959), 216.

4. Betsey Harvey Kraft, *Theodore Roosevelt: Champion of the American Spirit* (New York: Clarion Books, 2003), 31.

5. Stephanie Sammartino McPherson, *Theodore Roosevelt* (Minneapolis: Lerner Publications Company, 2005), 35.

6. Michael R. Canfield, *Theodore Roosevelt in the Field* (Chicago: University of Chicago Press, 2015), 157.

7. David McCullough, *Mornings on Horseback* (New York: Simon and Schuster, 1981), 333.

8. Theodore Roosevelt, *Hunting Trips of a Ranchman* (New York: G. P. Putnam's Sons, 1885), 139.

9. Roger L. DiSilvestro, *Theodore Roosevelt in the Badlands* (New York: Walker, 2011), 126.

10. Ibid., 125.

11. Roosevelt, *Hunting Trips of a Ranchman*, 101.

12. Ibid., 132.

13. Sarah Lyons Watts, *Rough Rider in the White House* (Chicago: University of Chicago Press, 2003), 131.

14. Theodore Roosevelt, *Ranch Life and the Hunting-Trail* (New York: The Century Company, 1899), 101.

15. Hermann Hagedorn, *Roosevelt in the Badlands* (New York: Houghton Mifflin Company, 1921), 183.

16. Ibid., 184.

CHAPTER 14

1. David McCullough, *Mornings on Horseback* (New York: Simon and Schuster, 1981), 209.
2. Ibid., 210.
3. Ibid., 211.
4. Edmund Morris, *The Rise of Theodore Roosevelt* (New York: Random House, 1979), 36.
5. Nathan Miller, *Theodore Roosevelt: A Life* (New York: William Morrow, 1992), 68.
6. McCullough, *Mornings on Horseback*, 215.
7. William Roscoe Thayer, *Theodore Roosevelt: An Intimate Biography* (Boston: Houghton Mifflin, 1919), 21.
8. McCullough, *Mornings on Horseback*, 183.
9. Theodore Roosevelt, *The Selected Letters of Theodore Roosevelt*, ed. H. W. Brands (New York: Cooper Square Press, 2001), 14.
10. McCullough, *Mornings on Horseback*, 187.
11. Dan Elish, *Theodore Roosevelt* (New York: Marshall Cavendish Benchmark, 2008), 15.
12. Theodore Roosevelt, *A Most Glorious Ride: The Diaries of Theodore Roosevelt*, ed. Edward P. Kohn (Albany: State University of New York Press, 2015), 26.
13. Ibid., 47.
14. Candice Millard, *The River of Doubt* (New York: Anchor Books, 2005), 17.

CHAPTER 15

1. Theodore Roosevelt, *The Wilderness Hunter* (New York: G. P. Putman's Sons, 1893), 173.
2. Hermann Hagedorn, *Roosevelt in the Badlands* (New York: Houghton Mifflin Company, 1921), 185.

3.   Theodore Roosevelt, *Theodore Roosevelt on Hunting*, ed.
     Lamar Underwood (Guilford, CT: Lyons Press, 2003), 180.
4.   Edmund Morris, *The Rise of Theodore Roosevelt* (New York:
     Random House, 1979), 280.
5.   Roger L. DiSilvestro, *Theodore Roosevelt in the Badlands*
     (New York: Walker, 2011), 132.
6.   Murat Halstead, *The Life of Theodore Roosevelt* (Akron,
     OH: The Saalfield Publishing Company, 1902), 49.
7.   Theodore Roosevelt, *Hunting Trips of a Ranchman* (New
     York: G. P. Putman's Sons, 1885), 338.
8.   Halstead, *The Life of Theodore Roosevelt*, 50.
9.   Michael R. Canfield, *Theodore Roosevelt in the Field*
     (Chicago: University of Chicago Press, 2015), 161.
10. Roosevelt, *The Wilderness Hunter*, 221.
11. Kathleen Dalton, *Theodore Roosevelt: A Strenuous Life* (New
     York: Alfred A. Knopf, 2002), 52.
12. Roosevelt, *Theodore Roosevelt on Hunting*, ed. Lamar
     Underwood, 162.
13. Ibid., 163.
14. Hagedorn, *Roosevelt in the Badlands*, 204.
15. Roosevelt, *Hunting Trips of a Ranchman*, 146.
16. Theodore Roosevelt, *The Selected Letters of Theodore
     Roosevelt*, ed. H. W. Brands (New York: Cooper Square
     Press, 2001), 40.
17. Theodore Roosevelt, *The Letters of Theodore Roosevelt*, ed.
     E. E. Morison (Cambridge, MA: Harvard University Press,
     1951), 82.

CHAPTER 16

1.   Edmund Morris, *The Rise of Theodore Roosevelt* (New York:
     Random House, 1979), 195.

2. Ibid., 196.
3. Hermann Hagedorn, *Roosevelt in the Badlands* (New York: Houghton Mifflin Company, 1921), 200.
4. Morris, *The Rise of Theodore Roosevelt*, 281.

CHAPTER 17

1. Theodore Roosevelt, *Ranch Life and the Hunting-Trail* (New York: The Century Company, 1899), 116.
2. Ibid., 115.
3. Ibid., 75.
4. Theodore Roosevelt, *Hunting Trips of a Ranchman* (New York: G. P. Putnam's Sons, 1885), 93.
5. Ibid., 100.
6. Edmund Morris, *The Rise of Theodore Roosevelt* (New York: Random House, 1979), 286.
7. Hermann Hagedorn, *Roosevelt in the Badlands* (New York: Houghton Mifflin Company, 1921), 218.
8. Ibid.
9. Roosevelt, *Ranch Life and the Hunting-Trail*, 73.

CHAPTER 18

1. Nathan Miller, *Theodore Roosevelt: A Life* (New York: William Morrow, 1992), 87.
2. David McCullough, *Mornings on Horseback* (New York: Simon and Schuster, 1981), 221.
3. Ibid., 220.
4. Ibid., 221.
5. Edmund Morris, *The Rise of Theodore Roosevelt* (New York: Random House, 1979), 102.
6. Ibid.
7. Ibid.

8.   H. W. Brands, *T. R.: The Last Romantic* (New York: Basic Books, 1997), 105.
9.   McCullough, *Mornings on Horseback*, 229.
10. Ibid., 230.
11. Ibid., 91.

CHAPTER 19

1.   Hermann Hagedorn, *Roosevelt in the Badlands* (New York: Houghton Mifflin Company, 1921), 222.
2.   Editorial, *Bismarck Weekly Tribune*, December 12, 1884.
3.   Hagedorn, *Roosevelt in the Badlands*, 224.
4.   Ibid., 227.
5.   Theodore Roosevelt, *The Selected Letters of Theodore Roosevelt*, ed. H. W. Brands (New York: Cooper Square Press, 2001), 38.
6.   Theodore Roosevelt, *Theodore Roosevelt on Hunting*, ed. Lamar Underwood (Guilford, CT: Lyons Press, 2003), 190.
7.   Hagedorn, *Roosevelt in the Badlands*, 232.
8.   Roger L. DiSilvestro, *Theodore Roosevelt in the Badlands* (New York: Walker, 2011), 154.

CHAPTER 20

1.   Edmund Morris, *The Rise of Theodore Roosevelt* (New York: Random House, 1979), 291.
2.   Theodore Roosevelt, *The Letters of Theodore Roosevelt*, ed. E. E. Morison (Cambridge, MA: Harvard University Press, 1951), 89.
3.   Theodore Roosevelt, "Frontier Types," *Century Illustrated Monthly Magazine* 14, no. 36 (May 1888–October 1888): 843.
4.   Morris, *The Rise of Theodore Roosevelt*, 291.

5. Theodore Roosevelt, *Theodore Roosevelt on Hunting*, ed. Lamar Underwood (Guilford, CT: Lyons Press, 2003), 103.
6. Theodore Roosevelt, *Ranch Life and the Hunting-Trail* (New York: The Century Company, 1899), 100.

CHAPTER 21

1. Hermann Hagedorn, *Roosevelt in the Badlands* (New York: Houghton Mifflin Company, 1921), 250.
2. Theodore Roosevelt, quoted in Carleton Putnam, *Theodore Roosevelt, vol. 1: The Formative Years* by (New York: Charles Scribner's Sons, 1958), 521.
3. Edmund Morris, *The Rise of Theodore Roosevelt* (New York: Random House, 1979), 294.
4. Hagedorn, *Roosevelt in the Badlands*, 240.
5. Roger L. DiSilvestro, *Theodore Roosevelt in the Badlands* (New York: Walker, 2011), 46.
6. Morris, *The Rise of Theodore Roosevelt*, 295.
7. Hagedorn, *Roosevelt in the Badlands*, 244.
8. Ibid., 245.
9. Ibid.
10. Ibid., 246.
11. Theodore Roosevelt, *An Autobiography* (New York: Charles Scribner's Sons, 1921), 135.
12. Hagedorn, *Roosevelt in the Badlands*, 253.
13. Ibid., 256.

CHAPTER 22

1. Jerome Alden, *Bully: An Adventure with Teddy Roosevelt* (New York: Crown Publishers, 1979), 25.
2. Edmund Morris, *The Rise of Theodore Roosevelt* (New York: Random House, 1979), 124.

3. Roger L. DiSilvestro, *Theodore Roosevelt in the Badlands* (New York: Walker, 2011), 24.
4. David McCullough, *Mornings on Horseback* (New York: Simon and Schuster, 1981), 255.
5. Ibid., 256.
6. Ibid.
7. Bellamy Partridge, *The Roosevelt Family in America* (New York: Hillman-Curl, 1936), 90.
8. Nathan Miller, *Theodore Roosevelt: A Life* (New York: William Morrow, 1992) 123.
9. Carleton Putnam, *Theodore Roosevelt, vol. 1: The Formative Years* by (New York: Charles Scribner's Sons, 1958), 274.
10. McCullough, *Mornings on Horseback*, 266.
11. Ibid., 266.
12. Morris, *The Rise of Theodore Roosevelt*, 291.
13. McCullough, *Mornings on Horseback*, 277.
14. William Henry Harbaugh, *Power and Responsibility: The Life and Times of Theodore Roosevelt* (New York: Farrar, Straus and Cudahy, 1961), 51.
15. Morris, *The Rise of Theodore Roosevelt*, 228.

CHAPTER 23

1. Hermann Hagedorn, *Roosevelt in the Badlands* (New York: Houghton Mifflin Company, 1921), 266.
2. Theodore Roosevelt, *Ranch Life and the Hunting-Trail* (New York: The Century Company, 1899), 67.
3. Ibid.
4. Edmund Morris, *The Rise of Theodore Roosevelt* (New York: Random House, 1979), 105.
5. Roger L. DiSilvestro, *Theodore Roosevelt in the Badlands* (New York: Walker, 2011), 165.

6.   Roosevelt, *Ranch Life and the Hunting-Trail*, 106.
7.   *Mandan Pioneer*, May 22, 1884.
8.   Hagedorn, *Roosevelt in the Badlands*, 287.
9.   Ibid., 288.
10. Ibid.
11. Roosevelt, *Ranch Life and the Hunting-Trail*, 50.
12. Hagedorn, *Roosevelt in the Badlands*, 291.
13. Ibid., 277.
14. Ibid., 280.
15. Michael R. Canfield, *Theodore Roosevelt in the Field* (Chicago: University of Chicago Press, 2015), 154.
16. Nancy Whitelaw, *Theodore Roosevelt Takes Charge* (Morton Grove, IL: A. Whitman, 1992), 48.
17. Fred J. Cook and Robert Boehmer, *Theodore Roosevelt: Rallying a Free People* (Chicago: Kingston House, 1961), 64.
18. Roosevelt, *Ranch Life and the Hunting-Trail*, 57.
19. Ibid., 59.
20. Ibid., 210.
21. Hagedorn, *Roosevelt in the Badlands*, 296.
22. Roosevelt, *Ranch Life and the Hunting-Trail*, 58.
23. Hagedorn, *Roosevelt in the Badlands*, 298.
24. DiSilvestro, *Theodore Roosevelt in the Badlands*, 175.
25. Harold Howland, *Theodore Roosevelt and His Times* (New Haven, CT: Yale University Press, 1921), 7.

CHAPTER 24

1.   Hermann Hagedorn, *Roosevelt in the Badlands* (New York: Houghton Mifflin Company, 1921), 308.
2.   Ibid., 308–9.
3.   Ibid., 309.
4.   Hagedorn, *Roosevelt in the Badlands*, 305.

5.   Theodore Roosevelt, *An Autobiography* (New York: Charles Scribner's Sons, 1921), 103.
6.   Hagedorn, *Roosevelt in the Badlands*, 306.

CHAPTER 25

1.   Hermann Hagedorn, *Roosevelt in the Badlands* (New York: Houghton Mifflin Company, 1921), 311.
2.   Ibid., 316.
3.   Carleton Putnam, *Theodore Roosevelt, vol. 1: The Formative Years* (New York: Charles Scribner's Sons, 1958), 561.
4.   Hagedorn, *Roosevelt in the Badlands*, 307.
5.   Ibid., 318.
6.   Ibid,. 321.
7.   Ibid., 117.
8.   Ibid., 317.

CHAPTER 26

1.   Hermann Hagedorn, *Roosevelt in the Badlands* (New York: Houghton Mifflin Company, 1921), 340.
2.   Ibid.
3.   Ibid., 341.
4.   Ibid., 343.
5.   Ibid., 342.
6.   Carleton Putnam, *Theodore Roosevelt, vol. 1: The Formative Years* (New York: Charles Scribner's Sons, 1958), 537.
7.   Hagedorn, *Roosevelt in the Badlands*, 350.
8.   Edmund Morris, *The Rise of Theodore Roosevelt* (New York: Random House, 1979), 303.
9.   Ibid.
10. Ibid.

CHAPTER 27

1. Theodore Roosevelt, *An Autobiography* (New York: Charles Scribner's Sons, 1921), 108–9.
2. Hermann Hagedorn, *Roosevelt in the Badlands* (New York: Houghton Mifflin Company, 1921), 355.
3. Theodore Roosevelt, *Hunting Trips of a Ranchman* (New York: G. P. Putnam's Sons, 1885), 18.
4. Roosevelt, *An Autobiography*, 112.
5. Edmund Morris, *The Rise of Theodore Roosevelt* (New York: Random House, 1979), 306.
6. Roosevelt, *An Autobiography*, 113.
7. Ibid.

CHAPTER 28

1. Edmund Morris, *The Rise of Theodore Roosevelt* (New York: Random House, 1979), 74.
2. Ibid., 80.
3. Ibid., 82.
4. Ibid.

CHAPTER 29

1. Hermann Hagedorn, *Roosevelt in the Badlands* (New York: Houghton Mifflin Company, 1921), 365.
2. Ibid., 367.
3. Ibid., 372.
4. Ibid.
5. Ibid.
6. Edmund Morris, *The Rise of Theodore Roosevelt* (New York: Random House, 1979), 319.
7. Theodore Roosevelt, *Ranch Life and the Hunting-Trail* (New York: The Century Company, 1899), 116–18.

8. Ibid.
9. Ibid.
10. Ibid., 116.
11. Hagedorn, *Roosevelt in the Badlands*, 374.
12. Morris, *The Rise of Theodore Roosevelt*, 321.
13. Hagedorn, *Roosevelt in the Badlands*, 374.
14. Ibid., 375.
15. Ibid.
16. Morris, *The Rise of Theodore Roosevelt*, 322.
17. Hagedorn, *Roosevelt in the Badlands*, 376.
18. Ibid.
19. Morris, *The Rise of Theodore Roosevelt*, 322.
20. Ibid.
21. Ibid.
22. Hagedorn, *Roosevelt in the Badlands*, 377.
23. Ibid.

CHAPTER 30

1. Edmund Morris, *The Rise of Theodore Roosevelt* (New York: Random House, 1979), 322.
2. Ibid., 323.
3. Ibid., 322.
4. Ibid.
5. Ibid.
6. Theodore Roosevelt, *Ranch Life and the Hunting-Trail* (New York: The Century Company, 1899), 123.
7. Hermann Hagedorn, *Roosevelt in the Badlands* (New York: Houghton Mifflin Company, 1921), 379.
8. Ibid., 124.
9. Morris, *The Rise of Theodore Roosevelt*, 323.
10. Ibid.

11. Theodore Roosevelt, *An Autobiography* (New York: Charles Scribner's Sons, 1921), 131.
12. Roosevelt, *Ranch Life and the Hunting-Trail*, 25.
13. Hagedorn, *Roosevelt in the Badlands*, 380.
14. Ibid.
15. Roosevelt, *Ranch Life and the Hunting-Trail*, 126.
16. Hagedorn, *Roosevelt in the Badlands*, 380.
17. Morris, *The Rise of Theodore Roosevelt*, 325.
18. Ibid.
19. Ibid.
20. Hagedorn, *Roosevelt in the Badlands*, 384.
21. Ibid.

CHAPTER 31

1. Hermann Hagedorn, *Roosevelt in the Badlands* (New York: Houghton Mifflin Company, 1921), 386.
2. Ibid., 395.
3. Ibid., 396.
4. Ibid.
5. Ibid., 397.
6. Ibid.
7. Ibid.
8. Theodore Roosevelt, *Ranch Life and the Hunting-Trail* (New York: The Century Company, 1899), 56.
9. Ibid.
10. Hagedorn, *Roosevelt in the Badlands*, 401.
11. Roger L. DiSilvestro, *Theodore Roosevelt in the Badlands* (New York: Walker, 2011), 219.
12. Theodore Roosevelt, *The Wilderness Hunter* (New York: G. P. Putnam's Sons, 1893), 118.
13. Ibid., 101.

14. Hagedorn, *Roosevelt in the Badlands*, 403.

15. Ibid., 404.

16. Edmund Morris, *The Rise of Theodore Roosevelt* (New York: Random House, 1979), 332.

17. Ibid., 333.

18. Ibid., 334.

19. Hagedorn, *Roosevelt in the Badlands*, 411.

CHAPTER 32

1. Hermann Hagedorn, *Roosevelt in the Badlands* (New York: Houghton Mifflin Company, 1921), 255.

2. Edmund Morris, *The Rise of Theodore Roosevelt* (New York: Random House, 1979), 337.

3. Jon A. Knokey, *Theodore Roosevelt and the Making of American Leadership* (New York: Skyhorse Publishing, 2015), 55.

4. Ibid.

5. Theodore Roosevelt, *The Hunting and Exploring Adventures of Theodore Roosevelt*, ed. Donald Day and E. E. Morison (New York: Dial, 1955), 132.

6. Hagedorn, *Roosevelt in the Badlands*, 422.

7. Ibid., 423.

8. Ibid., 428.

9. Ibid., 429.

10. Ibid., 431.

11. Morris, *The Rise of Theodore Roosevelt*, 338.

CHAPTER 33

1. Hermann Hagedorn, *Roosevelt in the Badlands* (New York: Houghton Mifflin Company, 1921), 432–33.

2. Edmund Morris, *The Rise of Theodore Roosevelt* (New York: Random House, 1979), 366.

3. Hagedorn, *Roosevelt in the Badlands*, 438.

4. Ibid.

5. Ibid.

6. Ibid., 441.

7. Ibid.

8. Theodore Roosevelt, *The Letters of Theodore Roosevelt*, ed. E. E. Morison (Cambridge, MA: Harvard University Press, 1951), 127.

CHAPTER 34

1. Hermann Hagedorn, *Roosevelt in the Badlands* (New York: Houghton Mifflin Company, 1921), 465.

2. Ibid., 466.

3. David McCullough, *Mornings on Horseback* (New York: Simon and Schuster, 1981), 113.

4. Ibid., 363.

5. Ibid., 365.

6. Ibid.

CHAPTER 35

1. Edmund Morris, *The Rise of Theodore Roosevelt* (New York: Random House, 1979), 378.

2. Theodore Roosevelt, *An Autobiography* (New York: Charles Scribner's Sons, 1921), 94–95.

SELECT BIBLIOGRAPHY

Abbott, Lawrence. *Impressions of Theodore Roosevelt*. New York: Doubleday, 1919.

Beale, Howard K. *Theodore Roosevelt and the Rise of America to World Power*. Baltimore: John Hopkins Press, 1956.

Bishop, Joseph Bucklin. *Theodore Roosevelt and His Time*. New York: Charles Scribner's Sons, 1920.

Brands, H. W. *T.R.: The Last Romantic*. New York: Basic Books, 1997.

Brinkley, Douglas. *The Wilderness Warrior*. New York: Harper Collins, 2009.

Burton, David. *Theodore Roosevelt: Confident Imperialist*. Philadelphia: University of Pennsylvania Press, 1968.

Canfield, Michael R. *Theodore Roosevelt in the Field*. Chicago: University of Chicago Press, 2015.

Cutright, Paul. *Theodore Roosevelt the Naturalist*. New York: Harper, 1956.

Dalton, Kathleen. *Theodore Roosevelt, A Strenuous Life*. New York: Alfred A. Knopf, 2002.

DiSilvestro, Roger L. *Theodore Roosevelt in the Badlands*. New York: Walker, 2011.

Elish, Dan. *Theodore Roosevelt*. New York: Marshall Cavendish Benchmark, 2008.

Hagedorn, Hermann. *Roosevelt in the Badlands*. New York: Houghton Mifflin Company, 1921.

———. *The Boy's Life of Theodore Roosevelt*. New York: Harper, 1928.

Iglehart, Ferdinand Cowle. *Theodore Roosevelt: The Man As I Knew Him*. New York: 1919.

Lorant, Stefan. *The Life and Times of Theodore Roosevelt*. New York: Doubleday, 1959.

McCullough, David. *Mornings on Horseback*. New York: Simon and Schuster, 1981.

Millard, Candice. *The River of Doubt*. New York: Anchor Books, 2005.

Miller, Nathan. *Theodore Roosevelt: A Life*. New York: William Morrow, 1992.

Morris, Edmund. *The Rise of Theodore Roosevelt*. New York: Random House, 1979.

Mowry, George. *The Era of Theodore Roosevelt and the Birth of Modern America*. New York: Harper and Row, 1958.

Putnam, Carleton. *Theodore Roosevelt, vol. 1: The Formative Years*. New York: Charles Scribner's Sons, 1958.

Renehan, Edward. *The Lion's Pride: Theodore Roosevelt and His Family*. New York: Oxford University Press, 1998.

Robinson, Corinne Roosevelt. *My Brother Theodore Roosevelt*. New York: Scribner's, 1921.

Roosevelt, Kermit. *The Long Trail*. New York: Metropolitan Publications, 1921.

Roosevelt, Theodore. *All in the Family*. New York: G. P. Putnam's Sons, 1929.

———. *An Autobiography*. New York: Charles Scribner's Sons, 1921.

———. *Hunting Trips of a Ranchman*. New York: G. P. Putnam's Sons, 1885.

————. *The Letters of Theodore Roosevelt*. Edited by E. E. Morison. Cambridge, MA: Harvard University Press, 1951.

————. *Ranch Life and the Hunting-Trail*. New York: The Century Company, 1899.

————. *The Selected Letters of Theodore Roosevelt*. Edited by H. W. Brands. New York: Cooper Square Press, 2001.

————. *The Strenuous Life*. New York: The Century Company, 1904.

————. *Theodore Roosevelt's Diaries of Boyhood and Youth*. New York: Charles Scribner's Sons, 1924.

————. *The Wilderness Hunter*. New York: G. P. Putnam's Sons, 1893.

————. *The Works of Theodore Roosevelt*. New York: G. P. Putnam's Sons, 1893.

Sewall, William. *Bill Sewall's Story of TR*. New York: Harper and Brothers, 1919.

Thayer, William Roscoe. *Theodore Roosevelt: An Intimate Biography*. Boston: Houghton Mifflin, 1919.

Turner, Frederick Jackson. *The Frontier in American History*. New York: Henry Holt and Company, 1921.

Wagenknecht, Edward. *The Seven Worlds of Theodore Roosevelt*. New York: Longman's, 1958

Warren, Louis. *Buffalo Bill's America*. New York: Alfred A. Knopf, 2005.

Wister, Owen. *Roosevelt: The Story of a Friendship*. New York: The Macmillan Company, 1930.

INDEX

READ ANOTHER VIVID HISTORY FROM AUTHOR WILLIAM HAZELGROVE...

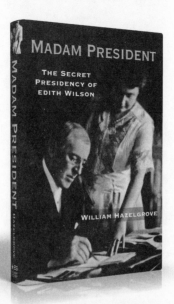

MADAM PRESIDENT
THE SECRET PRESIDENCY OF
EDITH WILSON

After President Woodrow Wilson suffered a paralyzing stroke in the fall of 1919, his wife, First Lady Edith Wilson, began to handle the day-to-day responsibilities of the Executive Office. She was a woman with little formal education who had been married to President Wilson for only four years; yet, in the tenuous peace following World War II, she became the acting president of the United States—months before women officially won the right to vote.

"...a lively, engaging narrative..." — *Foreword Reviews*

AVAILABLE NOW IN HARDCOVER, EBOOK, AND AUDIO FROM BOOKSTORES EVERYWHERE.

PUBLISHED BY REGNERY HISTORY.